Advanced Christian Prayer Book Collection
Over 100 Authentic Christian Prayers and Much More.

Editor: *Marshal Mason*

Note from the Editor

This book is a collection of four works and compiled to help you on your journey of faith and prayer. The four books herein are:

1. Prayers of the Early Church: Over 100 authentic Christian prayers

2. On Prayer and The Contemplative Life. By St. Thomas Aquinas.

3. The Only Teacher: Lord, teach us how to pray. By Andrew Murray.

4. The Prayers of St. Paul. By W. H. Griffith Thomas.

Prayers of the Early Church: Over 100 authentic Christian prayers

On Prayer and The Contemplative Life

By St. Thomas Aquinas

The Only Teacher: Lord, teach us how to pray

By Andrew Murray

The Prayers of St. Paul

By W. H. Griffith Thomas

Marshal Mason

Prayers of the Early Church
Over 100 authentic Christian prayers

Editor: *J. Manning Potts*
(Originally published 1953)

Marshal Mason

TABLE OF CONTENTS

Preface

Chapter - I FIRST CENTURY PRAYERS

1. New Testament Prayers
The Prayer of Simeon
The Magnificat
Jesus in the Garden of Gethsemane
Jesus' High Priestly Prayer
Jesus Prays From the Cross
Prayer of Stephen
That Christ May Dwell in Your Hearts
For Friends and Relatives
For a Knowledge of God's Will
Persecuted for Righteousness' Sake
For Spiritual Desires
Patience and Longsuffering
Begotten to a Lively Hope

2. Other First Century Prayers
For All Kings and Rulers
A Morning Prayer
For Rulers and Governors
For Blessings
For Forgiveness
Prayer Before Partaking of the Holy Sacrament
A Pure Heart
For Joy and Gladness

Chapter II - SECOND CENTURY PRAYERS

Intercession
A Dying Prayer of Polycarp, the Martyr
A Prayer for the Privilege of Martyrdom

For Soul Cleansing
To Witness for Christ
For a Pure Heart
Sanctify Us, O Lord
For Stewardship
Stewardship
Prayer to the Teacher
For Growth in Grace

Chapter III - THIRD CENTURY PRAYERS

For Blessings
For Light
For the Peace of Christ's Flock
Before the Holy Communion
For Divine Strength
For Blessings
A Morning Prayer
Thanksgiving and Prayer for Pardon
For Friends and Relations
For Christian Graces
A Table Grace
Morning Prayer
A Table Grace
For Ministers
For Illumination

Chapter IV - FOURTH CENTURY PRAYERS

For Charity
For Protection
For Pardon
For Trust and Fuller Knowledge
For Salvation
For Freedom From Sin
For Pardon

For Purity
Confession of Sin
For Protection
A Prayer for Spiritual Blessings
For Those Gathered in Worship
For Right Blessings
For Converts in Mission Fields
For Light and Guidance
For Two or Three
For All People
Invocation
For Refreshment
Adoration
The Holy Spirit
For Entire Love
For Steadfastness
For Perseverance
For Mercy
Refuge and Peace
Perfect Love
For Perfect Light
For More Love
For Mercy and Grace
For a Safe Voyage
For Perfect Love
For Obedience and Love
For Light
For Illumination
Obligation to Others
For Refreshment
For Increased Godly Knowledge
Praise
For Grace
For Peace
Evening Prayer
For Perfection

For Light
Communion with God
Rest in Thee
For Light
A Morning Prayer
The Thanksgiving for the Morning
A Morning Prayer
An Evening Prayer
An Evening Prayer
An Evening Prayer
Table Grace
For the First-Fruits
Thanks For Thy Mercies
For The Holy Spirit
For the Faithful
On the Lord's Day
For the Holy Communion
After the Holy Communion

Chapter V - FIFTH CENTURY PRAYERS

For Thy Peace
Intercession
An Evening Thanksgiving
For Blessing
For Communicants
For Right Living
For Heavenly-Mindedness
For Love of God's Law
For Christ's Presence
For National Peace
For Light and Guidance
For Acceptable Petitions
For Peace
For Those Who Minister
For Good Use of Blessings

For Cleansing
For Grace and Protection
A Morning Prayer
For the Sorrowing
For Protection
For Love of God
For God's Guidance
For Refreshment
For Light
For True Joy
For Goodness
On a Fast-Day
A Prayer for Divine Help
Praise
For Light
For the Holy Spirit
For Thy Will
For Forgiveness
To Serve Thee
For Thy Presence
General Petitions
For Christ's Servants Everywhere
For the Spread of Christianity
For Grace
For Enlightenment

Marshal Mason

Preface

Within are prayers of our Lord, the apostles, the martyrs, and the saints covering the period of the Early Church from its beginning through the fifth century. There are some prayers from each of the first five centuries. The treasure house from which to choose is almost unlimited. It is a vast and fruitful field and anyone is amply rewarded who delves into it.

The prayers have been selected primarily for their spiritual and devotional content. Many have been laid aside with regret that they could not be included in this book, but its compass in size is set and only so many can be used.

The prayers are arranged chronologically. Some other method of arrangement might have been chosen but this seemed good in order to represent each century. There are questions about the date and authorship of the prayers. They are the same questions that arise in reference to the Books of the Bible.

This book of prayers is published with the hope and prayer that it may have wide use. It has been prepared for individual and family devotions. It can be used with prayer groups in prayer meetings, for cells, and, of course, for the development of one's own personal spiritual life. The material is perfect for use in the devotional services of young people's groups, women's groups, and men's clubs. The prayers are excellent for insertion in church bulletins. Other ways will be found of making these great prayers usable.

The prayers have been collected from many old books of prayers and devotional materials. The editor is deeply indebted to all those who have ploughed the field before. They have labored and we have entered into their labors. It has been a joy to search out the material, to arrange the prayers, to put them in order, and to index them under so many subjects.

J. Manning Potts

Editor, THE UPPER ROOM

Nashville, Tennessee

Chapter I
FIRST CENTURY PRAYERS

Marshal Mason

1. New Testament Prayers

The Prayer of Simeon

Lord, now lettest thou thy servant depart in peace, according to thy word; for mine eyes have seen thy salvation, which thou hast prepared before the face of all people; a light to lighten the Gentiles, and the glory of thy people Israel.

—Luke 2:29.

The Magnificat

And Mary said, My soul doth magnify the Lord, and my spirit hath rejoiced in God my Saviour. For he hath regarded the low estate of his handmaiden: for, behold, from henceforth all generations shall call me blessed. For he that is mighty hath done to me great things; and holy is his name. And his mercy is on them that fear him from generation to generation. He hath shewed strength with his arm; he hath scattered the proud in the imagination of their hearts. He hath put down the mighty from their seats, and exalted them of low degree. He hath filled the hungry with good things; and the rich he hath sent empty away. He hath holpen his servant Israel, in remembrance of his mercy.

—Luke 1:46-54.

Jesus in the Garden of Gethsemane

O my Father, if it be possible, let this cup pass from me: nevertheless not as I will, but as thou wilt. O my Father, if this cup may not pass away from me, except I drink it, thy will be done.

—Matt. 26:39, 42.

Jesus' High Priestly Prayer

These words spake Jesus, and lifted up his eyes to heaven, and said, Father, the hour is come; glorify thy Son, that thy Son also may glorify thee: as thou hast given him power over all flesh, that he should give eternal life to as many as thou hast given him. And this is life eternal, that they might know thee the only true God, and Jesus Christ, whom thou hast sent. I have glorified thee on the earth: I have finished the work which thou gavest me to do. And now, O Father, glorify thou me with thine own self with the glory which I had with thee before the world was. I have manifested thy name unto the men which thou gavest me out of the world: thine they were, and thou gavest them me; and they have kept thy word. Now they have known that all things whatsoever thou hast given me are of thee. For I have given unto them the words which thou gavest me; and they have received them, and have known surely that I came out from thee, and they have believed that thou didst send me.

—John 17:1-8.

Jesus Prays From the Cross

Father, forgive them; for they know not what they do.

—Luke 23:34.

Father, into Thy hands I commend my spirit.

—Luke 23:46.

Prayer of Stephen

And they stoned Stephen, calling upon God, and saying, Lord Jesus, receive my spirit.

And he kneeled down, and cried with a loud voice, Lord, lay not this sin to their charge. And when he had said this, he fell asleep.

—Acts 7:59-60.

That Christ May Dwell in Your Hearts

Wherefore I also, after I heard of your faith in the Lord Jesus, and love unto all the saints, cease not to give thanks for you, making mention of you in my prayers; that the God of our Lord Jesus Christ, the Father of glory, may give unto you the spirit of wisdom and revelation in the knowledge of him: the eyes of your understanding being enlightened; that ye may know what is the hope of his calling, and what the riches of the glory of his inheritance in the saints, and what is the exceeding greatness of his power to us-ward who believe, according to the working of his mighty power, which he wrought in Christ, when he raised him from the dead, and set him at his own right hand in the heavenly places.

For this cause I bow my knees unto the Father of our Lord Jesus Christ, of whom the whole family in heaven and earth is named, that he would grant you, according to the riches of his glory, to be strengthened with might by his Spirit in the inner man; that Christ may dwell in your hearts by faith; that ye, being rooted and grounded in love, may be able to comprehend with all saints what is the breadth, and length, and depth, and height; and to know the love of Christ, which passeth knowledge, that ye might be filled with all the fulness of God.

Now unto him that is able to do exceeding abundantly above all that we ask or think, according to the power that worketh in us, unto him be glory forever and ever. Amen.

—Epistle to the Ephesians 1:15-20; 3:14-21.

For Friends and Relatives

O God, the Father of glory, the God of our Lord Jesus Christ, of whom every family in heaven and earth is named, thou who hast set the solitary in families, grant to all members of this family and to all the members of our different families, that, according to the riches of thy glory, we may be strengthened with might by thy Spirit in the inner man; that Christ may dwell in our hearts by faith; that we, being rooted and grounded in love, may be able to comprehend with all saints what is the breadth, and length, and depth, and height; and to know the love of Christ, which passeth knowledge, that we may be filled with all the fulness of God; through the eternal Christ our Saviour. Amen.

—*Adapted*: Ephesians 1:17; 3:15-19.

For a Knowledge of God's Will

O Almighty God, we are confident of this very thing, that he which hath begun a good work in us, will perform it until the day of Jesus Christ: we pray that our love may abound yet more and more in knowledge and in all judgment; that we may approve things that are excellent; that we may be sincere and without offense, till the day of Christ, being filled with the fruits of righteousness, which are by Jesus Christ, unto the glory and praise of God. Amen.

—*Adapted*: Philippians 1:6-11.

Persecuted for Righteousness' Sake

O Lord, our heavenly Father, grant to thy children who are persecuted for righteousness' sake that our conversation may be as becometh the Gospel of Christ; that we may stand fast in one spirit, with one mind striving together for the faith of the Gospel; that in nothing terrified by our adversaries we may be steadfast in behalf of Christ, not only to believe on him, but also to suffer for his sake, who liveth forever and ever. Amen.

—*Adapted*: Philippians 1:27-29.

For Spiritual Desires

Our Father, we most humbly beseech Thee to give unto this house, and unto each member of it in particular, to stand fast in the Lord. May we be of the same mind in the Lord. May we rejoice in the Lord alway. Grant that whatsoever things are true, whatsoever things are honest, whatsoever things are just, whatsoever things are pure, whatsoever things are lovely, if there be any praise, may we think on these things, may we know both how to be abased, and how to abound. May we do all things through Christ which strengtheneth us, knowing that God shall supply all our need according to his riches in glory by Christ Jesus. Amen.

—*Adapted*: Philippians 4.

Patience and Longsuffering

For this cause we also, ... do not cease to pray for you, and to desire that ye might be filled with the knowledge of his will in all wisdom and spiritual understanding; that ye might walk worthy of the Lord unto all pleasing, being fruitful in every good work and increasing in the knowledge of God; strengthened with all might according to his glorious power, unto all patience and longsuffering with joyfulness; giving thanks unto the Father, which hath made us meet to be partakers of the inheritance of the saints in light: who hath delivered us from the power of darkness, and hath translated us unto the kingdom of his dear Son: in whom we have redemption through his blood, even the forgiveness of sins.

Now unto God and our Father be glory for ever and ever. Amen.

—*Adapted*: Epistles to the Colossians 1:9-14 and Philippians 4:20.

Begotten to a Lively Hope

Blessed be the God and Father of our Lord Jesus Christ, which according to his abundant mercy hath begotten us again unto a lively hope by the resurrection of Jesus Christ from the dead, to an inheritance incorruptible, and undefiled, and that fadeth not away, reserved in heaven for us. Keep us by the power of God through faith unto salvation; that the trial of our faith, being much more precious than of gold that perisheth, though it be tried with fire, might be found unto praise and honour and glory at the appearing of Jesus Christ. Amen.

—*Adapted*: First Peter 1:3-7.

2. Other First Century Prayers

For All Kings and Rulers

Grant unto all Kings and Rulers, O Lord, health, peace, concord, and stability, that they may administer the government which Thou hast given them without failure. For Thou, O heavenly Master, King of the Ages, givest to the sons of men glory and honour, and power over all things that are upon the earth. Do Thou, Lord, direct their counsel according to that which is good and well pleasing in Thy sight, that administering in peace and gentleness, with godliness, the power which Thou hast given them, they may obtain Thy favour. O Thou Who alone art able to do these things, and things far more exceeding good than these, for us, we praise Thee, through the High Priest and Guardian of our souls, Jesus Christ; through Whom be the glory and the majesty, unto Thee, both now and for all generations, and forever and ever. Amen.

—Clement of Rome.

A Morning Prayer

O God, Who art the unsearchable abyss of peace, the ineffable sea of love, the fountain of blessings, and the bestower of affection, Who sendest peace to those that receive it; open to us this day the sea of Thy love, and water us with the plenteous streams from the riches of Thy grace. Make us children of quietness, and heirs of peace. Enkindle in us the fire of Thy love; sow in us Thy fear; strengthen our weakness by Thy power; bind us closely to Thee and to each other in one firm bond of unity; for the sake of Jesus Christ. Amen.

—Syrian Clementine Liturgy.

For Rulers and Governors

To our rulers and governors on the earth—to them Thou, Lord, gavest the power of the kingdom by Thy glorious and ineffable might, to the end that we may know the glory and honour given to them by Thee and be subject to them, in nought resisting Thy will; to them, Lord, give health, peace, concord, stability, that they may exercise the authority given to them without offence. For Thou, O heavenly Lord and King eternal, givest to the sons of men glory and honour and power over the things that are on the earth; do Thou, Lord, direct their counsel according to that which is good and well-pleasing in Thy sight, that, devoutly in peace and meekness exercising the power given them by Thee, they may find Thee propitious. O Thou, who only hast power to do these things and more abundant good with us, we praise Thee through the High Priest and Guardian of our souls Jesus Christ, through whom be glory and majesty to Thee both now and from generation to generation and forevermore. Amen.

—Clement of Rome.

For Blessings

May God, who seeth all things, and who is the Ruler of all spirits and the Lord of all flesh—who chose our Lord Jesus Christ and us through Him to be a peculiar people—grant to every soul that calleth upon His glorious and holy Name, faith, peace, patience, long-suffering, self-control, purity, and sobriety, to the well-pleasing of His Name, through our High Priest and Protector, Jesus Christ, by whom be to Him glory, and majesty, and power, and honour, both now and forevermore. Amen.

—Clement of Rome.

For Forgiveness

Thou didst make to appear the enduring fabric of the world by the works of Thy hand; Thou, Lord, didst create the earth on which we dwell,—Thou, who art faithful in all generations, just in judgments, wonderful in strength and majesty, with wisdom creating and with understanding fixing the things which were made, who art good among them that are being saved and faithful among them whose trust is in Thee; O merciful and Compassionate One, forgive us our iniquities and offences and transgressions and trespasses. Reckon not every sin of Thy servants and handmaids, but Thou wilt purify us with the purification of Thy truth; and direct our steps that we may walk in holiness of heart and do what is good and well-pleasing in Thy sight and in the sight of our rulers. Yea, Lord, make Thy face to shine upon us for good in peace, that we may be shielded by Thy mighty hand and delivered from every sin by Thine uplifted arm, and deliver us from those who hate us wrongfully. Give concord and peace to us and all who dwell upon the earth, even as Thou gavest to our fathers, when they called upon Thee in faith and truth, submissive as we are to Thine almighty and all-excellent Name. **Amen.**

—Clement of Rome.

Prayer Before Partaking of the Holy Sacrament

O God, who art great, great in name and counsel, powerful in Thy works, the God and Father of Thy Holy Son Jesus, our Saviour, look upon us, Thy flock, which Thou hast chosen through Him to the glory of Thy Name; sanctify us in body and soul, and grant that we, being purified from all filthiness of flesh and spirit, may partake of the mystic blessings now going before Thee, and judge none of us unworthy of them, but be Thou our Supporter, our Helper, and Defender, through Thy Christ, with whom glory, honour, laud, praise, thanksgiving, be to Thee and the Holy Ghost forever. **Amen.**

—The Clementine Liturgy.

A Pure Heart

O God Almighty, Father of our Lord Jesus Christ, Thine only begotten Son, give me a body unstained, a pure heart, a watchful mind, and an upright understanding, and the presence of Thy Holy Spirit, that I may obtain and ever hold fast to an unshaken faith in Thy Truth, through Jesus Christ, Thy Son, our Lord; through whom be glory to Thee in the Holy Ghost, forever and ever. Amen.

—The Clementine Liturgy.

For Joy and Gladness

Blessed art Thou, O Lord, who hast nourished me from my youth up, who givest food to all flesh. Fill our hearts with joy and gladness, that we, always having all sufficiency in all things, may abound to every good work in Christ Jesus our Lord, through whom to Thee be glory, honour, might, majesty, and dominion, forever and ever. Amen.

—The Clementine Liturgy.

Chapter II
SECOND CENTURY PRAYERS

Intercession

May God the Father, and the Eternal High Priest Jesus Christ, build us up in faith and truth and love, and grant to us our portion among the saints with all those who believe on our Lord Jesus Christ. We pray for all saints, for kings and rulers, for the enemies of the Cross of Christ, and for ourselves we pray that our fruit may abound and we may be made perfect in Christ Jesus our Lord. Amen.

—Polycarp.

A Dying Prayer of Polycarp, the Martyr

O Father of Thy well-beloved and blessed Son Jesus Christ, through whom we have known Thee; O God of the angels and powers and of every living creature, and of all sorts of just men which live in Thy presence, I thank Thee that Thou hast graciously vouchsafed this day and this hour to allot me a portion among the number of martyrs, among the people of Christ unto the resurrection of the everlasting life, both of body and soul, in the incorruption of the Holy Ghost; among whom I shall be received in Thy sight this day, as a fruitful and acceptable sacrifice, as Thou hast heretofore prepared, often revealed and now fulfilled, most faithful God who canst not lie. Wherefore for all things I praise Thee, I bless Thee, I glorify Thee, through the everlasting High Priest, Jesus Christ, Thy well-beloved Son, to whom with Thee and the Holy Ghost, be all glory, world without end. Amen.

—The Martyrdom of Polycarp.

A Prayer for the Privilege of Martyrdom

Ask for me this only in your prayers, that strength may be given me of the Lord that I may not be called but proved to be a Christian. Then shall I be seen to be faithful when the world no longer sees me. For nothing that appeareth is eternal. For the things which are perceived are temporal, but the things which are not seen are eternal. I write to the Churches and charge you all that willingly I die for Christ, if you prevent me not. I ask of you that your love for me be not untimely; allow me to be devoured of wild beasts, through whom I may attain unto God. I am the grain of God ground between the teeth of wild beasts, that I may be found to be the pure bread of Christ. Then indeed shall I be the true disciple of Christ when the world shall no longer behold my body. Beseech Christ on my behalf that through these means I may be found a perfect sacrifice. Not as Peter and Paul do I command you. They were apostles, I am the least of them; they were free, but I am a slave even unto this day, but, if you wish, I shall be the freedman of Jesus Christ, and in Him I shall rise again and be free. Amen.

—Ignatius.

For Soul Cleansing

O God, who hast taught us Thy divine and saving oracles, enlighten the souls of us sinners for the comprehension of the things which have been before spoken, so that we may not only be seen to be hearers of spiritual things, but also doers of good deeds, striving after guileless faith, blameless life, and pure conversation.

Release, pardon, and forgive, O God, all our voluntary and involuntary sins, such as we have committed in action and in word, knowingly and ignorantly, by night and by day, in mind and thought, forgive us all in goodness and love.

Sanctify, O Lord, our souls, bodies and spirits; examine our minds and search our consciences; take from us all evil imaginations, all impurity of thought, all inclinations to lust, all depravity of conception, all envy, pride and hypocrisy, all falsehood, deceit and irregular living, all covetousness, vain glory and sloth; all malice, anger and wrath, all remembrance of injuries, all blasphemy and every motion of flesh and spirit that is contrary to the purity of Thy Will. Amen.

—Liturgy of St. James.

To Witness for Christ

Grant, O merciful God, that as Thy holy Apostle St. James, leaving his father and all that he had, without delay, was obedient to the call of Thy son Jesus Christ, and followed Him, and at last cheerfully laid down his life for His gospel's sake, so I, forsaking all worldly and carnal affections, may be evermore ready to follow Thy holy commandments, and, whenever Thy providence shall make it my duty, may readily and cheerfully embrace death, though armed with his utmost terror, rather than forsake or deny Thee. Let me rejoice in every happy occasion of testifying the sincerity of my love, by suffering for Thy truth, and let the firm belief of those glorious eternal rewards which Thou hast prepared for them who lay down their lives for Thy sake, support me under all the cruelties of the most merciless persecutors. Grant this, O blessed Lord, who didst die for me, and didst rise again, and now sittest at the right hand of the Father, to intercede for me, and all Thy faithful disciples. Amen.

—Liturgy of St. James.

For a Pure Heart

O God, the Father of our Saviour Jesus Christ, whose name is great, whose nature is blissful, whose goodness is inexhaustible, God and Ruler of all things, who art blessed forever; before whom stand thousands and thousands, and ten thousand times ten thousand, the hosts of holy angels and archangels; sanctify, O Lord, our souls and bodies and spirits, search our consciences, and cast out of us every evil thought, every base desire, all envy and pride, all wrath and anger, and all that is contrary to Thy holy will. And grant us, O Lord, Lover of men, with a pure heart and contrite soul, to call upon Thee, our holy God and Father who art in heaven. Amen.

—Liturgy of St. James.

Sanctify Us, O Lord

God and Father of our Lord and God and Saviour Jesus Christ, the glorious Lord, the blessed essence, the bounteous goodness, the God and Sovereign of all, who art blessed to all eternity, who sittest upon the cherubim, and art glorified by the seraphim, before whom stand thousand thousands and ten thousand times ten thousand hosts of angels and archangels: Thou hast accepted the gifts, offerings, and fruits brought unto Thee as an odour of a sweet spiritual smell, and hast been pleased to sanctify them, and make them perfect, O good One, by the grace of Thy Christ, and by the presence of Thy all-holy Spirit.

Sanctify also, O Lord, our souls, and bodies, and spirits, and touch our understandings, and search our consciences, and cast out from us every evil imagination, every impure feeling, every base desire, every unbecoming thought, all envy, and vanity, and hypocrisy, all lying, all deceit, every worldly affection, all covetousness, all vainglory, all indifference, all vice, all passion, all anger, all malice, all blasphemy, every motion of the flesh and spirit that is not in accordance with Thy holy will: and count us worthy, O loving Lord, with boldness, without condemnation, in a pure heart, with a contrite spirit, with unshamed face, with sanctified lips, to dare to call upon Thee, the holy God, Father in heaven. Amen.

—Liturgy of St. James.

For Stewardship

O Lord God Almighty, who hast built Thy Church upon the foundation of the Apostles, under Christ the head corner-stone, and to this end didst endue Thy holy apostle St. Barnabas with the singular gift of the Holy Ghost; leave me not destitute, I humbly beseech Thee, of Thy manifold gifts and talents, nor yet of grace to make a right use of them always without any sordid self-ends, to Thy honour and glory; that, making a due improvement of all those gifts Thou graciously entrustest me with, I may be able to give a good account of my stewardship when the great Judge shall appear, the Lord Jesus Christ, who reigneth with Thee and the Eternal Spirit, one God, blessed forever. Amen.

—Barnabas.

Stewardship

O Lord God Almighty, who didst endue Thy holy apostle Barnabas with singular gifts of the Holy Ghost; leave us not, we beseech Thee, destitute of Thy manifold gifts, nor yet of grace to use them always to Thy honour and glory; through Jesus Christ our Lord. Amen.

—Barnabas.

Prayer to the Teacher

Be gracious, O Instructor, to us Thy children, Father, Charioteer of Israel, Son and Father, both in One, O Lord. Grant to us who obey Thy precepts, that we may perfect the likeness of the image, and with all our power know Him who is the good God and not a harsh judge. And do Thou Thyself cause that all of us who have our conversation in Thy peace, who have been translated into Thy commonwealth, having sailed tranquilly over the billows of sin, may be wafted in calm by Thy Holy Spirit, by the ineffable wisdom, by night and day to the perfect day; and giving thanks may praise, and praising thank the Alone Father and Son, Son and Father, the Son, Instructor and Teacher, with the Holy Spirit, all in One, in whom is all, for whom all is One, for whom is eternity, whose members we all are, whose glory the aeons are; for the All-good, All-lovely, All-wise, All-just One. To whom be glory both now and forever. Amen.

—Clement of Alexandria.

For Growth in Grace

Give perfection to beginners, O Father; give intelligence to the little ones; give aid to those who are running their course. Give sorrow to the negligent; give fervour of spirit to the lukewarm. Give to the perfect a good consummation; for the sake of Christ Jesus our Lord. Amen.

—Irenaeus, Old Gallican Sacramentary.

Chapter III
THIRD CENTURY PRAYERS

For Blessings

We most earnestly beseech Thee, O Thou Lover of mankind, to bless all Thy people, the flocks of Thy fold. Send down into our hearts the peace of heaven, and grant us also the peace of this life. Give life to the souls of all of us, and let no deadly sin prevail against us, or any of Thy people. Deliver all who are in trouble, for Thou art our God, who settest the captives free; who givest hope to the hopeless, and help to the helpless; who liftest up the fallen; and who art the Haven of the shipwrecked. Give Thy pity, pardon, and refreshment to every Christian soul, whether in affliction or error. Preserve us, in our pilgrimage through this life from hurt and danger, and grant that we may end our lives as Christians, well-pleasing to Thee and free from sin, and that we may have our portion and lot with all Thy saints. Amen.

—Liturgy of St. Mark.

For Light

O God of Light, Father of Life, Giver of Wisdom, Benefactor of our souls, who givest to the fainthearted who put their trust in Thee those things into which the angels desire to look; O Sovereign Lord, who hast brought us up from the depths of darkness to light, who hast given us life from death, who hast graciously bestowed upon us freedom from slavery, and who hast scattered the darkness of sin within us, do Thou now also enlighten the eyes of our understanding, and sanctify us wholly in soul, body, and spirit. Amen.

—Liturgy of St. Mark.

For the Peace of Christ's Flock

O Sovereign and Almighty Lord, bless all Thy people and all Thy flock. Give peace, Thy help, Thy love unto us, Thy servants the sheep of Thy fold, that we may be united in the bond of peace and love, one body and one spirit, in one hope of our calling, in Thy Divine and boundless love; for the sake of Jesus Christ, the great Shepherd of the sheep. Amen.

—Liturgy of St. Mark.

Before the Holy Communion

O God of light, Father of life, Author of grace, Creator of worlds, Founder of knowledge, Giver of wisdom, Treasure of holiness, Teacher of pure prayers, Benefactor of our souls, who givest to the faint-hearted who put their trust in Thee those things into which the angels desire to look: O Sovereign Lord, who hast brought us up from the depths of darkness to light, who hast given us life from death, who hast graciously bestowed upon us freedom from slavery, who hast scattered the darkness of sin within us, through the presence of Thine only-begotten Son, do Thou now also, through the visitation of Thy all-holy Spirit, enlighten the eyes of our understanding, that we may partake without fear of condemnation of this heavenly and immortal food, and sanctify us wholly in soul, body, and spirit, that with Thy holy disciples and apostles we may say this prayer to Thee: Our Father who art in heaven, hallowed be thy name. Thy kingdom come. Thy will be done in earth as it is in heaven. Give us this day our daily bread; And forgive us our trespasses, as we forgive them that trespass against us. And lead us not into temptation, but deliver us from evil; For thine is the kingdom, and the power, and the glory, for ever. Amen.

—Liturgy of St. Mark.

For Divine Strength

O mightiest King, co-eternal with the Father, who by Thy might hast vanquished hell and trodden death under foot, who hast bound the strong man, and by Thy miraculous power and the enlightening radiance of Thy unspeakable Godhead hast raised Adam from the tomb, send forth Thy invisible right hand, which is full of blessing, and bless us all.

Pity us, O Lord, and strengthen us by Thy divine power.

Take away from us the sinful and wicked influence of carnal desire.

Let the light shine into our souls, and dispell the surrounding darkness of sin.

Unite us to the all-blessed assembly that is well-pleasing unto Thee; for through Thee and with Thee, all praise, honour, power, adoration, and thanksgiving are due unto the Father and the Holy Spirit, now, henceforth, and for evermore. Amen.

—Liturgy of St. Mark.

For Blessings

O Sovereign and Almighty Lord, bless all Thy people, and all Thy flock. Give Thy peace, Thy help, Thy love unto us Thy servants, the sheep of Thy fold, that we may be united in the bond of peace and love, one body and one spirit, in one hope of our calling, in Thy divine and boundless love. Amen.

—Liturgy of St. Mark.

A Morning Prayer

We give Thee thanks—yea, more than thanks O Lord our God, for all Thy goodness at all times, and in all places, because Thou hast shielded, rescued, helped, and guided us all the days of our lives, and brought us unto this hour. We pray and beseech Thee, merciful God, to grant in Thy goodness that we may spend this day, and all the time of our lives, without sin, in fullness of joy, holiness, and reverence of Thee. But drive away from us, O Lord, all envy, all fear, and all temptations. Bestow upon us what is good and meet. Whatever sin we commit in thought, word, or deed, do Thou in Thy goodness and mercy be pleased to pardon. And lead us not into temptation, but deliver us from evil; through the grace, mercy, and love of Thine only begotten Son. Amen.

—Liturgy of St. Mark.

Thanksgiving and Prayer for Pardon

We render unto Thee our thanksgiving, O Lord our God, Father of our Lord and Saviour Jesus Christ, by all means, at all times, in all places. For that Thou hast sheltered, assisted, supported, and led us on through the time past of our life, and brought us to this hour. And we pray and beseech Thee, O God and loving Lord, grant us to pass this day, this year, and all the time of our life without sin, with all joy, health, and salvation. But all envy, all fear, all temptation, all the working of Satan, do Thou drive away, O God, from us, and from Thy holy Church. Supply us with things good and profitable. Whereinsoever we have sinned against Thee, in word, or deed, or thought, be Thou pleased in Thy love and goodness to forgive, and forsake us not, O God, who hope in Thee, neither lead us into temptation, but deliver us from the evil one and from his works; by the grace and compassion of Thine only begotten Son, Jesus Christ. Amen.

—Liturgy of St. Mark.

For Friends and Relations

Have mercy, O Lord, upon all those whom Thou hast associated with us in the bonds of friendship and kindredship, and grant that they, with us, may be so perfectly conformed to Thy Holy Will, that being cleansed from all sin, we may be found worthy, by the inspiration of Thy love, to be partakers together of the blessedness of Thy heavenly kingdom; through Jesus Christ our Lord. Amen.

—Old Gallican Sacramentary.

For Christian Graces

Grant Thy servants, O God, to be set on fire with Thy Spirit, strengthened by Thy power, illuminated by Thy splendour, filled with Thy grace, and to go forward by Thine aid. Give them, O Lord, a right faith, perfect love, true humility. Grant, O Lord, that there may be in us simple affection, brave patience, persevering obedience, perpetual peace, a pure mind, a right and honest heart, a good will, a holy conscience, spiritual strength, a life unspotted and unblamable; and after having manfully finished our course, may we be enabled happily to enter into Thy kingdom; through Jesus Christ our Lord. Amen.

—Old Gallican Sacramentary.

A Table Grace

Abba, Father, fulfill the office of Thy Name towards Thy servants; do Thou govern, protect, preserve, sanctify, guide, and console us. Let us be so enkindled with love for Thee, that we may not be despised by Thee, O most merciful Lord, most tender Father; for Jesus Christ's sake. Amen.

—Old Gallican Sacramentary.

Morning Prayer

We give thee hearty thanks for the rest of the past night, and for the gift of a new day, with its opportunities of pleasing thee. Grant that we may so pass its hours in the perfect freedom of thy service, that at eventide we may again give thanks unto thee; through Jesus Christ our Lord. Amen.

—The Eastern Church.

A Table Grace

In the evening and morning and noonday we praise Thee, we thank Thee, and pray Thee, Master of all, to direct our prayers as incense before Thee. Let not our hearts turn away to words or thoughts of wickedness, but keep us from all things that might hurt us; for to Thee, O Lord, our eyes look up, and our hope is in Thee: confound us not, O our God; for the sake of Jesus Christ our Lord. Amen.

—Eastern Church Vespers.

For Ministers

O God, great in power, unsearchable in understanding, wondrous in counsels towards the children of men, do Thou fill with the gift of Thy Holy Spirit those whom Thou dost will to undertake the degree of the priesthood that they may be worthy to stand before Thy holy altar unblamably, to announce the Gospel of Thy kingdom, to administer the Word of Thy Truth, to offer gifts and spiritual sacrifices unto Thee, and to renew Thy people in the laver of regeneration; that at the second coming of our great God and Saviour Jesus Christ, Thine only begotten Son, they may go forth to meet Him, and by the multitude of Thy mercies receive their reward; for Thy venerable and majestic Name is blessed and glorified. Amen.

—Eastern Church Liturgy.

For Illumination

Shine into our hearts, O loving Master, by the pure light of the knowledge of Thyself, and open the eyes of our mind to the contemplation of Thy teaching, and put into us the fear of Thy blessed commandments; that trampling down all that is worldly, we may follow a spiritual life, thinking and doing all things according to Thy good pleasure. For Thou art our sanctification, and our illumination, and to Thee we render glory, Father, Son, and Holy Spirit, now and ever, and unto ages of ages. Amen.

—Eastern Church Liturgy.

Chapter IV
FOURTH CENTURY PRAYERS

For Charity

O God of love, Who hast given a new commandment through Thine only begotten Son, that we should love one another, even as Thou didst love us, the unworthy and the wandering, and gavest Thy beloved Son for our life and salvation; we pray Thee, Lord, give to us, Thy servants, in all time of our life on the earth, a mind forgetful of past ill-will, a pure conscience and sincere thoughts, and a heart to love our brethren; for the sake of Jesus Christ, Thy Son, our Lord and only Saviour. Amen.

—Coptic Liturgy of St. Cyril.

For Protection

Be gracious to our prayers, O merciful God, and guard Thy people with loving protection; that they who confess Thine only begotten Son as God, born in our bodily flesh, may never be corrupted by the deceits of the devil; through the same Jesus Christ our Lord. Amen.

—Ambrose.

For Pardon

O Lord, who hast mercy upon all, take away from me my sins, and mercifully kindle in me the fire of Thy Holy Spirit. Take away from me the heart of stone, and give me a heart of flesh, a heart to love and adore Thee, a heart to delight in Thee, to follow and to enjoy Thee, for Christ's sake. Amen.

—Ambrose.

For Trust and Fuller Knowledge

Merciful Lord, the Comforter and Teacher of Thy faithful people, increase in Thy Church the desires which Thou hast given, and confirm the hearts of those who hope in Thee by enabling them to understand the depth of Thy promises, that all Thine adopted sons may even now behold, with the eyes of faith, and patiently wait for, the light which as yet Thou dost not openly manifest; through Jesus Christ our Lord. Amen.

—Ambrose.

For Salvation

O God, Who didst look on man when he had fallen down into death, and resolve to redeem him by the advent of Thine only begotten Son; grant, we beseech Thee, that they who confess His glorious Incarnation may also be admitted to the fellowship of Him their Redeemer; through the same Jesus Christ our Lord. Amen.

—Ambrose.

For Freedom From Sin

O Lord, my Saviour, in whose power it is to remit sins, I beseech Thee say unto me, "Loose thee from thy chains, come out of the bonds of thy sins"; and when Thou sayest it, loose those cords of my errors wherewith I am entangled and bound; for, though I am the most wicked of all men, and to be abhorred by reason of my continuance in sins, yet when thou commandest, I shall be free from them. Amen.

—Ambrose.

For Pardon

Lord Jesus Christ, who didst stretch out Thine hands on the Cross, and redeem us by Thy Blood, forgive me, a sinner, for none of my thoughts are hid from Thee. Pardon I ask, pardon I hope for, pardon I trust to have. Thou who art pitiful and merciful, spare and forgive me. Amen.

—Ambrose.

For Purity

O Holy Spirit of God, very God, Who didst descend upon Christ at the River Jordan, and upon the Apostles in the upper chamber, we have sinned against heaven and before Thee; purify us again, we beseech Thee, with Thy Divine fire, and have mercy upon us; for Christ's sake. Amen.

—Nerses of Clajes.

Confession of Sin

O Thou that beholdest all things, we have sinned against Thee in thought, word, and deed; blot out our transgressions, be merciful to us sinners, and grant that our names may be found written in the book of life, for the sake of Christ Jesus our Saviour. Amen.

—Nerses of Clajes.

For Protection

Lord Jesus Christ, Keeper and Preserver of all things, let Thy right hand guard us by day and by night, when we sit at home, and when we walk abroad, when we lie down and when we rise up, that we may be kept from all evil, and have mercy upon us sinners. Amen.

—Nerses of Clajes.

A Prayer for Spiritual Blessings

Most high God, our loving Father, infinite in majesty, we humbly beseech Thee for all Thy servants everywhere, that Thou wouldst give us a pure mind, perfect love, sincerity in conduct, purity in heart, strength in action, courage in distress, self-command in character. May our prayers ascend to Thy gracious ears, and Thy loving benediction descend upon us all, that we may in all things be protected under the shadow of Thy wings. Grant us pardon of our sins; perfect our work; accept our prayers; protect us by Thine own Name, O God of Jacob; send us Thy saving help from Thy holy place, and strengthen us out of Zion. Remember all Thy people everywhere, give us all the grace of devotion to Thy will; fulfill our desires with good gifts, and crown us with Thy mercy. When we serve Thee with faithful devotion, pardon our sins and correct us with Fatherly tenderness. Grant that, being delivered from all adversity, and both here and eternally justified, we may praise Thee forever and ever, saying Holy, Holy, Holy; through Jesus Christ our Lord and Saviour, Who with Thee and the Holy Ghost, liveth and reigneth, ever one God, world without end. Amen.

—Gallican Sacramentary.

For Those Gathered in Worship

O Lord God, Who hast taught us to pray all together, and hast promised to hear the united voices of two or three invoking Thy Name; hear now, O Lord, the prayers of Thy servants unto their salvation, and give us in this world knowledge of Thy Truth, and in the world to come life everlasting; for the sake of Jesus Christ our Lord. Amen.

—Armenian Liturgy.

For Right Blessings

O Lord our God, teach us, we beseech Thee, to ask Thee aright for the right blessings. Steer Thou the vessel of our life toward Thyself, Thou tranquil Haven of all storm-tossed souls. Show us the course wherein we should go. Renew a willing spirit within us. Let Thy Spirit curb our wayward senses, and guide and enable us unto that which is our true good, to keep Thy laws, and in all our works evermore to rejoice in Thy glorious and gladdening Presence. For Thine is the glory and praise from all Thy saints forever and ever. Amen.

—Basil.

For Converts in Mission Fields

Remember, O Lord, all who in heathen lands are under instruction for Holy Baptism; have mercy upon them and confirm them in the faith; remove all the remains of idolatry and superstition from their hearts, that being devoted to Thy law, Thy precepts, Thy fear, Thy truths, and Thy commandments, they may grow to a firm knowledge of the word in which they have been instructed, and may be found worthy to be made an habitation of the Holy Ghost, by the laver of regeneration, for the remission of their sins, through Jesus Christ our Lord. Amen.

—Basil.

For Light and Guidance

Eternal God, Thou uncreate and primal Light, Maker of all created things, Fountain of pity, Thou Sea of Bounty, fathomless deep of Loving-Kindness: lift Thou up the light of Thy countenance upon us! Lord, shine in our hearts, true Sun of Righteousness, and fill our souls with Thy beauty.

Teach us always to keep in mind Thy judgments, and to discourse of them, and own Thee continually as our Lord and Friend. Govern by Thy will the works of our hands; and lead us in the right way, that we may do what is well-pleasing and acceptable to Thee, that through us unworthy Thy holy name may be glorified.

To Thee alone be praise and honor and worship eternally. Amen.

—Basil.

For Two or Three

Almighty God, who hast given us grace at this time to make our common supplications unto Thee; and dost promise that when two or three are gathered together in Thy name Thou wilt grant their requests: fulfill now, O Lord, the desires and petitions of Thy servants, as may be most expedient for them, granting us in this world knowledge of Thy truth, and in the world to come, life everlasting. Amen.

—Chrysostom.

For All People

Remember, O Lord, this city wherein we dwell and every other city and country, and all the faithful who dwell in them. Remember, O Lord, all who travel by land or water, all that labour under sickness or slavery; remember them for health and safety. Remember, O Lord, those in Thy Holy Church who bring forth good fruit, are rich in good works and forget not the poor. Grant unto us all Thy mercy and loving-kindness, and grant that we may with one mouth and one heart praise and glorify Thy great and glorious name, Father, Son, and Holy Ghost, now, henceforth, and forever. Amen.

—Chrysostom.

Invocation

Lord God, of might inconceivable, of glory incomprehensible, of mercy immeasurable, of benignity ineffable; do Thou, O Master, look down upon us in Thy tender love, and show forth, towards us and those who pray with us, Thy rich mercies and compassions. Amen.

—Liturgy of St. Chrysostom.

For Refreshment

O Lord our God, under the shadow of Thy wings let us hope. Thou wilt support us, both when little, and even to gray hairs. When our strength is of Thee, it is strength; but, when our own, it is feebleness. We return unto Thee, O Lord, that from their weariness our souls may rise towards Thee, leaning on the things which Thou hast created, and passing on to Thyself, who hast wonderfully made them; for with Thee is refreshment and true strength. Amen.

—Augustine.

Adoration

O Thou Good Omnipotent, Who so carest for every one of us, as if Thou caredst for him alone; and so for all, as if all were but one! Blessed is the man who loveth Thee, and his friend in Thee, and his enemy for Thee. For he only loses none dear to him, to whom all are dear in Him who cannot be lost. And who is that but our God, the God that made heaven and earth, and filleth them, even by filling them creating them. And Thy law is truth, and truth is Thyself. I behold how some things pass away that others may replace them, but Thou dost never depart, O God, my Father supremely good, Beauty of all things beautiful. To Thee will I intrust whatsoever I have received from Thee, so shall I lose nothing. Thou madest me for Thyself, and my heart is restless until it repose in Thee. Amen.

—Augustine.

The Holy Spirit

O holy Spirit, Love of God, infuse Thy grace, and descend plentifully into my heart; enlighten the dark corners of this neglected dwelling, and scatter there Thy cheerful beams; dwell in that soul that longs to be Thy temple; water that barren soil, over-run with weeds and briars, and lost for want of cultivating, and make it fruitful with Thy dew from heaven. Oh come, Thou refreshment of them that languish and faint. Come, Thou Star and Guide of them that sail in the tempestuous sea of the world; Thou only Haven of the tossed and shipwrecked. Come, Thou Glory and Crown of the living, and only Safeguard of the dying. Come, Holy Spirit, in much mercy, and make me fit to receive Thee. Amen.

—Augustine.

For Entire Love

O Lord, my God, Light of the blind and Strength of the weak; yea, also, Light of those that see, and Strength of the strong; hearken unto my soul, and hear it crying out of the depths.

O Lord, help us to turn and seek Thee; for Thou hast not forsaken Thy creatures as we have forsaken Thee, our Creator. Let us turn and seek Thee, for we know Thou art here in our hearts, when we confess to Thee, when we cast ourselves upon Thee, and weep in Thy bosom, after all our rugged ways; and Thou dost gently wipe away our tears, and we weep the more for joy; because Thou, Lord, who madest us dost remake and comfort us.

Hear, Lord, my prayer, and grant that I may most entirely love Thee, and do Thou rescue me, O Lord, from every temptation, even unto the end. Amen.

—Augustine.

For Steadfastness

O God, the light of every heart that sees Thee, the Life of every soul that loves Thee, the strength of every mind that seeks Thee, grant me ever to continue steadfast in Thy holy love. Be Thou the joy of my heart; take it all to Thyself, and therein abide. The house of my soul is, I confess, too narrow for Thee; do thou enlarge it, that Thou mayest enter in; it is ruinous, but do Thou repair it. It has that within which must offend Thine eyes; I confess and know it; but whose help shall I implore in cleansing it, but Thine alone? To Thee, therefore, I cry urgently, begging that Thou wilt cleanse me from my secret faults, and keep Thy servant from presumptuous sins, that they never get dominion over me. Amen.

—Augustine.

For Perseverance

I know, O Lord, and do with all humility acknowledge myself an object altogether unworthy of Thy love; but sure I am, Thou art an object altogether worthy of mine. I am not good enough to serve Thee, but Thou hast a right to the best service I can pay. Do Thou then impart to me some of that excellence, and that shall supply my own want of worth. Help me to cease from sin according to Thy will, that I may be capable of doing Thee service according to my duty. Enable me so to guard and govern myself, so to begin and finish my course, that, when the race of life is run, I may sleep in peace, and rest in Thee. Be with me unto the end, that my sleep may be rest indeed, my rest perfect security, and that security a blessed eternity. Amen.

—Augustine.

For Mercy

Come, O Lord, in much mercy down into my soul, and take possession and dwell there. A homely mansion, I confess, for so glorious a Majesty, but such as Thou art fitting up for the reception of Thee, by holy and fervent desires of Thine own inspiring. Enter then, and adorn, and make it such as Thou canst inhabit, since it is the work of Thy hands. Give me Thine own self, without which, though Thou shouldst give me all that ever Thou hast made, yet could not my desires be satisfied. Let my soul ever seek Thee, and let me persist in seeking, till I have found, and am in full possession of Thee. Amen.

—Augustine.

Refuge and Peace

O Thou full of compassion, I commit and commend myself unto Thee, in whom I am, and live, and know. Be Thou the Goal of my pilgrimage, and my Rest by the way. Let my soul take refuge from the crowding turmoil of worldly thoughts beneath the shadow of Thy wings; let my heart, this sea of restless waves, find peace in Thee, O God. Thou bounteous Giver of all good gifts, give to him who is weary refreshing food; gather our distracted thoughts and powers into harmony again; and set the prisoner free. See, he stands at thy door and knocks; be it open to him, that he may enter with a free step, and be quickened by Thee. For Thou art the Well-spring of Life, the Light of eternal Brightness, wherein the just live who love Thee. Be it unto me according to Thy word. Amen.

—Augustine.

Perfect Love

Grant me, even me, my dearest Lord, to know Thee, and love Thee, and rejoice in Thee. And, if I cannot do these perfectly in this life, let me at least advance to higher degrees every day, till I can come to do them in perfection. Let the knowledge of Thee increase in me here, that it may be full hereafter. Let the love of Thee grow every day more and more here, that it may be perfect hereafter; that my joy may be great in itself, and full in Thee. I know, O God, that Thou art a God of truth, O make good Thy gracious promises to me, that my joy may be full. Amen.

—Augustine.

For Perfect Light

O Thou holy and unspeakable, Thou wonderful and mighty God, whose power and wisdom hath no end, before whom all powers tremble, at whose glance the heavens and the earth flee away, Thou art Love, Thou art my Father, and I will love and worship Thee forever and ever!

Thou hast deigned to show pity on me, and a ray from Thy light hath shone upon mine inward eye. Guide me on into the perfect light, that it may illumine me wholly, and that all darkness may flee away. Let the holy flame of Thy love so burn in my heart that it be made pure, and I may see Thee, O God; for it is the pure in heart who see Thee. Thou hast set me free; Thou hast drawn me to Thee; therefore forsake me not, but keep me always in Thy grace. Guide me, and rule me, and perfect me for Thy kingdom. Amen.

—Augustine.

For More Love

Thee, most merciful God, do I now invoke to descend into my soul, which Thou hast prepared for Thy reception by the desire which Thou hast breathed into it. Ere ever I cried to Thee, Thou, most Merciful, hadst called and sought me, that I might find Thee, and finding love Thee. Even so I sought and found Thee, Lord, and desire to love Thee. Increase my desire, and grant me what I ask. See, I love Thee, but too little; strengthen my love. When my spirit aspires to Thee, and meditates on Thine unspeakable goodness, the burden of the flesh becomes less heavy, the tumult of thought is stilled, the weight of mortality is less oppressive. Then fain would my soul find wings, that she might rise in tireless flight ever upwards to Thy glorious throne, and there be filled with the refreshing solace that belongs to the citizens of heaven. Amen.

—Augustine.

For Mercy and Grace

O God, our true Life, in whom and by whom all things live, Thou commandest us to seek Thee, and art ready to be found; Thou biddest us knock, and openest when we do so. To know Thee is life, to serve Thee is freedom, to enjoy Thee is a kingdom, to praise Thee is the joy and happiness of the soul. I praise, and bless, and adore Thee, I worship Thee, I glorify Thee, I give thanks to Thee for Thy great glory. I humbly beseech Thee to abide with me, to reign in me, to make this heart of mine a holy temple, a fit habitation for Thy Divine majesty. O Thou Maker and Preserver of all things, visible and invisible! keep, I beseech Thee, the work of Thine own hands, who trusts in Thy mercy alone for safety and protection. Guard me with the power of Thy grace, here and in all places, now and at all times, forevermore. Amen.

—Augustine.

For a Safe Voyage

Blessed are all Thy saints, my God and King, who have travelled over the tempestuous sea of mortality, and have at last made the desired port of peace and felicity. Oh, cast a gracious eye upon us who are still in our dangerous voyage. Remember and succor us in our distress, and think on them that lie exposed to the rough storms of troubles and temptations. Strengthen our weakness, that we may do valiantly in this spiritual war; help us against our own negligence and cowardice, and defend us from the treachery of our unfaithful hearts. We are exceeding frail, and indisposed to every virtuous and gallant undertaking. Grant, O Lord, that we may bring our vessel safe to shore, unto our desired haven. Amen.

—Augustine.

For Perfect Love

Look upon us, O Lord, and let all the darkness of our souls vanish before the beams of Thy brightness. Fill us with holy love, and open to us the treasures of Thy wisdom. All our desire is known unto Thee, therefore perfect what Thou hast begun, and what Thy Spirit has awakened us to ask in prayer. We seek Thy face, turn Thy face unto us and show us Thy Glory. Then shall our longing be satisfied, and our peace shall be perfect. Amen.

—Augustine.

For Obedience and Love

Thou, O Lord, who commandest me to ask, grant that I may receive; Thou hast put me upon seeking, let me be happy in finding; Thou hast bidden me knock, I pray Thee open unto me. Be graciously pleased to direct and govern all my thoughts and actions, that, for the future, I may serve Thee, and entirely devote myself to obeying Thee. Accept me, I beseech Thee, and draw me to Thyself, that I may henceforth be Thine by obedience and love, who am already all Thine own, as Thy creature. Even Thine, O Lord, who livest and reignest forever and ever. Amen.

—Augustine.

For Light

O God our Father, who dost exhort us to pray, and who dost grant what we ask, if only, when we ask, we live a better life; hear me, who am trembling in this darkness, and stretch forth Thy hand unto me; hold forth Thy light before me; recall me from my wanderings; and, Thou being my

Guide, may I be restored to myself and to Thee, through Jesus Christ. Amen.

—Augustine.

For Illumination

Late have I loved Thee, O Thou Eternal Truth and Goodness: late have I sought Thee, my Father! But Thou didst seek me, and when Thou shinedst forth upon me, then I knew Thee and learnt to love Thee. I thank Thee, O my Light, that Thou didst thus shine upon me; that Thou didst teach my soul what Thou wouldst be to me, and didst incline Thy face in pity unto me. Thou, Lord, hast become my Hope, my Comfort, my Strength, my All! In Thee doth my soul rejoice. The darkness vanished from before mine eyes, and I beheld Thee, the Son of Righteousness. When I loved darkness, I knew Thee not, but wandered on from night to night. But Thou didst lead me out of that blindness; Thou didst take me by the hand and call me to Thee, and now I can thank Thee, and Thy mighty voice which hath penetrated to my inmost heart. Amen.

—Augustine.

Obligation to Others

O Lord, our Saviour, who hast warned us that thou wilt require much of those to whom much is given; grant that we whose lot is cast in so goodly a heritage may strive together the more abundantly to extend to others what we so richly enjoy; and as we have entered into the labours of other men, so to labour that in their turn other men may enter into ours, to the fulfillment of Thy holy will; through Jesus Christ our Lord. Amen.

—Augustine.

For Refreshment

O Holy Spirit, Love of God, infuse Thy grace, and descend plentifully into my heart; enlighten the dark corners of this neglected dwelling, and scatter there Thy cheerful beams; dwell in that soul that longs to be Thy temple; water that barren soil, over-run with weeds and briars, and lost for want of cultivating, and make it fruitful with Thy dew from heaven. Oh come, Thou refreshment of them that languish and faint. Come, Thou Star and Guide of them that sail in the tempestuous sea of the world; Thou only Haven of the tossed and ship-wrecked. Come, Thou Glory and Crown of the living, and only Safeguard of the dying. Come, Holy Spirit, in much mercy, and make me fit to receive Thee. Amen.

—Augustine.

For Increased Godly Knowledge

Grant us, even us, O Lord, to know Thee, and love Thee, and rejoice in Thee. And if we cannot do these perfectly in this life, let us, at least, advance to higher degrees every day, till we can come to do them in perfection. Let the knowledge of Thee increase in us here, that it may be full hereafter. Let the love of Thee grow every day more and more here, that it may be perfect hereafter; that our joy may be great in itself and full in Thee. We know, O God, that Thou art a God of truth, O make good Thy gracious promises to us, that our joy may be full. To Thine honour and glory, Who with the Father and the Holy Ghost liveth and reigneth one God, world without end. Amen.

—Augustine.

Praise

Great art Thou, O Lord, and greatly to be praised; great is Thy power, and Thy wisdom is infinite. Thee would we praise without ceasing. Thou callest us to delight in Thy praise, for Thou hast made us for Thyself, and our hearts find no rest until we rest in Thee; Who with the Father and the Holy Ghost all glory, praise, and honour be ascribed, both now and forevermore. **Amen.**

—Augustine.

For Grace

We ask not of Thee, O Father, silver and gold, honour and glory, nor the pleasures of the world, but do Thou grant us grace to seek Thy Kingdom and Thy righteousness, and do Thou add unto us things necessary for the body and for this life. Behold, O Lord, our desire; may it be pleasing in Thy sight. We present our petition unto Thee through our Lord Jesus Christ, Who is at Thy right hand, our mediator and Advocate, through Whom Thou soughtest us that we might seek Thee; Thy Word, through Whom Thou madest us and all things; Thy only begotten Son, through Whom Thou callest us to adoption, Who intercedeth with Thee for us, and in Whom are hid all the treasures of wisdom and knowledge; to Him, with Thyself and the Holy Spirit, be all honour, praise, and glory, now and forever. **Amen.**

—Augustine.

For Peace

O Lord God, grant Thy peace to us, for Thou hast supplied us with all things—the peace of rest, the peace of the Sabbath, which hath no evening; through Jesus Christ our Lord. **Amen.**

—Augustine.

Evening Prayer

Watch Thou, dear Lord, with those who wake, or watch, or weep to night, and give Thine angels charge over those who sleep. Tend Thy sick ones, O Lord Christ. Rest Thy weary ones. Bless Thy dying ones. Soothe Thy suffering ones. Pity Thine afflicted ones. Shield Thy joyous ones. And all, for Thy Love's sake. Amen.

—Augustine.

For Perfection

Hear, Lord, my prayer; let not my soul faint under Thy discipline, nor let me faint in confessing unto Thee all Thy mercies whereby Thou hast drawn me out of all my most evil ways, that Thou mightest become a delight to me above all the allurements which I once pursued; that I may most entirely love Thee, and clasp Thy hand with all my affections, and Thou mayest yet rescue me from every temptation, even unto the end. For lo, O Lord, my King and my God, for Thy service be whatever useful thing my childhood learned; for Thy service that I speak, write, read, reckon. For Thou didst grant me Thy discipline while I was learning vanities; and my sin of delighting in those vanities Thou hast forgiven. In them, indeed, I learnt many a useful word, but these may as well be learned in things not vain; and that is the safe path for the steps of youth. Amen.

—Augustine.

For Light

O let the Light, the Truth, the Light of my heart, not mine own darkness, speak unto me. I fell off into that, and became darkened; but even thence, even thence I loved Thee. I went astray, and remembered Thee. I heard Thy voice behind me, calling me to return, and scarcely heard it, through the tumultuousness of the enemies of peace. And now, behold, I return in distress and panting after Thy fountain. Let no man forbid me! of this will I drink, and so live. Let me not be mine own life; from myself I lived ill, death was I to myself; and I revive in Thee. Do Thou speak unto me, do Thou discourse unto me. I have believed Thy Books, and their words be most full of mystery. Amen.

—Augustine.

Communion with God

O how shall I call upon God, my God and Lord, since, when I call for Him, I shall be calling Him into myself? And what room is there within me, whither my God can come into me? Whither can God come into me, God who made heaven and earth? Is there, indeed, O Lord my God, aught in me that can contain Thee? Do, then, heaven and earth, which Thou hast made, and wherein Thou hast made me, contain Thee? Or, because nothing which exists could exist without Thee, doth therefore whatever exists contain Thee? Since, then, I too exist, why do I seek that Thou shouldest enter into me, who were not, wert Thou not in me? Why? Because I am not gone down in hell, and yet Thou art there also. For if I go down into hell, Thou art there. I could not be, then, O my God, could not be at all, wert Thou not in me; or rather, unless I were in Thee, of whom are all things, by whom are all things, in whom are all things! Even so, Lord, even so. Whither do I call Thee, since I am in Thee? Or whence canst Thou enter into me? For whither can I go beyond heaven and earth, that thence my God should come into me, who hath said, "I fill the heaven and the earth"?

O God, the vessels which Thou fillest uphold Thee not, since, though they were broken, Thou wert not poured out, on us, Thou art not cast down, but Thou upliftest us; Thou art not dissipated, but Thou gatherest us.... Amen.

—Augustine.

Rest in Thee

O Lord God, give peace unto us (for Thou hast given us all things): the peace of rest, the peace of the Sabbath, which hath no evening: Yea, give us rest in Thee, the Sabbath of eternal life. For Thou shalt rest in us, as now Thou workest in us; and Thy rest shall be through us, as Thy works are through us. Amen.

—Augustine.

For Light

O Lord, who art the Light, the Way, the Truth, the Life; in whom there is no darkness, error, vanity, or death—the Light without which there is darkness; the Way without which there is wandering; the Truth without which there is error; the life without which there is Death; say, Lord, let there be Light, and I shall see Light, and eschew Darkness; I shall see the way and avoid wandering; I shall see the Truth and shun error; I shall see Life and escape Death: Illuminate, O illuminate my blind soul which sitteth in darkness and the shadow of Death; and direct my feet into the way of peace. Amen.

—Augustine.

A Morning Prayer

O God, who art faithful and true, who "hast mercy on thousands and ten thousands of them that love Thee," the lover of the humble, and the protector of the needy, of whom all things stand in need, for all things are subject to Thee; look down upon this Thy people, who bow down their heads to Thee, and bless them with spiritual blessing. "Keep them as the apple of an eye," preserve them in piety and righteousness, and vouchsafe them eternal life in Christ Jesus Thy beloved Son, with whom glory, honour, and worship be to Thee and to the Holy Spirit, now and always, and forever and ever. Amen.

—Apostolic Constitutions.

The Thanksgiving for the Morning

O God, the God of spirits and of all flesh, who art beyond compare, and standest in need of nothing, who hast given the sun to have rule over the day, and the moon and the stars to have rule over the night, do Thou now also look down upon us with gracious eyes, and receive our morning thanksgivings, and have mercy upon us; for we have not "spread out our hands unto a strange God;" for there is not among us any new God, but Thou, the eternal God, who art without end, who hast given us our being through Christ, and given us our well-being through Him. Do Thou vouchsafe us also, through Him, eternal life; with whom glory, and honour, and worship be to Thee and to the Holy Spirit forever. Amen.

—Apostolic Constitutions.

A Morning Prayer

"Glory be to God in the highest, and upon earth peace, good-will among men." We praise Thee, we sing hymns to Thee, we bless Thee, we glorify Thee, we worship Thee by Thy great High Priest; Thee who art the true God, who art the One Unbegotten, the only inaccessible Being. For Thy great glory, O Lord and heavenly King, O God the Father Almighty, O

Lord God, the Father of Christ the immaculate Lamb, who taketh away the sin of the world, receive our prayer, Thou that sittest upon the cherubim. For Thou only art holy, Thou only art the Lord Jesus, the Christ of the God of all created nature, and our King, by whom glory, honour, and worship be to Thee. Amen.

—Apostolic Constitutions.

An Evening Prayer

Save us, O God, and raise us up by Thy Christ. Let us stand up, and beg for the mercies of the Lord, and His compassions, for the angel of peace, for what things are good and profitable, for a Christian departure out of this life, an evening and a night of peace, and free from sin; and let us beg that the whole course of our life may be unblamable. Let us dedicate ourselves and one another to the living God through His Christ. Amen.

—Apostolic Constitutions.

An Evening Prayer

O God, who art without beginning and without end, the Maker of the whole world by Christ, and the Provider for it, but before all His God and Father, the Lord of the Spirit, and the King of intelligible and sensible beings; who hast made the day for the works of light, and the night for the refreshment of our infirmity,—for "the day is Thine, the night also is Thine: Thou hast prepared the light and the sun,"—do Thou now, O Lord, Thou lover of mankind, and Fountain of all good, mercifully accept of this our evening thanksgiving. Thou who hast brought us through the length of the day, and hast brought us to the beginnings of the night, preserve us by Thy Christ, afford us a peaceable evening, and a night free from sin, and vouchsafe us everlasting life by Thy Christ, through whom glory, honour, and worship be to Thee in the Holy Spirit forever. Amen.

—Apostolic Constitutions.

An Evening Prayer

"Ye children, praise the Lord: Praise the name of the Lord." We praise Thee, we sing hymns to Thee, we bless Thee for Thy great glory, O Lord our King, the Father of Christ the immaculate Lamb, who taketh away the sin of the world. Praise becomes Thee, hymns become Thee, glory becomes Thee, the God and Father, through the Son, in the most holy Spirit, forever and ever. Amen.

—Apostolic Constitutions.

Table Grace

Thou art blessed, O Lord, who nourishest me from my youth, who givest food to all flesh. Fill our hearts with joy and gladness, that having always what is sufficient for us, we may abound to every good work, in Christ Jesus our Lord, through whom glory, honour, and power be to Thee forever. Amen.

—Apostolic Constitutions.

For the First-Fruits

We give thanks to Thee, O Lord Almighty, the Creator of the whole world, and its Preserver, through Thy only begotten Son Jesus Christ our Lord, for the first-fruits which are offered to Thee, not in such a manner as we ought, but as we are able. For what man is there that can worthily give Thee thanks for those things Thou hast given them to partake of? The God of Abraham, and of Isaac, and of Jacob, and of all the saints, who madest all things fruitful by Thy word, and didst command the earth to bring forth various fruits for our rejoicing and our food; who hast given to the duller and more sheepish sort of creatures juices—herbs to them that feed on herbs, and to some flesh, to others seeds, but to us corn, as advantageous and proper food, and many other things—some for our necessities, some for our health, and some for our pleasure. On all these accounts, therefore, art Thou worthy of exalted hymns of praise for Thy beneficence by Christ, through whom glory, honour, and worship be to Thee, in the Holy Spirit, forever. Amen.

—Apostolic Constitutions.

Thanks For Thy Mercies

We give Thee thanks for all things, O Lord Almighty, that Thou hast not taken away Thy mercies and Thy compassions from us; but in every succeeding generation Thou dost save, and deliver, and assist, and protect: for Thou didst assist in the days of Enos and Enoch, in the days of Moses and Joshua, in the days of the judges, in the days of Samuel and of Elijah and of the prophets, in the days of David and of the kings, in the days of Esther and Mordecai, and in our days hast Thou assisted us by Thy great High Priest, Jesus Christ Thy Son. For He has delivered us from the sword, and hath freed us from famine, and sustained us; has delivered us from sickness, has preserved us from an evil tongue. For all which things do we give Thee thanks through Christ, who has given us an articulate voice to confess withal, and added to it a suitable tongue as an instrument to modulate withal, and a proper taste, and a suitable touch, and a sight for contemplation, and the hearing of sounds, and the smelling of vapours, and hands for work, and feet for walking. Thou hast instructed [man] by Thy laws, improved him by Thy statutes; and when Thou bringest on a dissolution for a while, Thou hast promised a resurrection. Wherefore what life is sufficient, what length of ages will be long enough, for men to be thankful? To do it worthily it is impossible, but to do it according to our ability is just and right. Thou hast delivered us from error and ignorance; Thou hast sent Christ among men as a man, being the only begotten God; Thou hast made the Comforter to inhabit among us; Thou hast set angels over us; Thou hast put the devil to shame; Thou hast brought us into being when we were not; Thou takest care of us when made; Thou measurest out life to us; Thou affordest us food; Thou hast promised repentance. Glory and worship be to Thee for all these things, through Jesus Christ, now and ever, and through all ages. Amen.

—Adapted: Apostolic Constitutions.

For The Holy Spirit

O God Almighty, the Father of Thy Christ, Thy only begotten Son, give me a body undefiled, a heart pure, a mind watchful, an unerring knowledge, the influence of the Holy Ghost for the obtaining and assured enjoying of the truth, through Thy Christ, by whom glory be to Thee, in the Holy Spirit, for ever. Amen.

—Apostolic Constitutions.

For the Faithful

O Lord Almighty, the Most High, who dwellest on high, the Holy One, that restest among the saints, without beginning, the Only Potentate, who hast given to us by Christ the preaching of knowledge, to the acknowledgment of Thy glory and of Thy name, which He has made known to us, for our comprehension, do Thou now also look down through Him upon this Thy flock, and deliver it from all ignorance and wicked practice, and grant that we may fear Thee in earnest, and love Thee with affection, and have a due reverence of Thy glory. Be gracious and merciful to them, and hearken to them when they pray unto Thee; and keep them, that they may be unmoveable, unblameable, and unreprovable, that they may be holy in body and spirit, not having spot or wrinkle, or any such thing; but that they may be complete, and none of them may be defective or imperfect. O our support, our powerful God, who dost not accept persons, be Thou the assister of this Thy people, which Thou hast redeemed with the precious blood of Thy Christ; be Thou their protector, aider, provider, and guardian, their strong wall of defence, their bulwark and security. For "none can snatch out of Thy hand:" for there is no other God like Thee; for on Thee is our reliance. "Sanctify them by Thy truth: for Thy word is truth." **Amen.**

—Apostolic Constitutions.

On the Lord's Day

O Lord Almighty, Thou hast created the world by Christ, and hast appointed the Sabbath in memory thereof, because that on that day Thou hast made us rest from our works, for the meditation upon Thy laws. Thou hast also appointed festivals for the rejoicing of our souls, that we might come into the remembrance of that wisdom which was created by Thee; how He submitted to be made of a woman on our account; He appeared in life, and demonstrated Himself in His baptism; how he that appeared is both God and man; He suffered for us by Thy permission, and died, and rose again by Thy power: on which account we solemnly assemble to celebrate the feast of the resurrection on the Lord's day, and rejoice on account of Him who has conquered death, and hast brought life and immortality to light. **Amen.**

—Apostolic Constitutions.

For the Holy Communion

We thank Thee, our Father, for that life which Thou hast made known to us by Jesus Thy Son, by whom madest all things, and takest care of the whole world; whom Thou hast sent to become man for our salvation; whom Thou hast permitted to suffer and to die; whom Thou hast raised up, and been pleased to glorify, and hast set Him down on Thy right hand; by whom Thou hast promised us the resurrection of the dead. Do Thou, O Lord Almighty, everlasting God, so gather together Thy Church from the ends of the earth into Thy kingdom, as this corn was once scattered, and is now become one loaf. We also, our Father, thank Thee for the precious blood of Jesus Christ, which was shed for us, and for His precious body, whereof we celebrate this representation, as Himself appointed us, "to show forth His death." For through Him glory is to be given to Thee for ever. Amen.

—Apostolic Constitutions.

After the Holy Communion

We thank Thee, O God and Father of Jesus our Saviour, for Thy holy name, which Thou hast made to inhabit among us; and that knowledge, faith, love, and immortality which Thou hast given us through Thy Son Jesus. Thou, O Almighty Lord, the God of the universe, hast created the world, and the things that are therein by Him; and hast planted a law in our souls, and beforehand didst prepare things for the convenience of men. O God of our holy and blameless fathers, Abraham, and Isaac, and Jacob, Thy faithful servants; Thou, O God, who art powerful, faithful and true, and without deceit in Thy promises; who didst send upon earth Jesus Thy Christ to live with men, as a man, when He was God the Word, and man, to take away error by the roots: do Thou even now, through Him, be mindful of this Thy holy Church, which Thou hast purchased with the precious blood of Thy Christ, and deliver it from all evil, and perfect it in Thy love and Thy truth, and gather us all together into Thy kingdom which Thou hast prepared. Let this Thy kingdom come. Amen.

—Apostolic Constitutions.

Chapter V
FIFTH CENTURY PRAYERS

For Thy Peace

Make Thy tranquillity, O Lord, to dwell amongst us, and Thy peace to abide in our hearts. May our voices proclaim Thy truth, and may Thy cross be the guardian of our souls. Account us worthy, O Lord, with boldness which is of Thee, to offer unto Thee of Thy grace a pure and holy prayer through Jesus Christ our Lord. Amen.

—Liturgy of The Nestorians.

Intercession

Almighty God, we beseech Thee to hear our prayers for all who sin against Thee, or neglect to serve Thee, all who forget Thee, all who leave Thee out of their lives. O Lord, have mercy upon them; bestow upon us all true repentance and an earnest longing for Thyself. Vouchsafe, we beseech Thee, O Lord, to strengthen and confirm all Thy faithful people, and to lift up the light of Thy face upon them, giving them continually heavenly desires; through Jesus Christ our Lord. Amen.

—An Ancient Collect.

An Evening Thanksgiving

Accept, we beseech Thee, our evening thanksgiving, O Thou Fountain of all good, who hast led us in safety through the length of the day; Who daily blessest us with so many temporal mercies, and hast given us the hope of resurrection to eternal life; through Jesus Christ our Lord. Amen.

—An Ancient Collect.

For Blessing

Bless all who worship Thee, from the rising of the sun unto the going down of the same. Of Thy goodness, give us; with Thy love, inspire us; by Thy spirit guide us; by Thy power, protect us; in Thy mercy, receive us now and always. Amen.

—An Ancient Collect.

For Communicants

Hear us, O merciful Father, we most humbly beseech Thee, and grant to all communicants of Thy Church this day, true repentance and living faith. And we pray that all those who shall from time to time receive Thy creatures of bread and wine, according to Thy Son our Saviour Jesus Christ's Holy Institution, in remembrance of His Death and Passion, may be partakers of His most blessed Body and Blood; to Whom with Thee and the Holy Ghost, be all honour and glory, world without end. Amen.

—An Ancient Liturgy.

For Right Living

Grant to us, Lord, we beseech thee, the spirit to think and do always such things as be rightful; that we, who cannot do anything that is good without thee, may by thee be enabled to live according to thy will; through Jesus Christ our Lord. Amen.

—Leonine Sacramentary.

For Heavenly-Mindedness

Grant us, O Lord, not to mind earthly things, but to love things heavenly; and even now, while we are placed among things that are passing away, to cleave to those that shall abide; through Jesus Christ our Lord. **Amen.**

—Leonine Sacramentary.

For Love of God's Law

We beseech Thee, O Lord, be gracious to Thy people, that we, leaving day by day the things which displease Thee, may be more and more filled with the love of Thy commandments, and being supported by Thy comfort in this present life, may advance to the full enjoyment of life immortal; through Jesus Christ our Lord. **Amen.**

—Leonine Sacramentary.

For Christ's Presence

Be present, O Lord, to our supplications; that as we trust that the Saviour of mankind is seated with Thee in Thy Majesty, so we may feel that, according to His promise, He abideth with us unto the end of the world; through the same Jesus Christ our Lord. **Amen.**

—Leonine Sacramentary.

For National Peace

We beseech Thee, O Lord, be gracious to our times; that both national quietness and Christian devotion may be duly maintained by Thy bounty; through Jesus Christ our Lord. Amen.

—Leonine Sacramentary.

For Light and Guidance

We beseech Thee, O Lord, let our hearts be graciously enlightened by Thy holy radiance, that we may serve Thee without fear in holiness and righteousness all the days of our life; that so we may survive the storms of this world, and with Thee for our Pilot attain the haven of eternal brightness; through Thy mercy, O blessed Lord, Who dost live and govern all things, world without end. Amen.

—Leonine Sacramentary.

For Acceptable Petitions

Let the prayers of Thy children, O Lord, come up to the ears of Thy mercy; and that we may obtain what we ask, make us ever to ask what pleaseth Thee; through Jesus Christ our Lord. Amen.

—Leonine Sacramentary.

For Peace

Mercifully receive, O Lord, the prayers of Thy people, that all adversities and errors may be destroyed, and they may serve Thee in quiet freedom, and give Thy peace in our times; through Jesus Christ our Lord. Amen.

—Leonine Sacramentary.

For Those Who Minister

O God, Whose ways are all mercy and truth, carry on Thy gracious work, and bestow, by Thy benefits, what human frailty cannot attain; that they who attend upon the heavenly mysteries may be grounded in perfect faith, and shine forth conspicuous by the purity of their souls; through Jesus Christ our Lord. Amen.

—Leonine Sacramentary.

For Good Use of Blessings

Almighty and everlasting God, who healest us by chastening, and preservest us by pardoning; grant unto Thy suppliants, that we may both rejoice in the comfort of the tranquillity which we desired, and also use the gift of Thy peace for the effectual amendment of our lives; through Jesus Christ our Lord. Amen.

—Leonine Sacramentary.

For Cleansing

Cleanse us, O Lord, from our secret faults, and mercifully absolve us from our presumptuous sins, that we may receive Thy holy things with a pure mind; through Jesus Christ our Lord. Amen.

—Leonine Sacramentary.

For Grace and Protection

Incline mercifully Thine ear, O Lord, to these our prayers, and fill our hearts with Thy grace, that loving Thee with an unfeigned love we may evermore be defended under Thy most gracious protection, and be accepted in all our prayers and services; through Jesus Christ our Lord. Amen.

—An Ancient Collect.

A Morning Prayer

Almighty God, who fillest all things with Thy presence, we meekly beseech thee, of thy great love, to keep us near unto thee this day; grant that in all our ways and doings we may remember that thou seest us, and may always have grace to know and perceive what things thou wouldst have us to do, and strength to fulfil the same; through Jesus Christ our Lord. Amen.

—An Ancient Collect.

For the Sorrowing

Almighty and everlasting God, the Comfort of the sad, the Strength of sufferers, let the prayers of those that cry out of any tribulation come unto Thee, that all may rejoice to find that Thy mercy is present with them in their afflictions; through Jesus Christ our Lord. Amen.

—Gelasian Sacramentary.

For Protection

O Lord, give ear unto our prayers and dispose the way of Thy servants in safety under Thy protection, that amid all the changes of this our pilgrimage, we may ever be guarded by Thine Almighty aid; through Jesus Christ our Lord. Amen.

—Gelasian Sacramentary.

For Love of God

O God, Who hast prepared for them that love Thee such good things as pass man's understanding; pour into our hearts such love towards Thee, that we, loving Thee above all things, may obtain Thy promises, which exceed all that we can desire; through Jesus Christ our Lord. Amen.

—Gelasian Sacramentary.

For God's Guidance

O Lord, from Whom all good things do come; grant to us, Thy humble servants, that by Thy holy inspiration we may think those things that be good, and by Thy merciful guiding may perform the same, through Jesus Christ our Lord. Amen.

—Gelasian Sacramentary.

For Refreshment

We beseech Thee, Almighty God, to behold our prayers, and to pour out upon us Thy loving tenderness; that we who are afflicted by reason of our sins, may be refreshed by the coming of our Saviour; through the same Jesus Christ our Lord. Amen.

—Gelasian Sacramentary.

For Light

Incline, O Lord, Thy merciful ears, and illuminate the darkness of our hearts by the light of Thy visitation; through Jesus Christ our Lord. Amen.

—Gelasian Sacramentary.

For True Joy

Almighty God, who alone canst order the unruly wills and affections of sinful men; grant unto thy people that they may love the thing which thou commandest, and desire that which thou dost promise; that so, among the sundry and manifold changes of the world, our hearts may surely there be fixed, where true joys are to be found; through Jesus Christ our Lord. Amen.

—Gelasian Sacramentary.

For Goodness

Lord of all Power and Might, who art the Author and Giver of all good things; graft in our hearts the love of thy name, increase in us true religion, nourish us with all goodness, and of thy great mercy keep us in the same; through Jesus Christ our Lord. Amen.

—Gelasian Sacramentary.

On a Fast-Day

O God, who in Thy deep counsel and foresight for mankind hast appointed holy fasts, whereby the hearts of the weak might receive salutary healing, do Thou purify our souls and bodies, O Saviour of body and soul, O loving Bestower of eternal happiness! through Jesus Christ our Lord. Amen.

—Gelasian Sacramentary.

A Prayer for Divine Help

Stretch forth, O Lord, Thy mercy over all Thy servants everywhere, even the right hand of heavenly help, that they may seek Thee with their whole heart, and obtain what they rightly ask for; through Jesus Christ our Lord. Amen.

—Gelasian Sacramentary.

Praise

O God of hope, the true Light of faithful souls and perfect Brightness of the Blessed, Who art verily the Light of the world, grant that our hearts may both render Thee a worthy prayer, and always glorify Thee with the offering of praises; through Jesus Christ our Lord. **Amen.**

—Gelasian Sacramentary.

For Light

Shed forth, O Lord, we pray Thee, Thy light into our hearts, that we may perceive the light of Thy commandments, and walking in Thy way may fall into no error; through Jesus Christ our Lord. **Amen.**

—Gelasian Sacramentary.

For the Holy Spirit

We beseech Thee, Almighty God, let our souls enjoy this their desire, to be enkindled by Thy Spirit, that being filled, as lamps, by the Divine gift, we may shine like blazing lights before the Presence of Thy Son Christ at His coming; through the same Jesus Christ our Lord. **Amen.**

—Gelasian Sacramentary.

For Thy Will

Into thy hands, O Lord, we commit ourselves this day. Give to each of us a watchful, humble, and a diligent spirit, that we may seek in all things to know thy will, and when we know it may perform it perfectly and gladly, to the honor and glory of thy Name; through Jesus Christ our Lord. **Amen.**

—Gelasian Sacramentary.

For Forgiveness

We beseech Thee, Almighty God, to receive with Fatherly tenderness Thy people fleeing from Thine anger to Thyself; that they who dread the scourge that comes from Thy Majesty may be enabled to rejoice in Thy forgiveness; through Jesus Christ our Lord. **Amen.**

—Gelasian Sacramentary.

To Serve Thee

O God, who art the light of the minds that know thee, the life of the souls that love thee, the strength of the thoughts that seek thee, help us so to know thee that we may truly love thee, so to love thee that we may fully serve thee, whose service is perfect freedom; through Jesus Christ our Lord. **Amen.**

—Gelasian Sacramentary.

For Thy Presence

Into Thy hands, O God, we commend ourselves and all who are dear to us this day. Let the gift of Thy special Presence be with us even to its close. Grant us never to lose sight of Thee all the day long, but to worship and pray to Thee, that at eventide we may again give thanks unto Thee; through Jesus Christ our Lord. **Amen.**

—Gelasian Sacramentary.

General Petitions

O God, from whom all holy desires, all good counsels, and all just works do proceed; give unto thy servants that peace which the world cannot give; that our hearts may be set to obey thy commandments, and also that by thee, we, being defended from the fear of our enemies, may pass our time in rest and quietness; through the merits of Jesus Christ our Saviour. Amen.

—Gelasian Sacramentary.

For Christ's Servants Everywhere

O God of infinite mercy and boundless majesty, Whom no distance can part from those for whom Thou carest, be present to Thy servants who everywhere confide in Thee, and through all the way in which they are to go be pleased to be their Guide and Companion. May no adversity harm them, no difficulty oppose them; may all things turn out happily and prosperously for them; that by the aid of Thy right hand, whatsoever they have asked for with reasonable desire they may speedily find brought to good effect; through Jesus Christ our Lord. Amen.

—Gelasian Sacramentary.

For the Spread of Christianity

O God of unchangeable power and eternal light, look favourably on Thy whole Church, that wonderful and sacred mystery; and by the tranquil operation of Thy perpetual providence, carry out the work of man's salvation; let the whole world feel and see that things which were cast down are being raised up, that those which had grown old are being made new, and that all things are returning to perfection; through Him from Whom they took their origin, even Jesus Christ Thy Son our Lord. Amen.

—Gelasian Sacramentary.

For Grace

O our Lord and God, look not on the multitude of our sins, and let not Thy dignity be turned away on account of the heinousness of our iniquities; but through Thine unspeakable grace sanctify this sacrifice of Thine, and grant through it power and capability, so that Thou mayest forget our many sins, and be merciful when Thou shalt appear at the end of time, in the man whom Thou hast assumed from among us, and we may find before Thee grace and mercy, and be rendered worthy to praise Thee with spiritual assemblies. Amen.

—Liturgy of the Blessed Apostles.

For Enlightenment

Enlighten, O our Lord and God, the movements of our meditations to hear and understand the sweet listenings to Thy life-giving and divine commands; and grant unto us through Thy grace and mercy to gather from them the assurance of love, and hope, and salvation suitable to soul and body, and we shall sing to Thee everlasting glory without ceasing and always, O Lord of all. Amen.

—Liturgy of the Blessed Apostles.

On Prayer
and
The Contemplative Life

By *St. Thomas Aquinas*
Translator: *Hugh Pope*

(Originally published in 1914)

TABLE OF CONTENTS

PREFACE

INTRODUCTION
Footnotes

QUESTION 1 - OF THE VIRTUE OF RELIGION
Footnotes

QUESTION 2 - OF DEVOTION
Footnotes

QUESTION 3 - OF PRAYER
Footnotes

QUESTION 4 - OF THE PRAYERS OF THE SAINTS WHO ARE IN HEAVEN
Footnotes

QUESTION 5 - OF THE DIVISION OF LIFE INTO THE ACTIVE AND THE CONTEMPLATIVE
Footnotes

QUESTION 6 - OF THE CONTEMPLATIVE LIFE
Footnotes

QUESTION 7 - OF THE ACTIVE LIFE
Footnotes

QUESTION 8 - OF THE COMPARISON BETWEEN THE ACTIVE AND THE CONTEMPLATIVE LIFE
Footnotes

QUESTION 9 - ON THE RELIGIOUS STATE
Footnotes

PREFACE

The present generation in the fervour of its repentance is like to cast off too much. So many false principles and hasty deductions have been offered to its parents and grandparents in the name of science that it is becoming unduly suspicious of the scientific method.

A century ago men's minds were sick unto death from too much science and too little mysticism. To-day the danger is that even the drawing-rooms are scented with a mysticism that anathematizes science.

At no time since the days of S. Thomas was the saint's scientific method more lacking. Everywhere there is need for a mystic doctrine, which in itself is neither hypnotism nor hysteria, and in its expression is neither superlative nor apostrophic, lest the hungered minds of men die of surfeit following on starvation.

The message and method of S. Thomas are part of that strange rigidity of the thirteenth century which is one of the startling paradoxes of the ages of faith. It is surely a consolation that these ages of a faith which moved mountains, or at least essayed to remove the Turk, were minded to express their beliefs in the coat of mail of human reason! The giants of those days, who in the sphere of literature were rediscovering verse and inventing rhyme, and who in every sphere of knowledge were bringing forth the sixteenth and nineteenth centuries, were not so blinded by the white light of vision as to disown the Greeks. They made the Ethics of Aristotle the four-square walls of the city of God; they expressed the mysteries of the Undivided Three in terms of the Syllogism. Thus they refused to cut themselves off from the aristocracy of human genius. They laid hands—but not violent hands—on the heritage of the ages. No philosophers have ever equalled their bold and lowly-minded profession of faith in the solidarity of human reason. For this cause S. Thomas, who is their spokesman, has now become an absolute necessity of thought. Unless the great Dumb Ox is given a hearing, our mysticism will fill, not the churches, but the asylums and the little self-authorized Bethels where every man is his own precursor and messiah.

That S. Thomas is to be accepted as a master of mysticism may be judged from the following facts in the life of a mystic of the mystics, S. John of the Cross:

"It has been recorded that during his studies he particularly relished psychology; this is amply borne out by his writings. S. John was not what one could term a scholar. He was, however, intimately acquainted with the Summa of S. Thomas Aquinas, as almost every page of his works proves.... He does not seem to have ever applied himself to the study of the Fathers.... As has already been stated, the whole work (The Ascent of Mount Carmel) is based upon the view S. Thomas Aquinas takes of the essence and operations of the senses and of the faculties of the soul, and upon his treatise on the virtues."[1]

S. Thomas hardly needs an imprimatur after six centuries of full trust. But in the hard matters of mysticism, which he has treated as a scholar should, it is reassuring to know that he has the approval, not only of the scholars, but of the mystics.

VINCENT McNABB, O.P.

INTRODUCTION

The pages which follow call for little introduction. S. Thomas has left us no formal treatise on Mystical Theology, though his teachings on this subject have been collected from his various works and combined to form such a treatise. Especially noteworthy is the work of the Spanish Dominican Valgornera.[2] No such synthesis has been attempted here. We have simply taken from the Summa Theologica the treatises on Religion, on Devotion, Prayer, and the Contemplative Life, and presented them in an English dress. When occasion offered we have added to each portion appropriate passages from S. Augustine, S. Thomas's master, and more rarely from the Commentary on the Summa by the illustrious Cardinal Cajetan.

And we have been led to do this for several reasons. The Mystical life is the life of union with God, and it is based essentially on Prayer and Contemplation. But prayer and contemplation, though simple in themselves, are yet fraught with difficulties and dangers unless we be wisely guided. And as Father Faber shrewdly says: when we ask for instruction in these things, let us by all means make appeal to those whose names begin with S—let us, in other words, go to God's Saints. And the reason is simple: these Saints are no mere idle sign-posts who point the way but stand still themselves; they themselves have been where they would have us go; they speak from no mere theoretical knowledge; they themselves have tasted and seen that the Lord is sweet!

Further, it would have been easy to cull from S. Thomas's writings the salient points of his teaching on these points, and to have presented them in an attractive form. But had we done so the teachings of the Saint would have lost much of their force, and readers might well have doubted at times whether they really had before them the mind of S. Thomas or that of the translator. It is preferable to read the Bible than what men have said about the Bible. Unfortunately, it is the fashion nowadays to consider S. Thomas's writings "out of date"! If the perusal of these pages shall have induced some few at least to go to the original and study it for themselves they will have more than fulfilled the translator's desires.

Another reason which has weighed much with the translator and encouraged him to undertake this task has been the suddenly awakened interest in Mysticism and Mystical studies during the last decade. It has become the fashion to talk about Mysticism, even to pose as Mystics, and—need it be said?—those who talk the most on such subjects are those who know the least. For those who have entered into the secret of the King are ever the most reticent on such matters. At the same time we may welcome this recent development, if only as a set-off against the Spiritualism and occultism which have played such havoc with souls during a space of over fifty years. The human soul, "naturally Christian," as Tertullian would say, is also naturally Divine in the sense that, as S. Augustine so often insists, no rest is possible for it save in God. Now those who are familiar with the Summa Theologica are aware that Union with God is its keynote, or rather is the dominant note which rings out clear again and again with its ever-repeated Sursum Corda! It is this that gives such special value to the treatises here presented on Prayer and the Contemplative Life. They flow from the pen of one who was literally steeped in God and Divine things, and who is speaking to us of things which he had himself tasted and seen. It is this that gives such simplicity and charm to the whole of his teaching. He is not experimenting; he is not speaking of theories; he is portraying to us what was his everyday life.

Perhaps one of the commonest errors regarding the Spiritual life is the confusion between the ordinary and the extraordinary ways of God. For how many does not the Contemplative Life mean the life of ecstasy and vision with which we are familiar in the lives of the Saints? For S. Thomas, on the contrary, the Contemplative Life is but the natural life of a man who is serving God and who devotes a certain portion of his time to the study and contemplation of Divine things. Ecstasy and vision he treats of in another place. They occupy a sphere apart. They belong to God's extraordinary dealings with favoured souls, and while they presuppose prayer and contemplation on the part of those so visited they themselves form no integral part of the Contemplative Life; indeed, they are the exception. Hence in these pages we shall find nought touching Supernatural manifestations, such as visions, ecstasies, and revelations; but we shall find what is of far greater use to us—a Catechism on Devotion, Prayer, and Contemplation.

The main features of the Life of S. Thomas of Aquin are known to most of those who are likely to read this book. His life at first sight seems of such an even tenor that there is but little to record. Yet when we penetrate beneath the surface we realize that he lived in stirring days, and that his short span of fifty years was passed in the full light of the world of the thirteenth century. Thomas was born in the beginning of the year 1225 in the castle of Rocca-Secca, the ancestral home of the Counts of Aquino, in the kingdom of Sicily. His future glory was foretold to his mother, the Countess Theodora, by a hermit of that neighbourhood who also foretold that his parents would endeavour to make him a monk in the Benedictine Abbey of Monte Cassino, but that God had other designs for him, since he was to be a Friar Preacher, a member of the Order of the great S. Dominic who had just gone to his reward. The prophecy was fulfilled to the letter. At the early age of five years he was sent to the Abbey to be educated among the young nobles of the day, as was then the custom. Even thus early he showed a remarkable maturity of character, and his biographer, William of Tocco, dwells with delight on the calm reserve of his childish days and on that eager seeking after God which was to be his future glory.[3]

From Monte Cassino Thomas passed to Naples to complete his studies. Here he became conscious of his vocation, and offered himself to the Dominicans. The Prior of the convent at Naples at that time was Father John of S. Julian, who later became Patriarch of Jerusalem[4]; he gave the habit of the Order to Thomas, who was then but fourteen years of age. His parents were indignant at this step, and did all in their power to shake his determination. Fearing their recourse to the violent methods then so common, the Dominicans sent Thomas to the convent of Santa Sabina at Rome. But S. Thomas's brothers, at their mother's bidding, seized upon the young man and carried him off in his religious habit to his mother who kept him imprisoned for nearly two years.[5] During this time of anxiety nothing disturbed the Saint's equanimity, and he made good use of his time by studying the Bible, the Book of the Sentences—the Theological Manual of those days—and also Aristotle's philosophical treatises. It was at this time that the diabolical attempt upon his virtue was made—an attempt which the Saint resisted effectually; in reward for his constancy he was miraculously girded with a cincture by two Angels from Heaven.[6] Failing in their attempt to shake his determination, his brothers permitted him to escape, and he returned to the convent at Naples in 1245. Thence he was sent by his superiors to Rome, and shortly afterwards to Paris and Cologne to study under Blessed Albert the Great. At Cologne he led the life of a simple student, a life of recollection, prayer, and study. But his extraordinary talents could not long remain hid. The post of Bachelor in the famous House of Studies at Paris was vacant, and at the suggestion of Cardinal Hugo à S. Caro, himself a Dominican, S. Thomas was appointed by the Master-General of the Order to the vacant post. This was a blow to the Saint's humility, but he accepted it under obedience. The impression made by his teaching was extraordinary, and the words of William of Tocco on this point are worth transcribing: "Erat enim novos in sua lectione movens articulos, novum modum et clarum determinandi inveniens, et novas reducens in determinationibus rationes: ut nemo qui ipsum audisset nova docere, et novis rationibus dubia definire dubitaret, quod eum Deus novi luminis radiis illustrasset, qui statim tam certi c[oe]pisset esse judicii, ut non dubitaret novas opiniones docere et scribere, quas Deus dignatus esset noviter inspirare." This novelty in method was evidently remarkable, but, while provoking the attacks of some, it attracted an immense crowd to his lectures, and this not simply by reason of the novelty which characterized them, but by reason of the supereminent sanctity of the teacher. "Dilectus Deo!" cries out his biographer. "Qui scientiam tribuit; et acceptus hominibus, quibus quasi novis radiis veritatis illuxit."[7]

In 1253 or 1254 Thomas was, again much against his will, created Master in Sacred Theology, and the remaining twenty years of his life were wholly devoted to teaching, studying, and preaching, whether at Paris or at Naples. Dignities and honours were frequently offered him, but he succeeded in avoiding them all. He felt that his vocation was to study and teach. And since his teaching was to be of things Divine, he felt that he must needs be absorbed in such things, and that his life must be wholly spent with God. This feature of his life is insisted on by his biographers: "Men ever saw him of joyful mien, gentle and sweet, not occupying himself with worldly affairs, but ever given to study, to reading, to writing, and to prayer for the enlightening of the faithful."[8] Thus we are told that when Brother Reginald, who had been Blessed Thomas's companion, returned from Fossa Nuova to Naples after the Master's death to resume the lectures he had been giving there, he burst into tears as he stood before the Brethren, and said:

"Brothers, I was forbidden by my Master to reveal during his life the marvels I had seen. One of those marvels was that his knowledge, which so wondrously surpassed that of other men, was not due to any human skill, but to the merits of his prayers. For whenever he would study, or dispute, or read, or write, or dictate, he would first betake himself to prayer in secret, and there with many tears would implore light wherewith to search rightly into the secret things of God. And by the merits of such prayer it came to pass that, whereas previous to his prayer he had been in doubt about the subject of his study, he always returned from it illumined. And when any doubtful point occurred to him before he had had recourse to prayer, he went to pray, and what had previously been obscure was then Divinely made clear to him."[9]

Truly characteristic of our Saint are those three petitions he was wont to make: that he might never learn to love things of earth; that he might never change his state of life; that God would reveal to him the state of his brother Reginald, who had been put to death, unjustly, as Thomas thought, by the Emperor Frederic. All three petitions were granted, two of them, as he himself told Brother Reginald on his deathbed, by the Blessed Virgin herself. "She appeared to him," says William of Tocco, "and assured him regarding his life and his knowledge, promised him, too, that God would grant him whatsoever he should ask through her intercession, and told him, moreover, that he would never change his state of life."[10]

The following story is well known, but is too illustrative of the Saint's character to be omitted: A dispute had arisen in the University of Paris regarding the Accidents of the Holy Eucharist, and the Doctors of the University decided to leave the decision with S. Thomas. The responsibility was great, but the Saint according to his custom betook himself to prayer and then wrote his answer to the difficulty. "But since he would not dare," says William of Tocco, "to expound his opinion in the Schools before the Masters of the University without first consulting Him of Whom he was treating and to Whom he had prayed that he might teach correctly, he came to the altar and there spread out the pages he had written before Him; then, lifting up his hands to the Crucifix, he prayed and said: 'O Lord Jesus Christ, Who art most truly contained in this wondrous Sacrament and Who as Supreme Artificer ever wondrously workest, I seek to understand Thee in this Sacrament and to teach truly concerning Thee. Wherefore I humbly pray Thee that if what I have written spring from Thee, and be true concerning Thee, then Thou wouldest enable me to declare it and clearly expound it. But if I have written ought which is not in harmony with Thy Faith and which accords not with the Mysteries of this Sacrament, then I pray Thee that nought may proceed from my mouth which deviates from the Catholic Faith.' Then those who watched saw on a sudden Christ standing before the Saint and on the paper he had written, and they heard Him say: 'Well hast thou written of Me in this Sacrament of My Body, and well and truly hast thou answered the question put to thee, as far, that is, as it can be understood by man in this life, or expressed in human words.'"[11]

And it was ever the same throughout his life: in God he sought God. Hence his incessant meditation on the Holy Scriptures; hence his diligent study of the writings of the Fathers of the Church. "Master," said a band of his students to him as they looked on Paris spread before them—"Master, see what a lovely city Paris is! Would you not like to be its owner?" And with a Saint's simplicity he replied: "Far rather would I have the Homilies of Chrysostom on S. Matthew! For if this city were mine then the task of governing it would take me away from the contemplation of things Divine and deprive my soul of its consolations!"[12]

And his companion Reginald has told us how he studied to know the things of God. For he tells us that when the Saint was occupied with his Commentary on Isaias and could not arrive at any satisfactory explanation of a certain passage he gave himself up to fasting and prayer. Then one night Reginald heard voices in the Saint's cell, and whilst he wondered what this might mean at that hour, S. Thomas came to him and said: "Reginald, get up, light a candle, and take the book in which you have been writing upon Isaias and make ready to write once more." Then Reginald wrote whilst the Saint dictated as though he were reading out of a book, with such facility did he speak. And then, at Reginald's insistent petition, he said to him: "My son, you have seen the affliction under which I have been of late owing to this passage of Isaias which I have just been expounding, and you know how I besought God with tears that I might understand it. God, then, this very night had pity upon me, and sent His Blessed Apostles Peter and Paul whom I had prayed to intercede for me, and they have most fully explained it all!"[13] How gladly would one know what passage of Isaias it was which was thus Divinely interpreted!

And so this truly marvellous life went on till the end drew near. Day by day he ascended the steps of the altar, his face bathed in tears; day by day he returned to his work more and more illumined regarding the Mysterium Fidei, and with his soul still more closely knit to its Maker. His ecstasies became more frequent, and in one of these he was told that the close of his life was at hand. For it was at San Severino, not far from Salerno, that he fell into so prolonged an ecstasy that his sister who was present appealed to Reginald to know what had happened to her brother. Even Reginald was astonished. "He is frequently rapt in spirit," he said, "but never before have I seen him thus abstracted!" "Then," says William of Tocco, "Master Reginald went to him, and, plucking him by the cloak, roused him from this deep sleep of contemplation. But he sighed and said: 'My son Reginald, I tell thee in secret, and I forbid thee to reveal it to anyone during my life, the close of my writing has come; for such things have been revealed to me that all I have written and taught seems to me of small account. Hence I hope in my God that as there is an end to my writing, so too will speedily come the end of my life.'"[14]

And S. Thomas was ready for the end, for not long previously, when he was in the convent at Naples and was praying in the Church, there appeared to him Brother Romanus, whom he had left teaching at Paris. Brother Thomas said to him: "Welcome! Whence dost thou come?" But Romanus said to him: "I have passed from this life, and I am allowed to come to thee by reason of thy merits." Then Brother Thomas, summoning up his courage, for he had been much disturbed by the sudden apparition, said to him: "If it be pleasing to God, I adjure you by God to answer my questions. First: How does it stand with me? and are my works pleasing to God?" And the other answered: "Thou art in a good state, and thy works are pleasing to God." Then the Master continued: "And what of thyself?" And Romanus answered: "I am in Eternal Life, but I was in Purgatory sixteen days because of some negligence of which I was guilty in the affair of a will which the Bishop of Paris entrusted to me for speedy execution; but I, through mine own fault, was tardy in executing it." Lastly S. Thomas asked: "What about that question we have so often discussed together: Do the habits we have acquired here abide with us when we are in our Fatherland?" But the other replied: "Brother Thomas, I see God, and you must ask me nought further on that question." But Thomas at once said:

"Since you see God, tell me whether you see Him with or without any intermediate image?" But Romanus replied: "As we have heard, so we have seen in the City of our God,"[15] and forthwith disappeared. But the Master remained astonished at that marvellous and unwonted apparition, and filled with joy at his favourable replies. "O Blessed Teacher!" ejaculates William of Tocco, who has left us this account, "to whom Heaven's secrets were thus familiar, to whom Heaven's citizens came with such sweet familiarity to lead him to those heavenly shores!"[16]

Nor was this the only warning. For just as in earlier years at Paris he had received Divine commendation for his writings, so now again at Naples. For Brother Dominic of Caserta tells us that at Naples he watched S. Thomas praying at night. He saw him, he says, absorbed in prayer, and then lifted up into the air about the height of two cubits from the ground. And whilst for a long space he marvelled at this, he suddenly heard this voice from the Crucifix: "Thomas, well hast thou written of Me! What reward wilt thou have from Me for all thy labour?" But he replied: "Lord, none save Thyself!" At that time the Saint was engaged upon the Third Part of the Summa, and was treating of the Passion and Resurrection of Christ. But after arriving at that point he wrote but little more by reason of the marvels that God had wondrously revealed to him.[17]

Since his soul, then, was thus united to God it is small wonder the Brethren saw him rapt in ecstasy and with his face bathed in tears as he stood in choir and sang the Antiphon wont to be sung according to the Dominican Office for Compline during Lent: "Ne projicias nos in tempore senectutis: cum defecerit virtus nostra, ne derelinquas nos Domine."[18]

In the year 1274 the Saint was summoned by Pope Gregory X. to the Council about to be held at Lyons. He set out, taking with him his Treatise against the Errors of the Greek Schismatics, for the great question which the Pope had at heart was the settlement of the Schism between the East and the West. But the Council was never to see Thomas, for he fell ill when traversing the Campagna, and though he was able to reach the Cistercian Abbey of Fossa Nuova he reached it only to die. "This is my rest for ever and ever," he said as he entered the gates. "Here will I dwell, for I have chosen it." And here, as he lay dying, he expounded to the monks who stood round that most sublime of all the Books of the Bible, the Canticle of Canticles: "Behold, my Beloved speaketh to me: Arise, make haste, my love, my dove, my beautiful one, and come.... I sleep, and my heart watcheth; the voice of my Beloved Who is knocking!... My Beloved to me and I to Him Who feedeth among the lilies: till the Day break and the shadows retire!"

As the time of his summons drew on he asked for the Holy Viaticum. And, in the words of William of Tocco, "when It was brought with devout reverence by the Abbot and the monks, he prostrated himself on the ground, weak indeed in body but mighty in spirit, and so came to meet his Lord with tears."

And when the priest asked him—as it is the custom to ask all Christians at death touching their faith in this mighty Sacrament—whether he believed that That Consecrated Host was the True Son of God, Who came forth from the Virgin's womb, Who hung upon the tree of the Cross, Who died for us and rose again on the third day:—with clear voice, with full attention, and with tears, he replied: "If fuller knowledge than that of faith could be had in this life touching this Sacrament, in that knowledge I reply that I believe it to be true, and that I know for certain that This is True God and Man, the Son of God the Father and of the Virgin Mother: so I believe in my heart and so I confess in word." After some other devout expressions he received the Sacred Host, and then said: "I receive Thee, the Price of my soul's redemption, for love of Whom I have studied, watched, and toiled; Thee have I preached and taught; nought contrary to Thee have I ever said, neither do I obstinately hold to any opinion of mine own. If, however, I have said ought wrongly concerning this Sacrament, I submit it all to the correction of the Holy Roman Church in Whose obedience I now pass from this life!" "O Blessed Teacher! who ran so swiftly in the race, who fought so manfully in the strife, who could so well say with the Apostle: 'I have fought a good fight, I have finished my course, I have kept the faith; as for the rest there is laid up for me a crown of justice'; and such indeed had he truly won by his study of inspired doctrine."[19]

O Sancte Thoma!
Scholarum Patrone,
Fidem invictam,
Charitatem fervidam,
Vitam castissimam,
Scientiam veram,

A Deo nobis obtine.
Per Christum Dominum nostrum. Amen.

No one who is at all familiar with the writings of S. Thomas can be surprised to find many extracts from S. Augustine in the following pages. For Augustine and Thomas are one. Their respective styles are different, but their thoughts and teachings are the same on the great essential points of theological teaching. Cardinal Aguirre has well said: "Owing to the clearness and acuteness of his angelic mind S. Thomas sheds a flood of light on many most obscure matters, and brings out very clearly even the most profound teachings contained in the works of the Fathers, especially in those of S. Augustine. I speak simply from my own experience, but I am certain that many another has felt the same: in controverted matters, if we look merely at the text of S. Augustine, we are brought face to face with a flood of difficulties which seem well-nigh insoluble; but the difficulty disappears and the solution becomes clear the moment we set to work to find out what was S. Thomas's teaching on the question; for he is the surest and the easiest interpreter of S. Augustine."[20]

And indeed Augustine is a deep well! "Man shall come to a deep heart!" he was fond of saying, and those words of the Psalmist might stand for a motto at the head of his works. Traditionary art represents him with his heart in his hand, and the sentiment is true, for "great-hearted" is the epithet which best suits him, and those who use these pages for meditation or spiritual reading will find that whereas S. Thomas teaches how we ought to pray, S. Augustine makes us pray; not in vain had he studied and taught rhetoric for so many years!

This likeness between the two great Saints forms the theme of one of the Responsories for the Office for S. Thomas in the Dominican Breviary. It is based on a famous vision. "There appeared to me as I watched in prayer," said Brother Albert of Brescia in his deposition, "two revered personages clothed in wondrous splendour. One of them wore a mitre on his head, the other was clad in the habit of the Friars Preachers. And this latter bore on his head a golden crown; round his neck he wore two rings, one of silver, the other of gold; and on his breast he had an immense precious stone, which filled the church with light. His cloak, too, was sewn with precious stones, and his tunic and his hood were of snowy white. And the one who wore the mitre said to me: 'Brother Albert, why art thou thus filled with wonder? Thy prayers are heard; for—listen: I am Augustine, the Doctor of the Church, and I am sent to thee to tell thee of the doctrine and of the glory of Brother Thomas of Aquin who is here with me. For he is my son; he in all things has followed my doctrine and that of the Apostles, and by his teaching he has illumined the Church of God. This is signified by the precious stones which you see, and especially by the one he carries on his breast, for it signifies the upright intention which he ever had in view in his defence of the faith and which he showed in his words. These precious stones, then, and especially that great one, signify the many books and works that he wrote, and they show that he is equal to me in glory save only that in the aureola of Virginity he surpasseth me.'"[21]

Cardinal Cajetan, from whose famous Commentary on the Summa we have occasionally quoted, is unfortunately too little known. Born in 1469, and dying in 1534, he was the contemporary of Luther and the Reformers, and, as was to be expected, their most formidable opponent. A great student, a man of prayer as well as a man of action, his was the striking figure of the early portion of the sixteenth century. But his was a bold and independent mind, and he was not afraid to advance views which, though now commonly accepted, brought his works into a certain disfavour. This is especially to be regretted in the case of his Commentaries on the Bible. A thorough Greek scholar, possessing no mean acquaintance with Hebrew, he deserves, by reason of the clearness and precision of his thought, the title of "Prince of Commentators." Here, however, we are concerned with the devotional rather than with the critical aspect of his writings, and the reader will gain from some of Cajetan's terse and pithy comments a very great deal of instruction.

In conclusion, a few words may be desirable regarding the method of S. Thomas.

S. Thomas divides his Summa Theologica into three main parts. The First Part treats of God, the Exemplar.[22] The Second, of man made to the image of God;[23] the Third, of God Incarnate, of His Sacraments by which we attain to union with Him in this life, and of Eternal Life to which we attain ultimately by our resurrection. Here we are solely concerned with the Second part.[24] It is subdivided into two portions, known as the Prima Secundæ and the Secunda Secundæ respectively, or as the First and Second portions of the Second part. In the Prima Secundæ the Saint treats of the principles of Morals—namely, of man's ultimate end and of the habits, acts, and principles by which he attains it. In the Secunda Secundæ, after having laid in the Prima Secundæ the foundations of Moral Theology, he proceeds to treat of the individual virtues, firstly of the Theological Virtues, Faith, Hope, and Charity; then of the Cardinal Virtues, Prudence, Justice, Fortitude, and Temperance. Under each of these heads he treats of the Gifts corresponding to each Virtue, of the vices opposed to them, and of the Precepts regarding them.[25] Apropos of the Cardinal Virtue of Justice, he treats of the Moral Virtue of Religion, which is comprised under Justice, since Religion may be defined as the offering to God the worship which is His due, Question LXXXI. He then treats of Devotion, Question LXXXII., and then of Prayer, Question LXXXIII. These three Questions we here present in an English dress.

After these Treatises on individual virtues, he passes to the consideration of those virtues which concern, not men as a whole, but only certain classes of men.[26] And first of all he treats of those Gifts which are bestowed upon certain men not so much for their own benefit as for the good of others—viz., of Prophecy, of Ecstasy, of the Gift of Tongues, and of the Gift of Miracles. He then discusses the two kinds of operations or "lives"—the active, namely, and the contemplative—which find a place in the Mystical Body of Christ, which is the Church. These treatises in reality constitute a commentary on 1 Cor. xii. 4-11. Question CLXXIX., On the Division of Life into the Active and the Contemplative, is here given; as also Question CLXXX., On the Contemplative Life; Question CLXXXI., On the Active Life; Question CLXXXII., On the Comparison of the Active with the Contemplative Life.

S. Thomas then proceeds to treat of various states of life—viz., of the state of perfection, of the Episcopal and of the Religious state. Only one question raised in this connection concerns us here: Whether, namely, Contemplative Religious Orders are superior to Active Orders? (Question CLXXXVIII. 6).

Each Question is, as will be seen from the Table of Contents, divided into Articles.

The framework of what is termed an "article" of the Summa is familiar to those who use that work, but it may not be amiss to explain S. Thomas's method in brief fashion. Each "article" is couched in the form of a question, thus: Has contemplation its joys? And the Saint at once sets forth in succession three, sometimes more, arguments which seem to militate against the view he himself holds. These are commonly known as the objections. He then gives us a short paragraph opening with the words: Sed contra, or But on the contrary; and in this paragraph he gives some authority, generally that of Holy Scripture or one of the Fathers, for the view he is going to hold. This paragraph is generally known from its opening words as the Sed contra; there is no argument in it save from authority. He then proceeds to discuss the question from the standpoint of pure reason. This portion is known as the Corpus articuli, or Body of the Article, and in it the Saint presents his reasoning in clear, precise fashion. It will be apparent, of course, that many questions cannot be answered with a categoric yes or no, but the precise sense in which certain terms in the discussion are to be used has to be clearly ascertained; according to the diverse ways in which they may be understood the answer will be affirmative or negative. It is important for those not familiar with S. Thomas' works to grasp this point; they must not, for instance, presume that because the opening "objections" seem to uphold one point of view S. Thomas is therefore going to hold the precise opposite. A good example of this will be found in the Article: Ought we to pray to God alone?

In the Treatises here presented the argument, though clear and precise, is hardly what we should call subtle, and this for the simple reason that the subject-matter does not call for subtle treatment. But what cannot fail to strike the most cursory reader is the tone of submission to authority and to the teachings of the Fathers which characterizes every page: "Summe veneratus est sacros Doctores," says Cajetan, "ideo intellectum omnium quodammodo sortitus est."[27] And the natural corollary of this is the complete self-effacement of the Saint. The first person is conspicuous by its absence all through the Summa, though the reader of the following pages will find one exception to this rule.

And the more we study these Articles of S. Thomas the more we marvel; the thought is so concentrated and yet so limpid in its expression, that as we read it it seems as though no one could ever have thought otherwise. But read it, and then try to reformulate the line of argument which you have been following with such ease—and your mind halts, your tongue stammers! It is one thing to understand the thought when expressed, quite another to think such thoughts and express them. Hence the declaration made by Pope John XXII. when the question of the holy Doctor's canonization was brought forward: "Such teaching," he exclaimed, "could only have been due to miracle!" And on the following day in the Consistory: "He has brought greater light to the Church than all other Doctors; by one year's study of his writings a man may make greater profit than if he spend his whole life studying the writings of others!"[28]

The reader will sometimes feel inclined to smile at the quaint etymologies which occur now and again. But he must remember that these are given by the Saint for what they are worth. It was not a philological age, and S. Thomas made use of the Book of Etymologies drawn up in the seventh century by S. Isidore of Seville.

Besides the writings of S. Augustine, two Patristic works are cited with considerable frequency by S. Thomas in these pages: the Opus Imperfectum of S. Chrysostom on S. Matthew's Gospel, and the works of Denis the Areopagite. The former is almost certainly not the work of S. Chrysostom, but rather of an Arian writer towards the close of the sixth century.[29] The writer known as Denis the Areopagite, owing to his being traditionally identified with S. Paul's convert at Athens, probably wrote about the close of the fifth century. Few works of Mystical Theology exercised a greater influence on the writers of the Middle Ages.[30] A word must also be said about the Gloss to which S. Thomas so often refers, and which he quotes as an authority. The term "Gloss" was applied to the brief running commentaries on the Bible which were in vogue in the Middle Ages. These brief paraphrases were also known as Postillæ, and they were frequently written in between the lines of the text of the Bible, whence the name Interlinear Gloss; or in the margins, whence the name Marginal Gloss. The Glossa Ordinaria, as it is called, is the best known of these commentaries. It is usually attributed to Walafrid Strabo, a monk of the Abbey of S. Gall, who died in 849; but it is probable that Strabo took down his Commentary from the lips of Rabanus Maurus, a monk of the Abbey of Fulda, and afterwards its abbot. Rabanus was a most prolific writer, and has left Commentaries on nearly all the Books of the Bible. Even when Abbot he reserved to himself the Chair of Scripture;[31] he had had the great advantage of living for a time in Palestine. Another Biblical scholar to whom the Glossa Ordinaria of S. Thomas's time apparently owed much, was Hugo à S. Caro, the Dominican Provincial in France, and afterwards Cardinal-Priest of S. Sabina. It was under his direction that the first Concordance of the Bible was formed, in which task he is said to have had the assistance of five hundred Friars.[32] He owes his title of Glossator to his well-known Postillæ, or Brief Commentaries on the whole Bible. The Glossa Interlinearis is due to Anselm, a Canon of Laudun, who died in 1117. Another famous Glossator was Nicolas de Lyra, a Franciscan who died in 1340—some sixty-six years, that is, subsequent to S. Thomas. Lastly, we should mention Peter the Lombard, commonly known as The Master of the Sentences, from his four books of Sentences, in which he presented the theological teaching of the Fathers in Scholastic fashion. This treatise became the Scholastic manual of the age. To him is due a Gloss on the Psalter and on Job, as well as a series of brief notes on the Epistles of S. Paul taken from the writings of the chief Fathers, S. Ambrose, S. Jerome, S. Augustine, etc. And the authority accorded to these Glosses in general is due to the fact that they constituted a running Commentary taken from the writings of the Fathers and Doctors of the Church.

THE BREVIARY HYMN TO S. AUGUSTINE.

Magne Pater Augustine
Preces nostras suscipe,
Et per eas Conditori
Nos placare satage,
Atque rege gregem tuum
Summum decus præsulum.
Amatorem paupertatis
Te collaudant pauperes:
Assertorem veritatis
Amant veri judices:
Frangis nobis favos mellis,
De Scripturis disserens.
Quæ obscura prius erant
Nobis plana faciens,
Tu de verbis Salvatoris
Dulcem panem conficis,
Et propinas potum vitæ

De Psalmorum nectare.
Tu de vita clericorum
Sanctam scribis Regulam,
Quam qui amant et sequuntur
Viam tenent regiam,
Atque tuo sancto ductu
Redeunt ad Patriam.
Regi regum salus, vita,
Decus et imperium:
Trinitati laus et honor
Sit per omne sæculum:
Qui concives nos adscribat
Supernorum civium. Amen.

FOOTNOTES 1

[1] The Ascent of Mount Carmel by S. John of the Cross. Prefatory Essay on the Development of Mysticism in the Carmelite Order, by Benedict Zimmerman, O.C.D., pp. 13-17. (London: Thomas Baker, 1906.)

[2] Valgornera, O.P., Mystica Theologia D. Thomæ, ed. Berthier. 2 Vols. Turin, 1890-91.

[3] "In ætate tam tenera et scibilium nescia, qui necdum se scire poterat, miro modo Deum adhuc nesciens, divino ductus instinctu scire quærebat. De quo futurum erat, ut, dum sic anxius maturius Deum præ aliis quæreret, clarius præ ceteris, quæ scire futurus erat, scriberet, quæ de Deo, ipso donante, studiosius et citius inveniret" (William of Tocco, Vita B. Thomæ in the Bollandists, March 7, No. 5). This William of Tocco had seen and heard S. Thomas, and in 1319 took a prominent part in the Saint's canonization (see Bollandists, p. 653).

[4] Bernard Guidonis, Boll., No. 7, p. 659, note.

[5] Boll., Nos. 12 and 76.

[6] Ibid., No. 11.

[7] Boll., p. 661.

[8] Ibid., p. 662.

[9] Boll., p. 668.

[10] Boll., pp. 668 and 710.

[11] Boll., No. 53.

[12] Ibid., p. 671.

[13] Boll., p. 668.

[14] Boll., p. 672.

[15] Ps. xlvii.

[16] Boll., p. 672.

[17] Boll., p. 669.

[18] Ibid., p. 667; cp. Ps. lxx, 20.

[19] Boll., p. 675.

[20] Touron, Vie de S. Thomas d'Aquin, Paris, 1740, p. 353.

[21] Boll., p. 706; cp. p. 665.

[22] Prol. to Ia., IIdæ.

[23] Prol. to III. Pars.

[24] Prol. to IIa., IIdæ.

[25] Prol. to IIa. IIdæ.
[26] Prol. to Qu. CLXXI. of the IIda., IIdæ.
[27] Comment. on IIa., IIæ., cxlviii. 4.
[28] Boll., p. 680.
[29] See Bardenhewer, Patrologie, i. 319.
[30] Smith and Wace, Dict. of Christian Biography, i. 847.
[31] Fabricius, Bibliotheca Latina, s.v. Walafridus and Rabanus.
[32] Ibid., s.v. Hugo à S. Caro.

QUESTION 1

OF THE VIRTUE OF RELIGION

I. Does the Virtue of Religion Direct a Man To God Alone?
   S. Augustine, sermon, cccxxxiv. 3
   on Psalm lxxvi.
   sermon, cccxi. 14-15
II. Is Religion a Virtue?
III. Is Religion One Virtue?
IV. Is Religion a Special Virtue Distinct From Others?
V. Is Religion One of the Theological Virtues?
VI. Is Religion To Be Preferred To the Other Moral Virtues?
VII. Has Religion, Or Latria, Any External Acts?
   S. Augustine, of Care for the Dead, V.
VIII. Is Religion the Same As Sanctity?
   Cardinal Cajetan, on the Distinction Between Sanctity and Religion

I

Does the Virtue of Religion direct a Man to God Alone?

Cicero says[33]: "Religion offers internal and external reverence to that Superior Nature which we term the Divine."

S. Isidore says[34]: "A religious man is, as Cicero remarks, so called from religion, for he is occupied with and, as it were, reads through again and again (relegit) the things that concern Divine worship." Thus religion seems to be so called from reading again (religendo) things concerning Divine worship; for such things are to be repeatedly revolved in the mind, according to those words of Proverbs iii. 6: In all thy ways think on Him. At the same time religion might be said to be so called because "we ought to choose again (re-eligere) those things which through our negligence we have lost," as S. Augustine has noted.[35] Or perhaps it is better derived from "binding again" (religando); thus S. Augustine says[36]: "Let religion bind us once more to the One Almighty God."

But whether religion be so called from frequent reading, or from fresh election of Him Whom we have negligently lost, or from rebinding, it properly implies a certain relation to God. For it is He to Whom we ought to be especially bound as our indefectible principle; to Him must we assiduously direct our choice as our ultimate end; He it is Whom we negligently lose by sin and Whom we must regain by believing in Him and by professing our faith in Him.

But some deny that religion directs a man to God alone, thus:

1. S. James says[37]: Religion clean and undefiled before God and the Father is this: to visit the fatherless and widows in their tribulation; and to keep oneself unspotted from this world. But to visit the fatherless and widows indicates relation to our neighbour, and to keep oneself unspotted from this world refers to ourselves. Hence religion is not confined to our relationship with God.

But religion has two sorts of acts. Some belong to it properly and immediately, those acts, namely, which it elicits and by which man is directed to God alone, as, for instance, to offer Him sacrifice, to adore Him, etc.

But there are other acts which religion produces through the medium of the virtues which it controls, directing them, that is, towards reverence to God; for that virtue which is concerned with the end directs those virtues which have to do with the means to the end. And in this sense to visit the fatherless and widows in their tribulation is said to be an act of religion because commanded by it, though actually elicited by the virtue of mercy. Similarly to keep oneself unspotted from this world is an act commanded by religion, though elicited by temperance or some other virtue.

2. S. Augustine says[38]: "Since according to the genius of the Latin speech—and that not merely of the unlearned, but even of the most learned—religion is said to be shown towards our human relatives and connexions and intimates, this word 'religion' cannot be used without some ambiguity when applied to the worship of God; hence we cannot say with absolute confidence that religion is nought else but the worship of God." Religion, then, is not limited to our relation to God, but embraces, our neighbour as well.

But it is only by an extension of the name "religion" that it is made to embrace our relations towards our human kin, it is not according to the proper signification of the word. Hence S. Augustine prefaced the words quoted from him above with the remark: "Religion, strictly speaking, seems to mean, not any kind of worship, but only that of God."

3. Further, latria seems to come under religion. But S. Augustine says[39]: "Latria is interpreted as service." But we ought to serve not God only, but our neighbour as well: By charity of the spirit serve one another.[40] Religion, then, implies relation to our neighbour.

But since a slave implies a master, it follows that where there exists a peculiar and special title of dominion there also will be found a peculiar and special ratio of servitude. It is clear, however, that dominion belongs to God in a peculiar and special fashion, since He it is Who has made all things and Who holds the chief rule over all things. Consequently a special kind of service is due to Him. And this service is by the Greeks designated latria, which is, in consequence, properly comprised under "religion."

4. Again, reverence comes under religion. But man has to reverence, not only God, but his neighbour as well; as Cato says: "Reverence parents." Hence religion establishes a relation between ourselves and our neighbour as well as between ourselves and God.

But we are said to reverence those men whom we honour or remember, or to whose presence we resort. So, too, even things which are subject to us are said to be "cultivated" by us (coli); thus husbandmen (agricolæ) are so called because they "cultivate" the fields; the inhabitants of a place, too (incolæ), are so called because they "cultivate" the spots where they dwell. But since special honour is due to God as the First Principle of all, a special kind of "cultus"[41] or "reverence" is His due, and this the Greeks call eusebia or theosebia, as S. Augustine says.[42]

5. Lastly, all who are in a state of salvation are subject to God. But not all who are in a state of salvation are called "religious," but those only who bind themselves by certain vows and observances and who undertake to obey certain men. Hence religion does not seem to mean the relationship of subjection of man to God.

But although, generally speaking, all those who worship God can be termed "religious," yet those are specially so called who dedicate their whole lives to the Divine worship and cut themselves off from worldly occupations.

Thus those are not termed "contemplatives" who merely contemplate, but they who devote their lives to contemplation. And such men do not subject themselves to men for man's sake, but for God's, as the Apostle says: You received me as an Angel of God, even as Christ Jesus.[43]

S. Augustine: We are to abide in Christ! How then shall That not be now our possession Where we are then to abide and Whence we are to draw Life? Let Holy Scripture speak for us lest we should seem in mere conjecture to be saying things contrary to the teaching of the Word of God. Hear the words of one who knew: If God be for us who is against us?[44] The Lord, he says, is the portion of my inheritance.[45] He saith not: Lord, what wilt Thou give me for mine inheritance? All that Thou canst give me is worthless! Be Thou mine inheritance! Thee do I love! Thee do I wholly love! With all my heart, with all my soul, with all my mind do I love Thee! What, then, shall be my lot? What wilt Thou give me save Thyself? This is to love God freely. This is to hope for God from God. This is to hasten to be filled with God, to be sated with Him. For He is sufficient for thee; apart from Him nought can suffice thee! (Sermon, cccxxxiv. 3).

S. Augustine: I cried to the Lord with my voice.[46] Many cry to the Lord that they may win riches, that they may avoid losses; they cry that their family may be established, they ask for temporal happiness, for worldly dignities; and, lastly, they cry for bodily health, which is the patrimony of the poor. For these and suchlike things many cry to the Lord; hardly one cries for the Lord Himself! How easy it is for a man to desire all manner of things from the Lord and yet not desire the Lord Himself! As though the gift could be sweeter than the Giver! (on Ps. lxxvi.).

S. Augustine: Picture God as saying to you—He Who re-created you and adopted you: "My son, why is it that day by day you rise and pray, and genuflect, and even strike the ground with your forehead, nay, sometimes even shed tears, while you say to Me: 'My Father, my God! give me wealth!' If I were to give it to you, you would think yourself of some importance, you would fancy you had gained something very great. Yet because you asked for it you have it. But take care to make good use of it. Before you had it you were humble; now that you have begun to be rich you despise the poor! What kind of a good is that which only makes you worse? For worse you are, since you were bad already. And that it would make you worse you knew not, hence you asked it of Me. I gave it to you and I proved you; you have found—and you are found out! You were hidden when you had nothing. Correct thyself! Vomit up this cupidity! Take a draught of charity!... Ask of Me better things than these, greater things than these. Ask of Me spiritual things. Ask of Me Myself!" (Sermon, cccxi. 14-15).

II

Is Religion a Virtue?

A virtue is that which both renders its possessor, as also his work, good. Hence we must say that every good act comes under virtue. And it is clear that to render to another what is his due has the character of a good act; for by the fact that a man renders to another his due there is established a certain fitting proportion and order between them. But order comes under the ratio of good, just as do measure and species, as S. Augustine establishes.[47] Since, then, it belongs to religion to render to some one, namely, God, the honour which is His due, it is clear that religion is a virtue.

Some, however, deny this, thus:

1. It belongs to religion to show reverence to God. But reverence is an act of fear, and fear is a gift.[48] Religion, then, is a gift, not a virtue.

To reverence God is indeed an act of the gift of fear. But to religion it belongs to do certain things by reason of our reverence for God. Hence it does not follow that religion is the same thing as the gift of fear, but it is related to it as to a higher principle. For the gifts are superior to the moral virtues.

2. All virtue consists in the free-will, and hence virtue is called an elective or voluntary habit. But latria belongs to religion, and latria implies a certain servitude. Hence religion is not a virtue.

But even a servant can freely give to his master the service that is his due and thus "make a virtue of necessity"[49] by voluntarily paying his debt. And similarly the payment of due service to God can be an act of virtue according as a man does it voluntarily.

3. Lastly, as is said in Aristotle's Ethics,[50] the aptitude for the virtues is implanted in us by nature; hence those things which come under the virtues arise from the dictates of natural reason; but it belongs to religion to offer external reverence to the Divine Nature. Ceremonial, however, or external

reverence, is not due to the dictates of natural reason. Hence religion is not a virtue.

But it is due to the dictates of natural reason that a man does certain things in order to show reverence to God. That he should do precisely this or that, however, does not come from the dictates of natural reason, but from Divine or human positive law.

III

Is Religion One Virtue?

S. Paul says to the Ephesians[51]: One God, one faith. But true religion maintains faith in one God. Consequently religion is one virtue.

Habits are distinguished according to the divers objects with which they are concerned. But it belongs to religion to show reverence for the One God for one particular reason, inasmuch, namely, as He is the First Principle, the Creator and Governor of all things; hence we read in Malachi[52]: If I am a Father, where is my honour? for it is the father that produces and governs. Hence it is clear that religion is but one virtue.

But some maintain that religion is not one virtue, thus:

1. By religion we are ordained[53] to God. But in God there are Three Persons, and, moreover, divers attributes which are at least distinguishable from one another by reason. But the diverse character of the objects on which they fall suffices to differentiate the virtues. Hence religion is not one virtue.

But the Three Divine Persons are but One Principle as concerns the creation and the government of things. And consequently They are to be served by one religion. And the divers attributes all concur in the First Principle, for God produces all and governs all by His Wisdom, His Will, and the power of His Goodness. Hence religion is but one virtue.

2. One virtue can have but one act; for habits are differentiated according to their acts. But religion has many acts, e.g., to worship, to serve, to make vows, to pray, to make sacrifices, and many other similar things. Consequently religion is not one virtue.

But by one and the same act does man serve God and worship Him; for worship is referred to God's excellence, to which is due reverence: service regards man's subjection, for by reason of his condition he is bound to show reverence to God. And under these two heads are comprised all the acts which are attributed to religion; for by them all man makes protestation of the Divine excellence and of his subjection of himself to God, either by offering Him something, or, again, by taking upon himself something Divine.

3. Further, adoration belongs to religion. But adoration is paid to images for one reason and to God for another. But since diversity of "reason" serves to differentiate the virtues, it seems that religion is not one virtue.

But religious worship is not paid to images considered in themselves as entities, but precisely as images bringing God Incarnate to our mind. Further, regarding an image precisely as an image of some one, we do not stop at it; it carries us on to that which it represents. Hence the fact that religious veneration is paid to images of Christ in no sense means that there are various kinds of latria, nor different virtues of religion.

IV

Is Religion a Special Virtue Distinct From Others?

Religion is regarded as a part of Justice, and is distinct from the other parts of Justice.

Since virtue is ordained to what is good, where there exists some special ratio of good there must be some special corresponding virtue. But the particular good towards which religion is ordained is the showing due honour to God. Honour, however, is due by reason of some excellency. And to God belongs pre-eminent excellence, since He in every possible way infinitely transcends all things. Hence special honour is due to Him; just as we note that in human concerns varying honours are due to the varying excellencies of persons; one is the honour of a father, another that of a king, and so on. Hence it is manifest that religion is a special virtue.

Some, however, maintain that religion is not a special virtue distinct from others, thus:

1. S. Augustine says[54]: "True sacrifice is every work undertaken in order that we may be joined to God in holy fellowship." But sacrifice comes under religion. Every work of virtue therefore comes under religion. And consequently it is not a special virtue.

But every work of virtue is said to be a sacrifice in so far as it is directed to showing God reverence. It does not thence follow that religion is a general virtue, but that it commands all the other virtues.

2. The Apostle says to the Corinthians[55]: Do all to the glory of God. But it belongs to religion to do some things for the glory of God. Hence religion is not a special virtue.

But all kinds of acts, in so far as they are done for the glory of God, come under religion; not, however, as though it elicited them, but inasmuch as it controls them. Those acts, however, come under religion as eliciting them which, by their own specific character, pertain to the service of God.

3. Lastly, the charity whereby we love God is not distinct from the charity by which we love our neighbour. But in the Ethics[56] it is said: "To be honoured is akin to being loved." Hence religion by which God is honoured is not a specifically distinct virtue from those observances, whether dulia or piety, whereby we honour our neighbour. Hence it is not a special virtue.

But the object of love is a good thing; whereas the object of honour or reverence is what is excellent. But it is God's Goodness that is communicated to His creatures, not the excellence of His Goodness. Hence while the charity wherewith we love God is not a distinct virtue from the charity wherewith we love our neighbour, yet the religion whereby we honour God is distinct from the virtues whereby we honour our neighbour.

V

Is Religion One of the Theological Virtues?

Religion is considered a part of Justice, and this is a moral virtue.

Religion is the virtue whereby we offer to God His due honour. Two things have therefore to be considered in religion. First we have to consider what religion offers God, namely, worship: this may be regarded as the material and the object with which religion is concerned. Secondly, we have to consider Him to Whom it is offered, namely, God Himself. Now, when worship is offered to God it is not as though our worshipful acts touched God, though this is the case when we believe God, for by believing in God we touch Him (and we have therefore said elsewhere[57] that God is the object of our faith not simply inasmuch as we believe in God, but inasmuch as we believe God). Due worship, however, is offered to God in that certain acts whereby we worship Him are performed as homage to Him, the offering sacrifice, for instance, and so forth. From all which it is evident that God does not stand to the virtue of religion as its object or as the material with which it is concerned, but as its goal. And consequently religion is not a theological virtue, for the object of these latter is the ultimate end; but religion is a moral virtue, and the moral virtues are concerned with the means to the end.

But some regard religion as a theological virtue, thus:

1. S. Augustine says[58]: "God is worshipped by faith, hope, and charity," and these are theological virtues. But to offer worship to God comes under religion. Therefore religion is a theological virtue.

But it is always the case that a faculty or a virtue whose object is a certain end, controls—by commanding—those faculties or virtues which have to do with those things which are means to that end. But the theological virtues—i.e., faith, hope, and charity—are directly concerned with God as their proper object. And hence they are the cause—by commanding it—of the act of the virtue of religion which does certain things having relation to God. It is in this sense that S. Augustine says that "God is worshipped by faith, hope, and charity."

2. Those are called theological virtues which have God for their object. But religion has God for its object, for it directs us to God alone. Therefore it is a theological virtue.

But religion directs man to God, not indeed as towards its object, but as towards its goal.

3. Lastly, every virtue is either theological or intellectual or moral. But religion is not an intellectual virtue, for its perfection does not consist in the consideration of the truth. Neither is it a moral virtue, for the property of the moral virtues is to steer a middle course betwixt what is superfluous and what is below the requisite; whereas no one can worship God to excess, according to the words of Ecclesiasticus[59]: For He is above all praise. Religion, then, can only be a theological virtue.

But religion is neither an intellectual nor a theological virtue, but a moral virtue, for it is part of justice. And the via media in religion lies, not between the passions, but in a certain harmony which it establishes in the acts which are directed towards God. I say "a certain," not an absolute harmony, for we can never show to God all the worship that is His due; I mean, then, the harmony arising from the consideration of our human powers and of the Divine acceptance of what we offer. Moreover, there can be excess in those things which have to do with the Divine worship; not indeed as regards quantity, but in certain other circumstances, as, for example, when Divine worship is offered to whom it should not, or at times when it should not, or in other unfitting circumstances.

VI

Is Religion to be preferred to the Other Moral Virtues?

In Exodus[60] the commandments which concern religion are put first, as though they were of primary importance. But the order of the commandments is proportioned to the order of the virtues; for the commandments of the Law fall upon the acts of the virtues. Hence religion is chief among the moral virtues.

The means to an end derive their goodness from their relation to that end; hence the more nigh they are to the end the better they are. But the moral virtues are concerned with those things which are ordained to God as their goal. And religion approaches more nearly to God than do the other moral virtues, inasmuch as it is occupied with those things which are directly and immediately ordained to the Divine honour. Hence religion is the chief of the moral virtues.

Some, however, deny that religion is pre-eminent among the moral virtues, thus:

1. The perfection of a moral virtue lies in this, that it keeps the due medium.[61] But religion fails to attain the medium of justice, for it does not render to God anything absolutely equal to Him. Hence religion is not better than the other moral virtues.

But the praiseworthiness of a virtue lies in the will, not in the power. Hence to fall short of equality—which is the midpath of justice—for lack of power, does not make virtue less praiseworthy, provided the deficiency is not due to the will.

2. Again, in our service of men a thing seems to be praiseworthy in proportion to the need of him whom we assist; hence it is said in Isaias:[62] Deal thy bread to the hungry. But God needs nothing that we can offer Him, according to the Psalmist: I have said: Thou art my God, for Thou hast no need of my goods.[63] Hence religion seems to be less praiseworthy than the other virtues, for by them man is succoured.

But in the service we render to another for his profit, that is the more praiseworthy which is rendered to the most needy, because it is of greater profit to him. But no service is rendered to God for His profit—for His glory, indeed, but for our profit.

3. Lastly, the greater the necessity for doing a thing the less worthy it is of praise, according to the words: For if I preach the Gospel, it is no glory to me, for a necessity lieth upon me.[64] But the greater the debt the greater the necessity. Since, then, the service which man offers to God is the greatest of debts, it would appear that religion is the least praiseworthy of all human virtues.

Where necessity comes in the glory of supererogation is non-existent; but the merit of the virtue is not thereby excluded, provided the will be present. Consequently the argument does not follow.

VII

Has Religion, That is Latria,[65] any External Acts?

In Ps. lxxxiii. 3 it is said: My heart and my flesh have rejoiced in the living God. Now interior acts belong to the heart, and in the same way exterior acts are referred to the members of the body. It appears, then, that God is to be worshipped by exterior as well as by interior acts.

We do not show reverence and honour to God for His own sake—for He in Himself is filled with glory to which nought can be added by any created thing—but for our own sakes. For by the fact that we reverence and honour God our minds are subjected to Him, and in that their perfection lies; for all things are perfected according as they are subjected to that which is superior to them—the body, for instance, when vivified by the soul, the air when illumined by the sun. Now the human mind needs—if it would be united to God—the guidance of the things of sense; for, as the Apostle says to the Romans[66]: The invisible things of Him are clearly seen, being understood by the things that are made. Hence in the Divine worship it is necessary to make use of certain corporal acts, so that by their means, as by certain signs, man's mind may be stirred up to those spiritual acts whereby it is knit to God. Consequently religion has certain interior acts which are its chief ones and which essentially belong to it; but it has also external acts which are secondary and which are subordinated to the interior acts.

Some deny, however, that exterior acts belong to religion or latria, thus:

1. In S. John iv. 24 we read: For God is a Spirit, and they that adore Him must adore Him in spirit and in truth. External acts belong, however, rather to the body than to the spirit. Consequently religion, which comprises adoration, has no exterior acts, but only interior.

But here the Lord speaks only of that which is chiefest and which is essentially intended in Divine worship.

2. The end of religion is to show reverence and honour to God. But it is not reverent to offer to a superexcellent person what properly belongs to inferiors. Since, then, what a man offers by bodily acts seems more in accordance with men's needs and with that respect which we owe to inferior created beings, it does not appear that it can fittingly be made use of in order to show reverence to God.

But such external acts are not offered to God as though He needed them, as He says in the Psalm: Shall I eat the flesh of bullocks? Or shall I drink the blood of goats?[67] But such acts are offered to God as signs of those interior and spiritual works which God accepts for their own sakes. Hence S. Augustine says: "The visible sacrifice is the sacrament—that is, the visible sign—of the invisible sacrifice."[68]

3. Lastly, S. Augustine praises Seneca[69] for his condemnation of those men who offered to their idols what they were wont to offer to men: on the ground, namely, that what belongs to mortal men is not fittingly offered to the immortals. Still less, then, can such things be fittingly offered to the True God Who is above all gods.[70] Therefore to worship God by means of bodily acts seems to be reprehensible. And consequently religion does not include bodily acts.

But idolaters are so called because they offer to their idols things belonging to men, and this not as outward signs which may excite in them spiritual affections, but as being acceptable by those idols for their own sake. And especially because they offered them empty and vile things.

S. Augustine: When men pray, they, as becomes suppliants, make use of their bodily members, for they bend the knee, they stretch forth their hands, they even prostrate on the ground and perform other visible acts. Yet all the while their invisible will and their heart's intention are known to God. He needs not these signs for the human soul to be laid bare before Him. But man by so doing stirs himself up to pray and groan with greater humility and fervour. I know not how it is that whereas such bodily movements can only be produced by reason of some preceding act on the part of the soul, yet when they are thus visibly performed the interior invisible movement which gave them birth is thereby itself increased, and the heart's affections—which must have preceded, else such acts would not have been performed—are thereby themselves increased.

Yet none the less, if a man be in some sort hindered so that he is not at liberty to make use of such external acts, the interior man does not therefore cease to pray; in the secret chamber of his heart, where lies compunction, he lies prostrate before the eyes of God (Of Care for the Dead, v.).

VIII

Is Religion the Same as Sanctity?

In S. Luke's Gospel[71] we read: Let us serve Him in holiness and justice. But to serve God comes under religion. Hence religion is the same as sanctity.

The word "sanctity" seems to imply two things. First, it seems to imply cleanness; and this is in accordance with the Greek word for it, for in Greek it is hagios,[72] as though meaning "without earth." Secondly, it implies stability, and thus among the ancients those things were termed sancta which were so hedged about with laws that they were safe from violation; similarly a thing is said to be sanctum because established by law. And even according to the Latins the word sanctus may mean "cleanness," as derived from sanguine tinctus, for of old those who were to be purified were sprinkled with the blood of a victim, as says S. Isidore in his Etymologies.[73]

And both meanings allow us to attribute sanctity to things which are used in the Divine worship; so that not men only, but also temples and vessels and other similar things are said to be sanctified by reason of their use in Divine worship. Cleanness indeed is necessary if a man's mind is to be applied to God. For the mind of man is stained by being immersed in inferior things, as indeed all things are cheapened by admixture with things inferior to them—silver, for instance, when mixed with lead. And for our minds to be knit to the Supreme Being they must needs be withdrawn from inferior things. Without cleanness, then, the mind cannot be applied to God. Hence in the Epistle to the Hebrews[74] it is said: Follow peace with all men, and holiness, without which no man shall see God.

Stability is also required if the mind is to be applied to God. For the mind is applied to Him as to the Ultimate End and First Principle, and consequently must be immovable. Hence the Apostle says: For I am sure that neither death nor life shall separate me from the love of God.[75]

Sanctity, then, is said to be that whereby man's mind and its acts are applied to God. Hence sanctity does not differ from religion essentially, but in idea only. For by religion we mean that a man offers God due service in those things which specially pertain to the Divine worship—sacrifices, for example, and oblations, etc.; but by sanctity we mean that a man not only offers these things, but also refers to God the works of the other virtues, and also that a man disposes himself by good works for the Divine worship.

Some, however, deny the identity of religion and sanctity, thus:
1. Religion is a certain special virtue. But sanctity is called a general virtue, for according to Andronicus,[76] sanctity is that which "makes men faithful observers of what is justly due to God." Hence sanctity is not the same as religion.

But sanctity is in its essence a special virtue, and as such is, in a sort, the same as religion. It has, however, a certain general aspect in that, by its commands, it directs all the acts of the virtues to the Divine Good. In the same way legal justice is termed a general virtue in that it directs the acts of all the virtues to the common good.

2. Sanctity seems to imply cleanness, for S. Denis says[77]: "Sanctity is freedom from all impurity; it is perfect and stainless cleanness." Cleanness, however, seems to come under temperance, for this it is which precludes bodily defilement. Since, then, religion comes under justice, sanctity cannot be identified with religion.

Temperance indeed worketh cleanness, but this has not the ratio of sanctity except it be referred to God. Hence S. Augustine says of virginity itself that "not because it is virginity is it held in honour, but because it is consecrated to God."[78]

3. Lastly, things that are contradistinguished are not identical. But in all enumerations of the parts of justice sanctity is set against religion.

But sanctity is set against religion because of the difference aforesaid; they differ indeed in idea, not in substance.

Cajetan: Religion is directly concerned with those things which specially pertain to the Divine worship—ceremonies, for example, sacrifices, oblations, etc. Whereas sanctity directly regards the mind, and through the mind the other virtuous works, including those of religion ... for it makes use of them so as thereby to apply the mind—and by consequence all acts that proceed from the human mind—to God. Thus we see that many religious people are not saints, whereas all saints are religious. For people who devote themselves to ceremonies, sacrifices, etc., can be termed religious; but they can only be called saints in so far as by means of these things they give themselves interiorly to God (on 2. 2. 81. 8).

FOOTNOTES 2

[33] De invent. Rhetor., ii. 53.
[34] Etymolog., x. sub litt. R.
[35] Of the City of God, x. 3.
[36] Of the True Religion, lv.
[37] St. Jas. i. 27.
[38] Of the City of God, x. 1.
[39] Of the City of God, x. 1.
[40] Gal. v. 13.
[41] The objection and its solution turn upon the Latin words cultus and colere, which cannot be consistently rendered in English; "reverence" is perhaps the most appropriate translation here.
[42] Of the City of God, x. 1.
[43] Gal. iv. 14.
[44] Rom. viii. 31.
[45] Ps. xv. 5.
[46] Ps. lxxvi. 1.
[47] Of the Nature of Good, iii.
[48] Fear is one of the "Gifts" of the Holy Ghost.
[49] S. Jerome, Ep. LIV., alias X., ad Furiam.
[50] II., vi. 15.
[51] iv. 5-6.
[52] i. 6.
[53] The Latin word ordinare means "to set in due order"; there is no precise English equivalent which can be consistently employed.
[54] Of the City of God, x. 6.
[55] II. x. 31.
[56] VIII. viii. 1.
[57] 2. 2. Qu. II., Art. 2.
[58] Enchiridion, iii.
[59] xliii. 33.
[60] xx. 1-17.
[61] Ethics, II. vi.
[62] lviii. 7.
[63] Ps. xv. 2.

[64] 1 Cor. ix. 16.
[65] See p. 30.
[66] i. 20.
[67] Ps. xlix. 13.
[68] Of the City of God, x. 5.
[69] Ibid., vi. 10.
[70] Ps. xciv. 3.
[71] i. 74-75.
[72] Thus Origen, Hom. XI, i. in Leviticum, where, however, he is not really giving an etymology.
[73] X., sub litt. S.
[74] xii. 14.
[75] Rom. viii. 38-39.
[76] De Affectibus.
[77] Of the Divine Names, xii.
[78] Of Virginity, viii.

QUESTION 2

OF DEVOTION

I. Is Devotion a Special Kind of Act?
   Cardinal Cajetan, On the Meaning of the Term "Devotion"
   S. Augustine, Confessions, XIII. viii. 2
II. Is Devotion an Act of the Virtue of Religion?
III. Is Contemplation, that is Meditation, the Cause of Devotion?
   Cardinal Cajetan, On the Causes of Devotion
   On the Devotion of Women
IV. Is Joy an Effect of Devotion?
   Cardinal Cajetan, On Melancholy
   S. Augustine, Confessions, II. x.

I

Is Devotion a Special Kind of Act?

It is by our acts that we merit. But devotion has a peculiarly meritorious character. Consequently devotion is a special kind of act.

Devotion is so termed from "devoting" oneself. Hence the "devout" are so named because they "devote" themselves to God and thus proclaim their complete subjection to Him. Thus, too, among the heathen of old those were termed "devout" who for the army's sake "devoted" themselves to their idols unto death, as Livy[79] tells us was the case with the two Decii. Hence devotion seems to mean nothing else than "the will to give oneself promptly to those things which pertain to God's service"; thus it is said in Exodus[80]: *The multitude of the children of Israel ... offered first-fruits to the Lord with a most ready and devout mind.* It is clear, however, that a wish to do readily what belongs to God's service is a special act. Hence devotion is a special act of the will.

But some argue that devotion is not a special kind of act, thus:

1. That which serves to qualify other acts cannot be itself a special act. But devotion appears to qualify certain other acts; thus it is said that all the multitude offered victims, and praises, and holocausts with a devout mind.[81]

But that which moves another gives a certain measure to the latter's movement. The will, however, moves the other faculties of the soul to their respective acts; and, moreover, the will, as aiming at an end in view, moves itself to the means towards that end. Consequently, since devotion is the act of a man who offers himself to serve Him Who is the Ultimate End, it follows that devotion gives a certain measure to human acts—whether they be the acts of the will itself with regard to the means to an end, or the acts of the other faculties as moved by the will.

2. Again, no act which finds a place in different kinds of acts can be itself a special kind of act. But devotion is to be found in acts of different kinds, both in corporal acts, for example, and in spiritual; thus a man is said to meditate devoutly, for instance, or to genuflect devoutly.

But devotion does not find a place in different kinds of acts as though it were a species coming under different genera, but in the same sense as the motive power of a moving principle is virtually discoverable in the movements of the things it sets in motion.

3. Lastly, all special kinds of acts belong either to the appetitive or to the cognoscitive faculties. But devotion comes under neither of these—as will be evident to anyone who will reflect upon the various acts of these faculties respectively.

But devotion is an act of the appetitive powers of the soul, and is, as we have said above, a movement of the will.

Cajetan: With regard to the proper meaning of the term devotion, note that since devotion is clearly derived from devoting, and since to devote—derived in its turn from to vow—means to promise something spontaneously to God: it follows that the principle in all such promises is the will; and further, not the will simply as such, but the will so affected as to be prompt. Hence in Latin those are said to be devoted to some superior whose will is so affected towards him as to make them prompt in his regard. And this seems to refer especially to God and to those who in a sense stand in His place, as, for instance, our rulers, our fatherland, and our principles of action. Hence in the Church's usage the term devotion is especially applied to those who are so affected towards God as to be prompt in His regard and in all that concerns Him. And so devotion is here taken to signify the act of a will so disposed, the act by which a man shows himself prompt in the Divine service.... Thus, then, devotion, the principal act of the virtue of religion, implies first of all the prompt desire of the Divine honour in our exercise of Divine worship; and hence comes the prompt choice of appropriate means to this end, and also the prompt carrying out of what we see to be suitable to that end. And the proof of possession of such devotion is that truly devout souls, the moment they perceive that some particular thing (or other) ought to be done for the service of God, are so promptly moved towards it that they rejoice in having to do or in actually doing it (on 2. 2. 82. 1).

S. Augustine: Give me, O Lord, Thyself; grant Thyself to me! For Thee do I love, and if my love be but weak, then would I love Thee more. For I cannot measure it so as to know how much my love falls short of that love which shall make my life run to Thy embraces nor ever turn away from Thee till I be hid in the hiding-place of Thy countenance. This only do I know: that it fares ill with me when away from Thee; and this not merely externally, but within me; for all abundance which is not my God is but penury for me! (Confessions, XIII. viii. 2).

II

Is Devotion an Act of the Virtue of Religion?

Devotion is derived from "devoting oneself" or making vows. But a vow is an act of the virtue of religion. Consequently devotion also is an act of the virtue of religion.

It belongs to the same virtue to wish to do a thing and to have a prompt will to do it, for the object of each of these acts is the same. For this reason the Philosopher says[82]: "Justice is that by which men will and perform just deeds." And it is clear that to perform those things which pertain to the Divine worship or service comes under the virtue of religion. Consequently it belongs to the same virtue of religion to have a prompt will to carry out these things—in other words, to be devout. Whence it follows that devotion is an act of the virtue of religion.

But some argue that devotion is not an act of the virtue of religion, thus:

1. Devotion means that a man gives himself to God. But this belongs to the virtue of charity, for, as S. Denis says[83]: "Divine love causes ecstasy since it permits not that those who love should belong any more to themselves, but to those things which they love." Whence devotion would seem to be rather an act of charity than of the virtue of religion.

It is indeed through charity that a man gives himself to God, clinging to Him by a certain union of soul; but that a man should give himself to God and occupy himself with the Divine service, is due directly to the virtue of religion, though indirectly it is due to the virtue of charity, which is the principle of the virtue of religion.

2. Again, charity precedes the virtue of religion. But devotion seems to precede charity; for charity is signified in Scripture by fire, and devotion by the fat of the sacrifices—the material on which the fire feeds. Consequently devotion is not an act of the virtue of religion.

But while the fat of the body is generated by the natural digestive heat, that natural heat finds its nourishment in that same fat. Similarly charity both causes devotion—since it is by love that a man becomes prompt to serve his friend—and at the same time charity is fed by devotion; just as all friendship is preserved and increased by the practice of friendly acts and by meditating upon them.

3. Lastly, by the virtue of religion a man turns to God alone. But devotion extends to men as well; people, for instance, are said to be devoted to certain Saints, and servants are said to be devoted to their masters, as S. Leo says of the Jews,[84] that being devoted to the Roman laws, they said: We have no king but Cæsar.[85] Consequently devotion is not an act of the virtue of religion.

But the devotion which we have to the Saints of God, whether living or dead, does not stop at them, but passes on to God, since we venerate God in God's ministers. And the devotion which subjects have to their temporal masters is of a different kind altogether, just as the service of temporal masters differs from the service of the Divine Master.

III

Is Contemplation, that is Meditation, the Cause of Devotion?

In Ps. xxxviii. 4 it is said: And in my meditation a fire shall flame out. But spiritual fire causes devotion. Therefore meditation causes devotion.

The extrinsic and principal cause of devotion is God Himself; thus S. Ambrose says[86]: "God calls those whom He deigns to call; and whom He wills to make religious He makes religious; and had He willed it He would have made the Samaritans devout instead of indevout."

But the intrinsic cause of devotion on our part is meditation or contemplation. For, as we have said, devotion is a certain act of the will by which a man gives himself promptly to the Divine service. All acts of the will, however, proceed from consideration, since the will's object is good understood. Hence S. Augustine says[87]: "The will starts from the understanding." Meditation must, then, be the cause of devotion inasmuch as it is from meditation that a man conceives the idea of giving himself up to God.

And two considerations lead a man to do this: one is the consideration of the Divine Goodness and of His benefits, whence the words of the Psalmist: But for me it is good to cling close to my God, to put my hope in the Lord God.[88] And this consideration begets love, which is the proximate cause of devotion. And the second is man's consideration of his own defects which compel him to lean upon God, according to the words: I have lifted up mine eyes to the mountains, from whence help shall come to me; my help is from the Lord Who made Heaven and earth.[89] This latter consideration excludes all presumption which, by making him lean upon himself, might prevent a man from submitting himself to God.

Some, however, argue that contemplation or meditation is not the cause of devotion, thus:

1. No cause hinders its own effect. But subtle intellectual meditations often hinder devotion.

But it is the consideration of those things which naturally tend to excite love of God which begets devotion; consideration of things which do not come under this head, but rather distract the mind from it, are a hindrance to devotion.

2. Again, if contemplation were the real cause of devotion, it should follow that the higher the matter of our contemplation the greater the devotion it begot. But the opposite is the case. For it frequently happens that greater devotion is aroused by the contemplation of the Passion of Christ and of the other mysteries of His Sacred Humanity than by meditation upon the Divine excellences.

It is true that things which concern the Godhead are of themselves more calculated to excite in us love, and consequently devotion, since God is to be loved above all things; yet it is due to the weakness of the human mind that just as it needs to be led by the hand to the knowledge of Divine things, so also must it be lead to Divine love by means of the things of sense already known to it; and the chief of these things is the Humanity of Christ, as is said in the Preface of the Mass: So that knowing God visibly in the flesh, we may thereby be carried away to the love of things invisible. Consequently the things that have to do with Christ's Humanity lead us, as it were, by the hand and are thus especially suited to stir up devotion in us; though, none the less, devotion is principally concerned with the Divinity.

3. Lastly, if contemplation were the real cause of devotion, it ought to follow that those who are the more fitted for contemplation are also the more fitted for devotion; whereas the contrary is the case, for greater devotion is often found among simple folk and in the female sex, where contemplation is wanting.

But knowledge, as indeed anything which renders a person great, occasions a man to trust in Himself, and hence he does not wholly give himself to God. It is for this reason that knowledge and suchlike things are sometimes a hindrance to a man's devotion, whereas among women and simple folk devotion abounds by the suppression of all elation. But if a man will only perfectly subject to God his knowledge and any other perfection he may have, then his devotion will increase.

Cajetan: Note these two intrinsic causes of devotion: one, namely, which arises from meditation upon God and His benefits, the other from meditation on our own defects. Under the first head I must consider God's goodness, mercy, and kindness towards mankind and towards myself; the benefits, for instance, of creation according to His own Likeness, of Redemption, of Baptism, of His inspirations, of His invitations—whether directly or through the medium of others; His patient waiting till I do penance; His Holy Eucharist; His preserving me from so many perils both of body and soul; His care of me by means of His Angels; and His other individual benefits. Under the second head come all my faults and the punishments due to me, whether in the past or now in the present; my proneness to sin; my misuse of my own powers by habituating my thoughts and desires—as well as the inclinations of my other various faculties—to evil; my sojourning in a region far away from His Friendship and from His Divine conversation[90]; my perverted affections which make me think far more of temporal than of spiritual advantages or disadvantages; my utter lack of virtue; the wounds of my ignorance, of my malice, of my weakness, of my concupiscence; the shackles on my hands and feet, on my good works, that is; the shackles, too, on my affections, so that I dwell amidst darkness and rottenness and bitterness, and shrink not from it! My deafness, too, to the inner voice of my Shepherd; and, what is far worse, that I have chosen God for my enemy and my adversary as often as I have chosen mortal sin, and that I have thus offered Him the grievous insult of refusing to have Him for my God, and choosing instead my belly, or money, or false delights—and called them my God!

Meditations such as these should be in daily use among spiritual and religious people, and for their sake they should put aside the "much-speaking" of vocal prayer, however much it may appeal to them. And it is of such meditations that devotion and, by consequence, other virtues, are begotten. And they who do not give themselves to this form of prayer at least once in the day cannot be called religious men or women, nor even spiritual people. There can be no effect without a cause, no end without means to it, no gaining the harbour on the island save by a voyage in a ship; and so there can be no real religion without repeated acts regarding its causes, the means to it, and the vehicle that is to bring us thither (on 2. 2. 82. 3).

Cajetan: Just as he who removes an obstacle is the occasion of the resulting effect—a man, for instance, who pulls down a pillar is the occasion of the resulting fall of what it supported, and a man who removes a water-dam is the occasion of the consequent flood—so in the same way have women and simple folk a cause of devotion within themselves, for they have not that obstacle which consists in self-confidence. And because God bestows His grace on those who put no obstacle to it, the Church therefore calls the female sex "devout." Hence we are not to find fault with the learned for their knowledge, nor are we to praise women for womanly weakness; but that abuse of knowledge which consists in self-exaltation is blameworthy, just as the right use of women's weakness in not being uplifted is praiseworthy (on 2. 2. 82. 3).

IV

Is Joy an Effect of Devotion?

In the Church's Collect for the Thursday after the Fourth Sunday of Lent we say: May holy devotion fill with joy those whom the fast they have undertaken chastises.

Of itself indeed, and primarily, devotion brings about a spiritual joy of the mind; but as an accidental result it causes sorrow. For, as we have said above, devotion arises from two considerations. Primarily it arises from the consideration of the Divine Goodness, and from this thought there necessarily follows gladness, in accordance with the words: I remembered God and was delighted.[91] Yet, as it were accidentally, this consideration begets a certain sadness in those who do not as yet fully enjoy God: My soul hath thirsted after the strong living God,[92] and he immediately adds: My tears have been my bread.

Secondarily, however, devotion arises from the consideration of our own defects, for we thus reflect upon that from which a man, by devout acts of the will, turns away, so as no longer to dwell in himself, but to subject himself to God.

And this consideration is the converse of the former: for of itself it tends to cause sadness since it makes us dwell upon our defects; accidentally, however, it causes joy, for it makes us think of the hope we have of God's assistance.

Hence joy of heart primarily and of itself follows from devotion; but secondarily and accidentally there results a sadness which is unto God.

Some, however, argue that joy is not an effect of devotion, thus:

1. Christ's Passion, as said before, is especially calculated to cause devotion. But from dwelling on it there follows a certain affliction of soul: Remember my poverty ... the wormwood and the gall[93]—that is, the Sacred Passion; and then follows: I will be mindful, and remember, and my soul shall languish within me.

In meditation on the Passion of Christ there is food for sadness—viz., the thought of the sins of men, and to take these away Christ had need to suffer. But there is also food for joy—viz., the thought of God's merciful kindness towards us in providing us such a deliverance.

2. Again, devotion principally consists in the interior sacrifice of the heart: A sacrifice to God is an afflicted spirit;[94] consequently affliction, rather than pleasure or joy, is the outcome of devotion.

But the soul which is on the one hand saddened because of its shortcomings in this present life, is on the other hand delighted at the thought of the goodness of God and of the hope of Divine assistance.

3. Lastly, S. Gregory of Nyssa says[95]: "Just as laughter proceeds from joy, so are sorrow and groaning signs of sadness." But out of devotion some burst into tears.

Yet tears spring not from sadness alone, but also from a certain tenderness of feeling: and especially is this the case when we reflect on something that, while pleasant, has in it a certain admixture of sadness; thus men are wont to weep from loving affection when they recover their children or others dear to them whom they had thought lost. And it is in this sense that tears spring from devotion.

Cajetan: Notice the proof here afforded that those are not devout persons who are habitually sad and gloomy, and who cannot mingle with others without getting into difficulties or dissolving into tears. For devout folk are cheerful, and are full of joy in their souls; and this not solely by reason of the principal cause, as is stated in the text, but also by reason of a secondary cause—the thought, namely, of their own failings. For the sadness of devout folk is according to God, and joy accompanies it; whence S. Augustine's remark: "Let a man grieve, but let him rejoice at his grief."[96] Therefore it is that we read of the Saints that they were joyful and bright; and rightly so, for they had begun upon earth their "heavenly conversation"[97] (on 2. 2. 82. 4).

S. Augustine: For Thee do I yearn, Justice and Innocence, Beautiful and Fair in Thy beauteous light that satisfies and yet never sates! For with Thee is repose exceedingly and life without disquiet! He that enters into Thee enters into the joy of his Lord; he shall know no fear, and in the Best shall be best. But I have deserted Thee and have wandered away, O Lord, my God! Too far have I wandered from Thee, the Steadfast One, in my youth, and I have become to myself a very land of want! (Confessions, II. x.).

FOOTNOTES 3

[79] VIII. 9 and X. 29.
[80] xxxv. 20-21.
[81] 2 Paral. xxix. 31.
[82] Ethics, V. i. 3.
[83] Of the Divine Names, chap. iv., part i., lect. 10.
[84] Sermon VIII.: On the Passion of Our Lord.
[85] S. John xix. 15.
[86] Commentary on S. Luke ix. 55.
[87] De Trinitate, ix. 12; xv. 23.
[88] Ps. lxxii. 28.
[89] Ps. cxx. 1, 2.
[90] S. Luke xv. 13, 16.
[91] Ps. lxxvi. 4.
[92] Ps. xli. 3.
[93] Lam. iii. 19.
[94] Ps. i. 19.
[95] De Homine, xii.
[96] De Vera et Falsa Poenitentia, xiii.
[97] Phil. iii. 20.

QUESTION 3

OF PRAYER

I. Is Prayer an Act of the Appetitive Powers?
   Cardinal Cajetan, On Prayer based on Friendship
II. Is it Fitting to Pray?
   Cardinal Cajetan, On Prayer as a True Cause
   S. Augustine, On the Sermon on the Mount, II. iii. 14
   On the Gift of Perseverance, vii. 15
III. Is Prayer an Act of the Virtue of Religion?
   Cardinal Cajetan, On the Humility of Prayer
   S. Augustine, On Psalm cii. 10
   Of the Gift of Perseverance, xvi. 39
IV. Ought We to Pray to God Alone?
   S. Augustine, Sermon, cxxvii. 2
V. Should We in our Prayers ask for anything Definite from God?
   S. Augustine, De Catechizandis Rudibus, xxv. 47
   Confessions, X. xxix.
   Confessions, XI. ii. 2
VI. Ought We in our Prayers to ask for Temporal Things from God?
   S. Augustine, On Psalm xxxvii. 10
   Confessions, I. xx. 2
   Confessions, IX. iv. 12
   S. Thomas is miraculously relieved from Toothache
   S. Augustine, Sermon, lxxx. 7
   Sermon, cccliv. 8
VII. Ought We to Pray for Others?
VIII. Ought We to Pray for our Enemies?
   S. Augustine, Sermon, xv., on Psalm xxv. 8
IX. On the Seven Petitions of the Lord's Prayer
   Cardinal Cajetan, On the Grouping of these Petitions
   S. Augustine, Confessions, VII. x. 2
   Sermon, lvii., on S. Matt. vi. 7
   Sermon, lvi. 9, on S. Matt. vi.
   Sermon, lvi. 8, on S. Matt. vi.

Of the City of God, xix. 27

S. Thomas's Rhythm, Adoro Te Devote

X. Is Prayer Peculiar to Rational Creatures?

XI. Do the Saints in Heaven Pray for Us?

Cardinal Cajetan, On the Saints in Limbo

XII. Should Prayer be Vocal?

Cardinal Cajetan, On the Conditions of Vocal Prayer

S. Augustine, Confessions, IX. iv. 8

Confessions, X. xxxiii. 50

On Psalm cxviii., Sermon xxix. 1

XIII. Must Prayer necessarily be Attentive?

Cardinal Cajetan, On the Varieties of Attention at Prayer

S. Augustine, On Psalm lxxxv. 7

On Psalm cxlv. 1

S. Thomas, On Distractions, Com. on 1 Cor. xiv. 14

XIV. Should our Prayers be Long?

XV. Is Prayer Meritorious?

S. Augustine, On Psalm xxvi.

Ep. cxxx. ad Probam.

XVI. Do Sinners gain Anything from God by their Prayers?

XVII. Can We rightly term "Supplications," "Prayers," "Intercessions," and "Thanksgivings," parts of Prayer?

Cardinal Cajetan, On the Prayer of the Consecration

S. Augustine, Of Divers Questions, iv.

I

Is Prayer an Act of the Appetitive Powers?

S. Isidore says[98]: "To pray is the same thing as to speak." Speaking, however, belongs to the intellect. Hence prayer is not an act of the appetitive, but of the intellectual faculties.

According to Cassiodorus, on those words of the Psalmist: Hear my prayer, O Lord, and my supplication, give ear to my tears,[99] prayer means "the lips' reasoning." Now there is this difference between the speculative and the practical reason, that the speculative reason merely apprehends things, while the practical reason not only apprehends things, but actually causes them. But one thing is the cause of another in two ways:

in one way, perfectly—namely, as inducing a necessity—as happens when the effect comes entirely under the power of a cause; in another way, imperfectly—namely, by merely disposing to it—as happens when an effect is not entirely under the power of a cause.

And so, too, reason is in two ways the cause of certain things: in one way as imposing a necessity; and in this way it belongs to the reason to command not merely the lower faculties and the bodily members, but even men who are subject to us, and this is done by giving commands. In another way as inducing, and in some sort disposing to, an effect; and in this way the reason asks for something to be done by those who are subject to it, whether they be equals or superiors.

But both of these—namely, to command something, or to ask or beg for something to be done—imply a certain arrangement—as when a man arranges for something to be done by somebody else. And in this respect both of these acts come under the reason whose office it is to arrange. Hence the Philosopher says[100]: "Reason asks for the best things."

Here, then, we speak of prayer as implying a certain asking or petition, for, as S. Augustine says[101]: "Prayer is a certain kind of petition"; so, too, S. John Damascene says[102]: "Prayer is the asking of fitting things from God."

Hence it is clear that the prayer of which we are here speaking is an act of the reason.

Some, however, think that prayer is an act of the appetitive powers, thus:

1. The whole object of prayer is to be heard, and the Psalmist says that it is our desires which are heard: The Lord hath heard the desire of the poor.[103] Prayer, then, is desire; but desire is an act of the appetitive powers.

But the Lord is said to hear the desires of the poor either because their desire is the reason why they ask—since our petitions are in a certain sense the outward expression of our desires; or this may be said in order to show the swiftness with which He hears them—even while things are only existing in the poor man's desire; God hears them even before they are expressed in prayer. And this accords with the words of Isaias: And it shall come to pass that before they shall call I will hear, as they are yet speaking I will hear.[104]

2. Again, Denis the Areopagite says: "But before all things it is good to begin with prayer, as thereby giving ourselves up to and uniting ourselves with God."[105] But union with God comes through love, and love belongs to the appetitive powers; therefore prayer, too, would seem to belong to the appetitive powers.

But the will moves the reason to its end or object. Hence there is nothing to prevent the reason, under the direction of the will, from tending to the goal of charity, which is union with God. Prayer, however, tends towards God—moved, that is, by the will, which itself is motived by charity—in two ways: in one way by reason of that which is asked for, since in prayer we have particularly to ask that we may be united with God, according to those words: One thing I have asked of the Lord, this will I seek after, that I may dwell in the house of the Lord all the days of my life.[106] And in another way prayer tends towards God—by reason, namely, of the petitioner himself; for such a one must approach him from whom he asks something, and this either bodily, as when he draws nigh to a man, or mentally, as when he draws nigh to God.

Hence the same Denis says: "When we invoke God in prayer we are before Him with our minds laid bare." In the same sense S. John Damascene says: "Prayer is the ascent of the mind towards God."

Cajetan: Prayer demands of the petitioner a twofold union with God: the one is general—the union, that is, of friendship—and is produced by charity, so that further on[107] we shall find the friendship arising from charity enumerated among the conditions for infallibly efficacious prayer. The second kind of union may be termed substantial union; it is the effect of prayer itself. It is that union of application by which the mind offers itself and all it has to God in service—viz., by devout affections, by meditations, and by external acts. By such union as this a man who prays is inseparable from God in his worship and service, just as when one man serves another he is inseparable from him in his service (on 2. 2. 83. 1).

"And now, O Lord, Thou art our Father, and we are clay: and Thou art our Maker, and we are all the works of Thy hands. Be not very angry, O Lord, and remember no longer our iniquity: behold, see we are all Thy people."[108]

II

Is It Fitting To Pray?

In S. Luke's Gospel we read: We ought always to pray and not to faint.[109]

A threefold error regarding prayer existed amongst the ancients; for some maintained that human affairs were not directed by Divine Providence; whence it followed that it was altogether vain to pray or to worship God; of such we read: You have said, he laboureth in vain that serveth God.[110] A second opinion was that all things, even human affairs, happened of necessity—whether from the immutability of Divine Providence, or from a necessity imposed by the stars, or from the connection of causes; and this opinion, of course, excluded all utility from prayer. A third opinion was that human affairs were indeed directed by Divine Providence, and that human affairs did not happen of necessity, but that Divine Providence was changeable, and that consequently its dispositions were changed by our prayers and by other acts of religious worship. These views, however, have elsewhere been shown to be wrong.

Consequently we have so to set forth the utility of prayer as neither to make things happen of necessity because subject to Divine Providence, nor to suggest that the arrangements of Divine Providence are subject to change.

To bring this out clearly we must consider that Divine Providence not merely arranges what effects shall take place, but also from what causes they shall proceed, and in what order.

But amongst other causes human acts are causes of certain effects. Hence men must do certain things, not so that their acts may change the Divine arrangement, but that by their acts they may bring about certain effects according to the order arranged by God; and it is the same with natural causes. It is the same, too, in the case of prayer. For we do not pray in order to change the Divine arrangements, but in order to win that which God arranged should be fulfilled by means of prayers; or, in S. Gregory's words: "Men by petitioning may merit to receive what Almighty God arranged before the ages to give them."[111]

Some, however, maintain that prayer is futile, thus:

1. Prayer seems to be necessary in order that we may bring our wants to the notice of Him to Whom we make the petition. But our Lord says: Your Father knoweth that ye have need of all these things.[112]

But it is not necessary for us to set forth our petitions before God in order to make known to Him our needs or desires, but rather that we ourselves may realize that in these things it is needful to have recourse to the Divine assistance.

2. Again, by prayer the mind of him to whom it is made is prevailed upon to grant what is asked of him; but the mind of God is unchangeable and inflexible: The Triumpher in Israel will not spare, and will not be moved to repentance; for He is not a man that He should repent.[113] Consequently it is unavailing to pray to God.

But our prayers do not aim at changing the Divine arrangements, but at obtaining by our prayers what God has arranged to give us.

3. Lastly, it is more generous to give to one who does not ask than to one who asks, for, as Seneca remarks: "Nothing is bought at a dearer price than what is bought with prayers."[114] Whereas God is most generous.

God, indeed, bestows on us many things out of His generosity, even things for which we do not ask; but He wishes to grant us some things on the supposition that we ask for them. And this is for our advantage, for it is intended to beget in us a certain confidence in having recourse to God, as well as to make us recognize that He is the Author of all good to us. Hence S. Chrysostom says: "Reflect what great happiness is bestowed upon you, what glory is given you, namely, to converse in your prayers with God, to join in colloquy with Christ, and to beg for what you wish or desire."[115]

Cajetan: Notice how foolish are some Christians who, when desirous of reaching certain ends attainable by nature or art, are most careful to apply such means, and would rightly regard their hopes as vain unless they applied them; and yet at the same time they have quite false notions of the fruits to be derived from prayer: as though prayer were no cause at all, or at least but a remote one! Whence it comes to pass that, having false ideas about the causes, they fail to reap any fruit (on 2. 2. 83. 2).

S. Augustine: But some may say: It is not so much a question whether we are to pray by words or deeds as whether we are to pray at all if God already knows what is needful for us. Yet the very giving ourselves to prayer has the effect of soothing our minds and purifying them; it makes us more fit to receive the Divine gifts which are spiritually poured out upon us. For God does not hear us because of a display of prayer on our part; He is always ready, indeed, to give us His light, not, indeed, His visible light, but the light of the intellect and the spirit. It is we who are not always prepared to receive it, and this because we are preoccupied with other things and swallowed up in the darkness resulting from desire of the things of earth. When we pray, then, our hearts must turn to God, Who is ever ready to give if only we will take what He gives. And in so turning to Him we must purify the eye of our mind by shutting out all thought for the things of time, that so—with single-minded gaze—we may be able to bear that simple light that shines divinely, and neither sets nor changes. And not merely to bear it, but even to abide in it; and this not simply without strain, but with a certain unspeakable joy. In this joy the life of the Blessed is truly and really perfected (On the Sermon on the Mount, II. iii. 14).

S. Augustine: He could have bestowed these things on us even without our prayers; but He wished that by our prayers we should be taught from Whom these benefits come. For from whom do we receive them if not from Him from Whom we are bidden to ask them? Assuredly in this matter the Church does not demand laborious disputations; but note Her daily prayers: She prays that unbelievers may believe: God then brings them to the Faith. She prays that the faithful may persevere: God gives them perseverance to the end. And God foreknew that He would do these things. For this is the predestination of the Saints whom He chose in Christ before the foundation of the world[116] (Of the Gift of Perseverance, vii. 15).

"Thou hast taught me, O God, from my youth; and till now I will declare Thy wonderful works. And unto old age and grey hairs, O God, forsake me not, until I shew forth Thy arm to all the generation that is to come."[117]

III

Is Prayer an Act of the Virtue of Religion?

In Ps. cxl. 2 we read: Let my prayer be directed as incense in Thy sight, and on these words the Gloss remarks: "According to this figure, in the Old Law incense was said to be offered as an odour of sweetness to the Lord." And this comes under the virtue of religion. Therefore prayer is an act of religion.

It properly belongs to the virtue of religion to give due reverence and honour to God, and hence all those things by which such reverence is shown to God come under religion. By prayer, however, a man shows reverence to God inasmuch as he submits himself to Him and, by praying, acknowledges that he needs God as the Author of all his good. Whence it is clear that prayer is properly an act of religion.

Some, however, maintain that prayer is not an act of the virtue of religion, thus:

1. Prayer is rather the exercise of the Gift of Understanding than of the virtue of religion. For the virtue of religion comes under Justice; it is therefore resident in the will. But prayer belongs to the intellectual faculties, as we have shown above.

But we must remember that the will moves the other faculties of the soul to their objects or ends, and that consequently the virtue of religion, which is in the will, directs the acts of the other faculties in the reverence they show towards God. Now amongst these other faculties of the soul the intellect is the noblest and the most nigh to the will; consequently, next to devotion, which belongs to the will itself, prayer, which belongs to the intellective part, is the chief act of religion, for by it religion moves a man's understanding towards God.

2. Again, acts of worship fall under precept, whereas prayer seems to fall under no precept, but to proceed simply from the mere wish to pray; for prayer is merely asking for what we want; consequently prayer is not an act of the virtue of religion.

Yet not only to ask for what we desire, but to desire rightly, falls under precept; to desire, indeed, falls under the precept of charity, but to ask falls under the precept of religion—the precept which is laid down in the words: Ask and ye shall receive.[118]

3. Lastly, the virtue of religion embraces due worship and ceremonial offered to the Divinity; prayer, however, offers God nothing, but only seeks to obtain things from Him.

In prayer a man offers to God his mind, which he subjects to Him in reverence, and which he, in some sort, lays bare before Him—as we have just seen in S. Denis's words. Hence, since the human mind is superior to all the other exterior or bodily members, and also to all exterior things which have place in the Divine worship, it follows that prayer, too, is preeminent among the acts of the virtue of religion.

Cajetan: In prayer or petition there are three things to be considered: the thing petitioned for, the actual petition, and the petitioner. As far, then, as the thing petitioned for is concerned, we give nothing to God when we pray; rather we ask Him to give us something. But if we consider the actual petition, then we do offer something to God when we pray. For the very act of petitioning is an act of subjection; it is an acknowledgment of God's power. And the proof of this is that proud men would prefer to submit to want rather than humble themselves by asking anything of others. Further, the petitioner, by the very fact that he petitions, acknowledges that he whom he petitions has the power to assist him, and is merciful, or just, or provident; it is for this reason that he hopes to be heard. Hence petition or prayer is regarded as an act of the virtue of religion, the object of which is to give honour to God. For we honour God by asking things of Him, and this by so much the more as—whether from our manner of asking or from the nature of what we ask for—we acknowledge Him to be above all things, to be our Creator, our Provider, our Redeemer, etc. And this is what S. Thomas points out in the body of the Article. But if we consider the petitioner: then, since man petitions with his mind—for petition is an act of the mind—and since the mind is the noblest thing in man, it follows that by petitioning we submit to God that which is noblest in us, since we use it to ask things of Him, and thereby do Him honour. Thus by prayer we offer our minds in sacrifice to God; so, too, by bending the knee to Him we offer to Him and sacrifice to Him our knees, by using them to His honour (on 2. 2. 83. 3).

S. Augustine: I stand as a beggar at the gate, He sleepeth not on Whom I call! Oh, may He give me those three loaves! For you remember the Gospel? Ah! see how good a thing it is to know God's word; those of you who have read it are stirred within yourselves! For you remember how a needy man came to his friend's house and asked for three loaves. And He says that he sleepily replied to him: "I am resting, and my children are with me asleep." But he persevered in his request, and wrung from him by his importunity what his deserts could not get. But God wishes to give; yet only to those who ask—lest He should give to those who understand not. He does not wish to be stirred up by your weariness! For when you pray you are not being troublesome to one who sleeps; He slumbereth not nor sleeps that keepeth Israel.[119] ... He, then, sleeps not; see you that your faith sleeps not! (Enarr. in Ps. cii. 10).

S. Augustine: Some there are who either do not pray at all, or pray but tepidly; and this because, forsooth, they have learnt from the Lord

Himself[120] that God knows, even before we ask Him, what is necessary for us. But because of such folk are we to say that these words are not true and therefore to be blotted out of the Gospel? Nay, rather, since it is clear that God gives some things even to those who do not ask—as, for instance, the beginnings of faith—and has prepared other things for those only who pray for them—as, for instance, final perseverance—it is evident that he who fancies he has this latter of himself does not pray to have it (Of the Gift of Perseverance, xvi. 39).

"I will sing to the Lord as long as I live; I will sing praise to my God while I have my being. Let my speech be acceptable to Him; but I will take delight in the Lord."[121]

IV

Ought We To Pray To God Alone?

In Job v. 1 we read: Call, now, if there be any that will answer thee, and turn to some of the Saints.

Prayer is addressed to a person in two ways: in one way as a petition to be granted by him; in another way as a petition to be forwarded by him. In the former way we only pray to God, for all our prayers ought to be directed to the attaining of grace and glory, and these God alone gives: The Lord will give grace and glory.[122] But in the latter way we set forth our prayers both to the holy Angels and to men; and this, not that through their intervention God may know our petitions, but rather that by their prayers and merits our petitions may gain their end. Hence it is said in the Apocalypse: And the smoke of the incense of the prayers of the Saints ascended up before God from the hand of the Angel.[123] And this is clearly shown, too, from the style adopted by the Church in her prayers: for of the Holy Trinity we pray that mercy may be shown us; but of all the Saints, whomsoever they may be, we pray that they may intercede for us.

Some, however, maintain that we ought to pray to God alone, thus:

1. Prayer is an act of the virtue of religion. But only God is to be worshipped by the virtue of religion. Consequently it is to Him alone that we should pray.

But in our prayers we only show religious worship to Him from Whom we hope to obtain what we ask, for by so doing we confess Him to be the Author of all our goods; but we do not show religious worship to those whom we seek to have as intercessors with us before God.

2. Again, prayer to those who cannot know what we pray for is idle. But God alone can know our prayers, and this because prayer is frequently a purely interior act of which God alone is cognizant, as the Apostle says: I will pray with the spirit. I will pray also with the understanding;[124] and also because, as S. Augustine says[125]: The dead know not, not even the Saints, what the living—not even excepting their own children—are doing.

It is true that the dead, if we consider only their natural condition, do not know what is done on earth, and especially do they not know the interior movements of the heart. But to the Blessed, as S. Gregory says,[126] manifestation is made in the Divine Word of those things which it is fitting that they should know as taking place in our regard, even the interior movements of the heart. And, indeed, it is most befitting their state of excellence that they should be cognizant of petitions addressed to them, whether vocally or mentally. Hence through God's revelation they are cognizant of the petitions which we address them.

3. Lastly, some say: if we do address prayers to any of the Saints, the sole reason for doing so lies in the fact that they are closely united to God. But we do not address prayers to people who, while still living in this world, are closely knit to God, nor to those who are in Purgatory and are united to Him. There seems, then, to be no reason why we should address prayers to the Saints in Paradise.

But they who are still in the world or in Purgatory do not as yet enjoy the vision of the Divine Word so as to be able to know what we think or say, hence we do not implore their help when we pray; though when talking with living people we do ask them to help us.

S. Augustine: It is no great thing to live long, nor even to live for ever; but it is indeed a great thing to live well. Oh, let us love eternal life! And we realize how earnestly we ought to strive for that eternal life when we note how men who love this present temporal life so work for it—though it is to pass away—that, when the fear of death comes, they strive all they can, not, indeed, to do away with death, but to put death off! How men labour when death approaches! They flee from it; they hide from it; they give all they have; they try to buy themselves off; they work and strive; they put up with tortures and inconveniences; they call in physicians; they do everything that lies within their power! Yet even if they spend all their toil and their substance, they can only secure that they may live a little longer, not that they may live for ever! If, then, men spend such toil, such endeavour, so much money, so much anxiety, watchfulness, and care, in order to live only a little longer, what ought we not to do that we may live for ever? And if we call them prudent who take every possible precaution to stave off death, to live but a few days more, to save just a few days, then how foolish are they who so pass their days as to lose the Day of Eternity! (Sermon, cxxvii. 2).

"May God have mercy on us, and bless us: may He cause the light of His countenance to shine upon us, and may He have mercy on us. That we may know Thy way upon earth: Thy salvation in all nations. Let people confess to Thee, O God: let all people give praise to Thee. Let the nations be glad and rejoice: for Thou judgest the people with justice, and directest the nations upon earth. Let the people, O God, confess to Thee: let all the people give praise to Thee: the earth hath yielded her fruit. May God, our God bless us, may God bless us: and all the ends of the earth fear Him."[127]

V

Should We in our Prayers ask for Anything Definite from God?

Our Lord taught the disciples to ask definitely for the things which are contained in the petitions of the Lord's Prayer: Thus shalt thou pray.[128]

Maximus Valerius tells of Socrates[129] that he "maintained that nothing further should be asked of the immortal gods save that they should give us good things; and this on the ground that they knew well what was best for each individual, whereas we often ask in our prayers for things which it would be better not to have asked for." And this opinion has some truth in it as regards those things which can turn out ill, or which a man can use well or ill, as, for example, riches which, as the same Socrates says, "have been to the destruction of many; or honours which have ruined many; or the possession of kingdoms, the issues of which are so often ill-fated; or splendid matrimonial alliances, which have sometimes proved the ruin of families." But there are certain good things of which a man cannot make a bad use—those, namely, which cannot have a bad issue. And these are the things by which we are rendered blessed and by which we merit beatitude; these are the things for which the Saints pray unconditionally: Show us Thy

Face and we shall be saved;[130] and again: Lead me along the path of Thy commandments.[131]

Some, however, say that we ought not in our prayers to ask for definite things from God, thus:

1. S. John Damascene defines prayer as "asking from God things that are fitting";[132] consequently prayer for things which are not expedient is of no efficacy, as S. James says: You ask and receive not, because you ask amiss.[133] Moreover, S. Paul says: We know not what we should pray for as we ought.[134]

But it is also true that though a man cannot of himself know what he ought to pray for, yet, as the Apostle says in the same place: In this the Spirit helpeth our infirmity—namely, in that, by inspiring us with holy desires, He makes us ask aright. Hence Our Lord says that the true adorers must adore in spirit and in truth.[135]

2. Further, he who asks from another some definite thing strives to bend that other's will to do what the petitioner wants. But we ought not to direct our prayers towards making God will what we will, but rather we should will what He wills—as the Gloss says on the words of Ps. xxxii. 1: Rejoice in the Lord, O ye just! It would seem, therefore, that we ought not to ask for definite things from God when we pray.

Yet when in our prayers we ask for things which appertain to our salvation, we are conforming our will to the will of God, for of His will it is said: He will have all men to be saved.[136]

3. Lastly, evil things cannot be asked from God; and He Himself invites us to receive good things. But it is idle for a person to ask for what he is invited to receive.

God, it is true, invites us to receive good things; but He wishes us to come to them—not, indeed, by the footsteps of the body—but by pious desires and devout prayers.

S. Augustine: Fly, then, by unwavering faith and holy habits, fly, brethren, from those torments where the torturers never desist, and where the tortured never die; whose death is unending, and where in their anguish they cannot die. But burn with love for and desire of the eternal life of the Saints where there is no longer the life of toil nor yet wearisome repose.

For the praises of God will beget no disgust, neither will they ever cease. There will there be no weariness of the soul, no bodily fatigue; there will there be no wants: neither wants of your own which will call for succour, nor wants of your neighbour demanding your speedy help. God will be all your delight; there will ye find the abundance of that Holy City that from Him draws life and happily and wisely lives in Him. For there, according to that promise of His for which we hope and wait, we shall be made equal to the Angels of God; and equally with them shall we then enjoy that vision of the Holy Trinity in which we now but walk by faith. For we now believe what we do not see, that so by the merits of that same faith we then may merit to see what we believe, and may so hold fast to it that the Equality of Father, Son, and Holy Ghost, and the Unity of the Trinity, may no longer come to us under the garb of faith, nor be the subject of contentious talk, but may rather be what we may drink in in purest and deepest contemplation amid the silence of Eternity (De Catechizandis Rudibus, xxv. 47).

S. Augustine: O Lord, my God, give me what Thou biddest and then bid what Thou wilt! Thou biddest us be continent. And I knew, as a certain one says, that I could not otherwise be continent save God gave it, and this also was a point of wisdom to know Whose gift it was. Now by continence we are knit together and brought back into union with that One from Whom we have wandered away after many things. For he loves Thee but little who loves other things with Thee, and loves them not for Thee! O Love that ever burnest and wilt never be extinguished! O Charity! O Lord, my God, set me on fire! Thou dost bid continence? Then give me what Thou biddest and bid what Thou wilt! (Confessions, X. xxix.).

S. Augustine: O Lord, my God, listen to my prayer and mercifully hear my desire! For my desire burns not for myself alone, but fraternal charity bids it be of use. And Thou seest in my heart that it is so; for I would offer to Thee in sacrifice the service of my thoughts and of my tongue. Grant me then what I may offer to Thee. For I am needy and poor, and Thou art rich towards all that call upon Thee; for in peace and tranquillity hast Thou care for us. Circumcise, then, my lips, within and without, from all rashness and all untruthfulness. May Thy Scriptures be my chaste delight; may I never be deceived in them nor deceive others out of them. Attend, O Lord, and have mercy upon me, O Lord, my God. Thou art the Light of the blind, the

Strength of the weak, and so, too, art Thou the Light of them that see and the Strength of them that are strong. Look, then, on my soul, and hear me when I cry from out the depths! (Confessions, XI. ii. 2).

"Look down from Heaven, and behold from Thy holy habitation and the place of Thy glory: where is Thy zeal, and Thy strength, the multitude of Thy bowels, and of Thy mercies? they have held back themselves from me. For Thou art our Father, and Abraham hath not known us, and Israel hath been ignorant of us: Thou, O Lord, art our Father, our Redeemer, from everlasting is Thy Name."[137]

VI

Ought We in our Prayers to ask for Temporal Things from God?

We have the authority of the Book of Proverbs for answering in the affirmative, for there we read[138]: Give me only the necessaries of life.

S. Augustine says to Proba[139]: "It is lawful to pray for what it is lawful to desire." But it is lawful to desire temporal things, not indeed as our principal aim or as something which we make our end, but rather as props and stays which may be of assistance to us in our striving for the possession of God; for by such things our bodily life is sustained, and such things, as the Philosopher says, co-operate organically to the production of virtuous acts.[140] Consequently it is lawful to pray for temporal things. And this is what S. Augustine means when he says to Proba: "Not unfittingly does a person desire sufficiency for this life when he desires it and nothing more; for such sufficiency is not sought for its own sake but for the body's health, and for a mode of life suitable to a man's position so that he may not be a source of inconvenience to those with whom he lives. When, then, we have these things we must pray that we may retain them, and when we have not got them we must pray that we may have them."[141]

Some, however, argue that we ought not to pray for temporal things, thus:

1. What we pray for we seek. But we are forbidden to seek for temporal things, for it is said: Seek ye therefore first the kingdom of God, and His justice, and all these things shall be added unto you,[142] those temporal things, namely, which He says are not to be sought but which are to be added to the things which we seek.

But temporal things are to be sought secondarily not primarily. Hence S. Augustine[143]: "When He says the former is to be sought first (namely the kingdom of God), He means that the latter (namely temporal good things) are to be sought afterwards; not afterwards in point of time, but afterwards in point of importance; the former as our good, the latter as our need."

2. Again, we only ask for things about which we are solicitous. But we are not allowed to be solicitous about temporal concerns: Be not solicitous for your life, what ye shall eat[144]....

But not all solicitude about temporal affairs is forbidden, only such as is superfluous and out of due order.

3. Further, we ought in prayer to uplift our minds to God. But by asking for temporal things in prayer our mind descends to things beneath it, and this is contrary to the teaching of the Apostle: While we look not at the things which are seen, but at the things which are not seen. For the things which are seen are temporal: but the things which are not seen are eternal.[145]

When our mind is occupied with temporal affairs so as to set up its rest in them then it remains in them, and is depressed by them; but when the mind turns to them as a means of attaining to eternal life it is not depressed by them, but rather uplifted by them.

4. Lastly, men ought not to pray except for things useful and good. But temporal possessions are at times hurtful, and this not merely spiritually but even temporally; hence a man ought not to ask them of God.

But it is clear that since we do not seek temporal things primarily or for their own sake, but with reference to something else, we consequently only ask them of God according as they may be expedient for our salvation.

S. Augustine: Lord, all my desire is before Thee, and my groaning is not hid from Thee![146] It is not before men who cannot see the heart, but before Thee is all my desire! And let your desires, too, be before Him, and your Father Who seeth in secret will repay thee. For your very desire is a prayer, and if your desire is continual your prayer, too, is continual. Not without reason did the Apostle say: Pray without ceasing.[147] Yet can we genuflect without ceasing? Can we prostrate without ceasing? Can we lift up our hands without ceasing? How, then, does he say: Pray without ceasing? If by prayer he meant such things as these then I think we could not pray without ceasing. But there is another prayer, an interior prayer, which is without ceasing—desire. Whatever else you do, if only you desire that rest[148] you cease not to pray. If you wish to pray without ceasing then desire without ceasing. Your continual desire is your continual voice; but you will be silent if you cease to love (Enarr. in Ps. xxxvii. 10).

S. Augustine: But all these things are the gifts of my God; I did not give them to myself; they are good, and all these things am I. He then is good Who made me; nay, He Himself is my Good, and in Him do I rejoice for all the good things which I had even as a boy! But in this did I sin that, not in Him but in His creatures did I seek myself and other pleasures, high thoughts and truths. Thus it was that I fell into sorrow, confusion, and error. Thanks be to Thee, my Sweetness, my Honour and my Trust, O my God! Thanks be to Thee for Thy gifts! But do Thou keep them for me! For so doing Thou wilt be keeping me, and those things which Thou hast given me will be increased and perfected, and I myself shall be with Thee, for even that I should be at all is Thy gift to me! (Confessions, I. xx. 2).

S. Augustine: But I forget not, neither will I keep silence regarding the severity of Thy scourge and the wondrous swiftness of Thy mercy. Thou didst torture me with toothache; and when the pain had become so great that I could not even speak, it came into my mind to tell all my friends who were there to pray to Thee for me, to Thee the God of all manner of succour. And I wrote my request on a wax tablet and I gave it them to read. And hardly had we bent the knee in humble prayer than the pain fled! But what a pain it was! And how did it disappear? I was terrified, I confess it, O Lord my God! Never in all my life had I felt anything like it! (Confessions, IX. iv. 12).

It is narrated of S. Thomas that when at Paris it happened that having to lecture at the University on a subject which he had commenced the day before, he rose at night to pray as was his wont, but discovered that a tooth had suddenly pushed its way through his gums in such a way that he could not speak. His companion suggested that since it was an inopportune time for procuring assistance a message should be sent to the University stating what had happened and pointing out that the lecture could not be given till the tooth had been removed by a surgeon. But S. Thomas, reflecting upon the difficulty in which the University would be placed, considering also the danger which might arise from the removal of the tooth in the way suggested, said to his companion: I see no remedy save to trust to God's

Providence. He then betook himself to his accustomed place of prayer, and for a long space besought God with tears to grant him this favour, leaving himself entirely in His hands. And when he had thus prayed he took the tooth between his fingers, and it came out at once without the slightest pain or wrench, and he found himself freed from the impediment to his speech which it had caused. This tooth he carried about with him for a long time as a reminder of an act of Divine loving-kindness such as he was anxious not to forget, for forgetfulness is the mother of ingratitude; he wished it, too, to move him to still greater confidence in the power of prayer which had on that occasion been so quickly heard (see Vita S. Thomæ, Bollandists, March 7, vol. i., 1865, pp. 673, 704, 712).

S. Augustine: But temporal things are sometimes for our profit, sometimes for our hurt. For many poverty was good, wealth did them harm. For many a hidden life was best, high station did them harm. And on the other hand money was good for some, and dignities, too, were good for them—good, that is, for those who used them well; but such things did harm when not taken away from those who used them ill. Consequently, brethren, let us ask for these temporal things with moderation, being sure that if we do receive them, He gives them Who knoweth what is best suited to us. You have asked for something, then, and what you asked for has not been given you? Believe in your Father Who would give it you if it were expedient for you (Sermon, lxxx. 7).

S. Augustine: Sometimes God in His wrath grants what you ask; at other times in His mercy He refuses what you ask. When, then, you ask of Him things which He praises, which He commands, things which He has promised us in the next world, then ask in confidence and be instant in prayer as far as in you lies, that so you may receive what you ask. For such things as these are granted by the God of mercy; they flow not from His wrath but from His compassion. But when you ask for temporal things, then ask with moderation, ask with fear; leave all to Him so that if they be for your profit He may give them you, if they be to your hurt He may refuse them. For what is for our good and what is to our hurt the Physician knoweth, not the patient (Sermon, cccliv. 8).

"Cast thy care upon the Lord, and He shall sustain thee; He shall not suffer the just to waver for ever."[149]

VII

Ought We To Pray for Others?

S. James, in his Epistle, says[150]: Pray for one another that ye may be saved.

As we said above, we ought in prayer to ask for those things which we ought to desire. But we ought to desire good things not for ourselves only but also for others, for this belongs to that charity which we ought to exercise towards our neighbour. Hence charity demands that we pray for others. In accordance with this S. Chrysostom says[151]: "Necessity compels us to pray for ourselves, fraternal charity urges us to pray for others. But that prayer is more pleasing before God which arises not so much from our needs as from the demands of fraternal charity."

Some, however, urge that we ought not to pray for others, thus:

1. We are bound in our prayer to follow the norm which our Lord delivered to us; but in the Lord's Prayer we pray for ourselves and not for others, for we say: Give us this day our daily bread, etc.

But S. Cyprian says:[152] "We do not say my Father, but our Father, neither do we say Give me, but give us; and this because the Teacher of Unity did not wish prayer to be made privately, viz., that each should pray for himself alone; for He wished one to pray for all since He in His single Person had borne all."

2. Again, we pray in order to be heard; but one of the conditions for our prayer to be heard is that a man should pray for himself. Thus on the words: If ye ask the Father anything in My Name He will give it you,[153] S. Augustine says:[154] "All are heard for themselves, but not for all in general, hence He does not say simply: He will give it, but He will give it you."

But to pray for oneself is a condition attaching to prayer; not indeed a condition affecting its merit, but a condition which is necessary if we would ensure the attainment of what we ask. For it sometimes happens that prayer made for another does not avail even though it be devout and persevering and for things pertaining to a man's salvation; and this is because of the existence of some hindrance on the part of him for whom we pray, as we read in Jeremias[155]: If Moses and Samuel shall stand before Me, My soul is not towards this people. None the less, such prayer will be meritorious on the part of him who prays, for he prays out of charity; thus on the words, And my prayer shall be turned into my bosom,[156] the Interlinear Gloss has: "That is, and even though it avail not for them, yet shall I not be without my reward."

3. Lastly, we are forbidden to pray for others if they are wicked, according to the words: Do not thou pray for this people ... and do not withstand Me, for I will not hear thee.[157] And, on the other hand, we ought not to pray for them if they are good, for in that case they will be heard when they pray for themselves.

But we have to pray even for sinners, that they may be converted, and for the good, that they may persevere and make progress. Our prayers for sinners, however, are not heard for all, but for some. For they are heard for those who are predestined, not for those who are foreknown as reprobate; just in the same way as when we correct our brethren, such corrections avail among the predestinate but not among the reprobate, according to the words: No man can correct whom He hath despised.[158] Wherefore also it is said: He that knoweth his brother to sin a sin that is not unto death, let him ask, and life shall be given to him who sinneth not to death.[159] But just as we can refuse to no one, as long as he liveth on this earth, the benefit of correction—for we cannot distinguish between the predestinate and the reprobate, as S. Augustine says[160]—so neither can we refuse to anyone the suffrage of our prayers.

And for good men we have to pray, and this for a threefold reason: firstly, because the prayers of many are more easily heard; thus on the words: I beseech ye therefore, help me in your prayers for me,[161] the Ordinary Gloss of S. Ambrose says: "Well does the Apostle ask his inferiors to pray for him; for even the very least become great when many in number, and when gathered together with one mind; and it is impossible that the prayers of many should not avail" to obtain, that is, what is obtainable. And secondly, that thanks may be returned by many for the benefits conferred by God upon the just, for these same benefits tend to the profit of many—as is evident from the Apostle's words to the Corinthians.[162] And thirdly, that those who are greater may not therefore be proud, but may realize that they need the suffrages of their inferiors.

"Father, I will that where I am they also whom Thou hast given Me may be with Me; that they may see My glory, which Thou hast given Me: because Thou hast loved Me before the foundation of the world."[163]

VIII
Ought We To Pray for Our Enemies?

But I say to you ... pray for them that persecute and calumniate you.[164]

To pray for others is a work of charity, as we have said above. Hence we are bound to pray for our enemies in the same way as we are bound to love them. We have already explained, in the Treatise on Charity, in what sense we are bound to love our enemies; namely, that we are bound to love their nature, not their fault; and that to love our enemies in general is of precept; to love them, however, individually, is not of precept save in the sense of being prepared to do so; a man, for instance, is bound to be ready to love an individual enemy and to help him in case of necessity, or if he comes to seek his pardon. But absolutely to love our individual enemies, and to assist them, belongs to perfection.

In the same way, then, it is necessary that in our general prayers for others we should not exclude our enemies. But to make special prayer for them belongs to perfection and is not necessary, save in some particular cases.

Some, however, argue that we ought not to pray for our enemies, thus:

1. It is said in the Epistle to the Romans[165]: What things soever were written were written for our learning. But in Holy Scripture we find many imprecations against enemies; thus, for instance[166]: Let all my enemies be ashamed, let them be turned back and be ashamed very speedily. From which it would rather seem that we ought to pray against our enemies than for them.

But the imprecations which find place in Holy Scripture can be understood in four different ways: first of all according as the Prophets are wont "to predict the future under the figure of imprecations," as S. Augustine says[167]; secondly, in that certain temporal evils are sometimes sent by God upon sinners for their amendment; thirdly, these denunciations may be understood, not as demanding the punishment of men themselves, but as directed against the kingdom of sin, in the sense that by men being corrected sin may be destroyed; fourthly, in that the Prophets conform their wills to the Divine Justice with regard to the damnation of sinners who persevere in their sin.

2. Further, to be revenged upon our enemies means evil for our enemies. But the Saints seek to be avenged upon their enemies: How long, O Lord, dost Thou not judge and revenge our blood on them that dwell on the earth?[168] And in accordance with this we find them rejoicing in the vengeance taken upon sinners: The just shall rejoice when he shall see the revenge.[169] It would seem, then, that we ought rather to pray against our enemies than for them.

But, on the contrary, as S. Augustine says:[170] "The vengeance of the martyrs is the overthrow of the empire of sin under whose dominion they suffered so much"; or, as he says elsewhere[171]: "They demand vengeance, not by word of mouth, but by very reason, just as the blood of Abel cried out from the earth." Moreover, they rejoice in this vengeance, not for its own sake, but because of the Divine Justice.

3. Lastly, a man's deeds and his prayers cannot be in opposition. But men sometimes quite lawfully attack their enemies, else all wars would be illegal. Hence we ought not to pray for our enemies.

But it is lawful to assail our enemies that so they may be hindered from sin; and this is for their good and for that of others. In the same way, then, it is lawful to pray for temporal evils for our enemies to the end that they may be corrected. In this sense our deeds and our prayers are not in opposition.

S. Augustine: If there were no wicked folk, then for whom could we be supposed to pray when we are told: Pray for your enemies? Perhaps you would like to have good enemies. Yet how could that be? For unless you yourself are bad you will not have good people for enemies; and if, on the contrary, you are good, then no one will be your enemy save the wicked folk (Sermon, xv., on Ps. xxv. 8).

"Have mercy upon us, O God of all, and behold us, and shew us the light of Thy mercies: And send Thy fear upon the nations, that have not sought after Thee: that they may know that there is no God beside Thee, and that they may shew forth Thy wonders. Lift up Thy hand over the strange nations, that they may see Thy power."[172]

On the Seven Petitions of the lord's Prayer.

The Lord's Prayer is the most perfect of all prayers, for, as S. Augustine says to Proba[173]: "If we pray rightly and fittingly we can say nothing else but what is set down in the Lord's Prayer." And since prayer is, in a sort, the interpreter of our desires before God, we can only rightly ask in prayer for those things which we can rightly desire. But in the Lord's Prayer not only do we have petitions for all those things which we can rightly desire, but they are set forth in the order in which they are to be desired. Hence this prayer not only teaches us how to pray, but serves as the norm of all our dispositions of mind.

For it is clear that we desire first the end and then the means to the attainment of that end. But our end is God, towards Whom our desires tend in two ways: first, in that we desire God's glory; secondly, in that we desire to enjoy that glory ourselves. The former of these pertains to that love wherewith we love God in Himself, the latter to that charity wherewith we love ourselves in God. Hence the first petition runs: Hallowed be Thy Name, wherein we pray for God's glory; and the second runs: Thy kingdom come, wherein we pray that we may come to the glory of His kingdom.

But to this said end things lead us in two ways: viz., either essentially or accidentally. Things which are useful for the attainment of that end essentially lead us to it. But a thing may be useful as regards that end which is the possession of God in two ways: namely, directly and principally, that is, according to the merits by which we merit the possession of God by obeying Him; and in accordance with this runs the petition: Thy Will be done on earth as it is in Heaven; also instrumentally as assisting us to merit, whence the petition: Give us this day our daily bread. And this is true whether we understand by this "bread" that Sacramental Bread, the daily use of Which profits man, and in Which are comprised all the other Sacraments; or whether we understand it of material bread so that "bread" here means all that is sufficient for the support of life—as S. Augustine explains it to Proba.[174] For both the Holy Eucharist is the chief of Sacraments, and bread is the chief of foods, whence in the Gospel of S. Matthew we have the term "super-substantial" or "special" applied to it, as S. Jerome explains it.[175]

And we are lead, as it were, accidentally to the possession of God by the removal of impediments from our path. Now there are three things which impede us in our efforts after the possession of God. The first of these is sin, which directly excludes us from the kingdom: Neither fornicators, nor idolaters, ... etc., shall possess the kingdom of God;[176] hence the petition: Forgive us our trespasses.... And the second impediment is temptation which hinders us from obeying the Divine Will; whence the petition: And lead us not into temptation; in which petition we do not pray that we may not be tempted, but that we may not be overcome by temptation, for this is the meaning of being led into temptation. And the third hindrance lies in our present penal state which prevents us from having "the sufficiency of life"; and for this reason we say: Deliver us from evil.

Some, however, argue that these seven petitions are not very appropriate, thus:

1. It seems idle to pray that that may be hallowed which is already hallowed or holy. But the Name of God is holy: And holy is His Name.[177] Similarly, His kingdom is everlasting: Thy kingdom, O Lord, is a kingdom of all ages.[178] God's Will, too, is always fulfilled: And all My Will shall be done.[179] Hence it is idle to pray that God's Name may be hallowed, that His kingdom may come, and that His Will may be done.

But, as S. Augustine says,[180] when we say, Hallowed be Thy Name, we do not make this petition as though God's Name were not holy, but that It may be held holy by men; in other words, that God's glory may be propagated amongst men. And when we say, Thy kingdom come, it is not as though we meant that God did not reign, but, as S. Augustine says to Proba[181]: "We stir up our desires for that kingdom, that it may come upon us and that we may reign in it." Lastly, when we say, Thy Will be done, this is rightly understood to mean: May Thy precepts be obeyed on earth as in Heaven—that is, as by Angels, so by men. These three petitions, then, will receive their perfect fulfilment in the life to come; but the remaining four, as S. Augustine says, refer to the necessities of the present life.[182]

2. But further, to depart from evil must precede the pursuit of what is good. Hence it hardly seems appropriate to place those petitions which are concerned with the pursuit of what is good before those which refer to the departing from evil.

Yet since prayer is the interpreter of our desires the order of these petitions does not correspond to the order of attainment but of desire or intention; in this order, however, the end precedes the means to the end, the pursuit of good comes before the departure from evil.

3. But once more, we ask for something in order that it may be given us. But the chief gift of God is the Holy Spirit and those things which are given us through Him. Hence these petitions do not seem to be very appropriate since they do not correspond to the Gifts of the Holy Spirit.

S. Augustine[183], however, adapts these seven petitions to the Gifts of the Holy Spirit and to the Beatitudes; he says: "If we have the fear of God by which the poor in spirit are blessed, we pray that God's Name may be hallowed among men by chaste fear. If we have piety, by which the meek are blessed, we pray that His kingdom may come, that we may be meek, and that we may not withstand It. If we have knowledge, by which they that mourn are blessed, we pray that His will may be done, and that so we may not mourn. If we have fortitude, by which they that hunger are blessed, we pray that our daily bread may be given us. If we have counsel, by which they that are merciful are blessed, let us forgive our debtors that we ourselves may be forgiven. If we have understanding, by which the clean of heart are blessed, let us pray that we may not have a double heart that pursues after temporal things whence temptations come to us. If we have wisdom, whence the peace-makers are blessed—for they shall be called the sons of God—let us pray that we may be delivered from evil, for that very deliverance will make us the free sons of God."

4. Again, according to S. Luke,[184] there are only five petitions in the Lord's Prayer. Hence it would seem superfluous to have seven in S. Matthew.

But, as S. Augustine says[185]: "S. Luke only includes five petitions and not seven in the Lord's Prayer, for he shows that the third petition is, in a sense, only a repetition of the two preceding ones; by omitting it he makes us see that God's will is more especially concerned with our knowledge of His sanctity and with our reigning with Him. But Luke has omitted Matthew's last petition, Deliver us from evil, in order to show us that we are delivered from evil just precisely as we are not led into temptation."

5. And lastly, it seems idle to try to stir up the benevolence of one who is beforehand with his benevolence. But God does forestall us with His benevolence, for He hath first loved us.[186] Consequently it seems

superfluous to preface our petitions with the words Our Father Who art in Heaven, words which seem intended to stir up God's benevolence.

But we must remember that prayer is not directed to God in order to prevail upon Him, but in order to excite ourselves to confidence in our petitions. And this confidence is especially excited in us by consideration of His love towards us whereby He wishes us well, wherefore we say, Our Father; and of His pre-eminent power whereby He is able to assist us, whence we say, Who art in Heaven.

Cajetan: The first three petitions of the Lord's Prayer can also be referred to that which we principally desire, so that all three regard mainly that love wherewith we love God in Himself, and secondarily that love wherewith we love ourselves in God. And the proof of this is that in each of the first three we have the pronoun Thine, but in the last four the pronoun our. Thus the first petition asks for the effective and enduring praise of God's Name; the second, that He—and not the devil, nor the world, nor the flesh, nor sin—may reign effectively; the third, that His Will may be effectively fulfilled. For these things are not now absolutely so with God, and this by reason of the multitude of sins, and also because the mode of their present fulfilment is hidden. And the word effectively is introduced into each clause by reason of the subjoined qualification on earth as it is in Heaven, for this qualifies each of the foregoing clauses. Hence rightly do our desires first of all aim at, wish for, and pray that—even as something good for God Himself—He may be sanctified in His Name; that He may be permanently uplifted above all things—on earth as in Heaven; that He—not sin—may reign—on earth as in Heaven; that His Will—none other—may be done—on earth as in Heaven (on 2. 2. 83. 9).

S. Augustine: O Eternal Truth, True Love and lovable Eternity! Thou art my God; for Thee do I sigh night and day! And when I first knew Thee Thou didst snatch me up so that I saw that That really was Which I saw, and that I who saw was really not—as yet. And Thou didst beat back my weak gaze, pouring out Thy light upon me in its intensity; and I trembled with love and with horror. For I found myself to be far away from Thee in a land that was unlike Thee; it was as though I heard Thy Voice from on high, saying: "I am the Food of grown men, grow, and thou shalt eat Me, but thou shalt not be changed into Me" (Confessions, VII. x. 2).

S. Augustine: And the faithful are well aware of that Spiritual Food Which you, too, will soon know and Which you are to receive from God's altar. It will be your food, nay, your daily food, needful for this life. For are we not about to receive the Eucharist wherein we come to Christ Himself, and begin to reign with Him for ever? The Eucharist is our daily Bread. But let us so receive it as to be thereby refreshed, not in body merely but in mind. For the power which we know to be therein is the power of Unity whereby we are brought into union with His Body and become His members. Let us be What we receive; for then It will be truly our daily bread.

Again, what I set before you is your daily bread; and what you hear read day by day in the church is your daily bread; and the hymns you hear and which you sing—they are your daily bread. For these things we need for our pilgrimage. But when we get There are we going to hear a book read? Nay, we are going to hear the Word Himself; we are going to see the Word Himself; we are going to eat Him, to drink Him, even as the Angels do already. Do the Angels need books, or disputations, or readers? Nay, not so. But by seeing they read, for they see the Truth Itself and are sated from that Fount whence we receive but the sprinkling of the dew (Sermon, lvii., on S. Matt. vi. 7).

S. Augustine: When ye say Give us this day our daily bread, ye profess yourselves God's beggars. Yet blush not at it! The richest man on earth is God's beggar. The beggar stands at the rich man's door. But the rich man in his turn stands at the door of one richer than he. He is begged from, and he, too, has to beg. If he were not in need he would not beseech God in prayer. But what can the rich man need? I dare to say it: he needs even his daily bread! For how is it that he abounds with all things, save that God gave them to him? And what will they have if God but withdraw His hand? (Sermon, lvi. 9, on S. Matt. vi.).

S. Augustine: Think not that you have no need to say Forgive us our trespasses as we forgive them that trespass against us.... He who looks with pleasure at what he should not—sins. Yet who can control the glance of the eye? Indeed, some say that the eye is so called from its swiftness (oculus a velocitate). Who can control his eyes or his ears? You can close your eyes when you like, but how quickly they open again! You can shut your ears with an effort; put up your hand, and you can touch them. But if someone holds your hands your ears remain open, and you cannot then shut out cursing words, impure words, flattering and deceitful words. When you hear something which you should not—do you not sin with your ears? What when you hear some evil thing with pleasure? And the death-dealing tongue! How many sins it commits! (Sermon, lvi. 8).

S. Augustine: Indeed, our whole righteousness—true righteousness though it be, by reason of the True Good to Whom it is referred, consists rather, as long as we are in this life, in the remission of our sins than in the perfection of our virtues. And the proof of this is the Prayer of the whole City of God which is in pilgrimage on this earth. For by all Its members It cries to God: Forgive us our trespasses as we forgive them the trespass against us! And this Prayer is of no avail for those whose faith is without works—dead; but only for those whose faith worketh through charity. For though our reason is indeed subject to God, yet in this our mortal condition, in this corruptible body which weigheth down the soul, our reason does not perfectly control our vices, and hence such prayer as this is needful for the righteous (Of the City of God, xix. 27).

"Father, the hour is come; glorify Thy Son, that Thy Son may glorify Thee. As Thou hast given Him power over all flesh, that He may give life everlasting to all whom Thou hast given Him. And this is life everlasting, that they may know Thee, the only true God, and Jesus Christ, Whom Thou hast sent."[187]

Rhythm in Honour of the Blessed Sacrament, said to have been composed by S. Thomas on his Death-Bed.[188]

Adoro Te devote, latens Deitas,
Quæ sub his figuris vere latitas;
Tibi se cor meum totum subjicit,
Quia Te contemplans totum deficit.
Visus, tactus gustus, in Te fallitur,
Sed auditu solo tuto creditur;
Credo quidquid dixit Dei Filius,
Nil hoc verbo veritatis verius.
In cruce latebat sola Deitas,
At hic latet simul et humanitas;
Ambo tamen credens atque confitens,
Peto quod petivit latro poenitens.

Plagas, sicut Thomas, non intueor,
Deum tamen meum Te confiteor;
Fac me Tibi semper magis credere,
In Te spem habere, Te diligere.
O memoriale mortis Domini,
Panis vivus, vitam præstans homini,
Præsta meæ menti de Te vivero,
Et Te illi semper dulce sapere.
Pie Pellicane Jesu Domine,
Me immundum munda Tuo Sanguine,
Cujus una stilla salvum facere
Totum mundum quit ab omni scelere.
Jesu Quem velatum nunc aspicio,
Oro fiat illud quod tam sitio,
Ut Te revelata cernens facie,
Visu sim beatus Tuæ gloriæ!

(An Indulgence of 100 days for the recitation of this rhythm. S. Congr. of Indulgences, December 20, 1884.)

X

Is Prayer Peculiar to Rational Creatures?

Prayer is an act of the reason, as we have shown above. And rational creatures are so termed because of the possession of reason. Consequently prayer is peculiar to them.

As we have said above, prayer is an act of the reason by which a person pleads with his superior, just in the same way as a command is an act of the reason by which an inferior is directed to do something. Prayer, then, properly pertains to one who has the use of reason and who also has a superior with whom he can plead. The Persons of the Trinity have no superior; the brute animals have no reason. Hence prayer belongs neither to the Divine Persons nor to the brute creation, but is peculiar to rational creatures.

Some, however, argue that prayer cannot be peculiar to rational creatures, thus:

1. To ask and to receive belong to the same person. But the Divine Persons receive: the Son, namely, and the Holy Spirit. Consequently They

can also pray; indeed it is the Son Himself Who says, I will ask the Father,[189] and the Apostle says of the Holy Spirit, The Spirit Himself asketh for us.[190]

But it belongs to the Divine Persons to receive by Their nature, whereas to pray belongs to one who receives through grace. The Son is said to ask or pray according to the nature He took upon Himself—that is according to His Human, and not according to His Divine, Nature; the Holy Spirit, too, is said to petition because He makes us petition.

2. But further, the Angels are superior to the rational creation since they are intellectual substances; but it belongs to the Angels to pray, for it is said in the Psalm[191]: Adore Him, all ye His Angels.

But the intellect and the reason are not different faculties in us, though they do differ in the sense that one is more perfect than the other. Consequently the intellectual creation, such as are the Angels, is sometimes distinguished from the rational creation, but at other times both are embraced under the one term "rational." And it is in this latter sense of the term "rational" that prayer is said to be peculiar to the rational creation.

3. Lastly, he prays who calls upon God; for it is chiefly by prayer that we call upon God. But the brute animals also call upon God, for the Psalmist says: Who giveth to beasts their food, and to the young ravens that call upon Him.[192]

But the young ravens are said to call upon God by reason of those natural desires by which all things, each in their own fashion, desire to obtain the Divine goodness. In the same way brute animals are said to obey God by reason of the natural instinct by which they are moved by God.

"Reward them that patiently wait for Thee, that Thy Prophets may be found faithful: and hear the prayers of Thy servants. According to the blessing of Aaron over Thy people, and direct us into the way of justice, and let all know that dwell upon the earth, that Thou art God the beholder of all ages."[193]

XI

Do the Saints in Heaven Pray for Us?

This is he who prayeth much for the people and for all the holy city, Jeremias the Prophet of God.[194]

As S. Jerome says,[195] Vigilantius's error lay in maintaining that "while we live we can mutually pray for one another; but after we are dead no one's prayer for another is heard, and this is especially clear in the case of the Martyrs who were unable to obtain by their prayers vengeance for their blood."

But this is altogether false; for since prayer for others springs from charity, the more perfect the charity of those who are in Heaven the more they pray for those wayfarers on earth who can be helped by their prayers. And the more knit they are to God the more efficacious are their prayers; for the Divine harmony demands that the superabundance of those who are in the higher position should redound upon those who are lower, just as the brightness of the sun renders the atmosphere itself luminous. Whence Christ Himself is said to be Approaching of Himself to God to intercede for us.[196] Whence, too, S. Jerome's reply to Vigilantius: "If the Apostles and Martyrs, when they were still in the body, and had still to be solicitous on their own account, prayed for others, how much more when they have won the crown, when they have gained the victory and the triumph?"

Yet some maintain that the Blessed in Heaven do not pray for us, thus:

1. A man's acts are more meritorious for himself than for another. But the Saints who are in Heaven neither merit for themselves nor pray for themselves, for they have already attained the goal of their desires. Hence neither do they pray for us.

But the Saints who are in our Fatherland lack no Blessedness—since they are Blessed—save the glory of the body, and for this they pray. But they pray for us who still lack the ultimate perfection of Blessedness; and their prayers are efficacious by reason of their previous merits and of the Divine acceptation of their prayers.

2. But once more: the Saints are perfectly conformed to the Will of God, and consequently will nothing but what He wills. But what God wills is always fulfilled. Hence it is idle for the Saints to pray for us.

But the Saints obtain that which God wills should come about through the medium of their prayers; and they ask for what they think is, by God's Will, to be fulfilled through their prayers.

3. And yet again: just as the Saints in Heaven are superior to us so also are they who are in Purgatory—for they cannot sin. Those, however, who

are in Purgatory do not pray for us, but rather we for them. It follows, then, that neither can the Saints in Heaven pray for us.

But though those who are in Purgatory are superior to us in that they cannot sin, yet are they our inferiors as regards the penalties they suffer; hence they are not in a state to pray for us, but rather we for them.

4. Once more: if the Saints in Heaven could pray for us it would follow that the prayers of the holiest Saints would be the most efficacious, and that consequently we ought not to ask the inferior Saints to pray for us, but only the greatest ones.

But God desires inferior things to be helped by all that are superior, and consequently we have to implore the aid of not only the chief Saints but also of the lesser; else it would follow that we ought to implore mercy from God alone. And it may sometimes happen that the petition made to a lesser Saint is more efficacious, either because we ask him more devoutly, or because God wishes thus to show forth his sanctity.

5. Lastly, Peter's soul is not Peter. Consequently if the souls of the Saints could pray for us, we ought—as long as their souls are separated from their bodies—to appeal, not to Peter to help us, but to Peter's soul; whereas the Church does the contrary. From which it would seem that the Saints, at all events previous to the Resurrection, do not pray for us.

But since the Saints merited when alive that they should pray for us, we therefore call upon them by the names they bore when here below, and by which they are best known to us; and we do this, too, in order to show our faith in the Resurrection, in accordance with the words I am the God of Abraham.[197]

Cajetan: The question arises: how could Jeremias, who in the days of the Maccabees was not yet in our Fatherland but still in the Limbo of the Fathers, pray for Jerusalem?

But if we carefully consider what it is at root which makes the prayers of the Saints in the Fatherland avail for us, we shall find that the same reason holds for the Saints who were in Limbo as for those who enjoy the Beatific Vision. For it is their charity in their state of absolute superiority to us which is the reason for their praying for us. Hence, in the reply to the third difficulty, those who are in Purgatory are excluded from the number of those who pray for us because they are not altogether our superiors, but by reason of their sufferings are inferior to us, and need our prayers.

But the Fathers in Limbo were, it is clear, confirmed in charity and were incapable of sin, neither were they liable to any peculiar or fresh suffering. For while the pain of loss was common to them and to the sojourners on earth, the former were free from all pain of sense, hence they could pray for us. There is, however, this difference to be noted between them and the Saints in the Fatherland—viz., that whereas the former had it in common with the latter to pray for those sojourning on earth, it is given only to the Saints in the Fatherland to see the prayers of us sojourners addressed to them. Hence Jeremias is here said to pray, he is not said to have heard their prayers or supplications (on 2. 2. 83. 11).

XII

Should Prayer be Vocal?

I cried to the Lord with my voice, with my voice I made supplication to the Lord.[198]

Prayer is of two kinds: public and private. Public or common prayer is that which is offered to God by the Church's ministers in the person of the whole body of the faithful. And it is necessary that such prayer should be known to the body of the faithful for whom it is offered; this, however, could not be unless it were vocal; consequently it is reasonably enacted that the Church's ministers should pronounce such prayers in a loud voice so as to reach the ears of all.

Private prayer, on the contrary, is that which is offered by private individuals, whether for themselves or for others; and its nature does not demand that it should be vocal. At the same time, we can use our voices in this kind of prayer, and this for three reasons: Firstly, in order to excite interior devotion whereby our minds may, when we pray, be lifted up to God; for men's minds are moved by external signs—whether words or acts—to understand, and, by consequence, also to feel. Wherefore S. Augustine says to Proba[199]: "By words and other signs we vehemently stir ourselves up so as to increase our holy desires." Hence in private prayer we must make such use of words and other signs as shall avail to rouse our minds interiorly. But if, on the other hand, such things only serve to distract the mind, or prove in any way a hindrance, then we must cease from them;

this is especially the case with those whose minds are sufficiently prepared for devotion without such incentives. Thus the Psalmist says: My heart hath said to Thee, My face hath sought Thee[200]; and of Anna we are told that she spoke within her heart.[201]

And secondly, we make use of vocal prayer in payment, as it were, of a just debt—in order, that is, to serve God with the entirety of what we have received from Him; consequently not with our mind alone but with our body as well; and this, as the Prophet Osee says, is especially suitable to prayer considered as a satisfaction for our sins: Take away all iniquity and receive the good, and we will render the calves of our lips.[202]

And thirdly, we sometimes make use of vocal prayer because the soul overflows, as it were, on to the body by reason of the vehemence of our feelings, as it is written: My heart hath been glad, and my tongue hath rejoiced.[203]

But it seems to some that prayer should not be vocal, thus:

1. Prayer is, as we have said, principally directed to God, and God knows the heart's speech. Consequently to add vocal prayer is idle.

But vocal prayer is not employed in order to manifest to God something which He did not know, but to stir up the mind of him who prays, and of others, too, towards God.

2. Again, man's mind is meant to rise by prayer towards God; but words, and other things pertaining to the senses, keep back a man from the ascent of contemplation.

Words appertaining to other things than God do indeed distract the mind and hinder the devotion of him who prays; but devotional words stir up the mind, especially if it be less devout.

3. Lastly, prayer ought to be offered to God in secret, according to the words: But thou when thou shalt pray, enter into thy chamber, and having shut the door, pray to thy Father in secret;[204] whereas to pray vocally means to publish it abroad.

But, as S. Chrysostom says[205]: "The Lord forbade us to pray in public with a view to being seen by the public. Consequently, when we pray we should do nothing novel to attract men's attention, whether by uttering cries which may be heard by them, or by openly beating our breasts, or by spreading out our hands, for the crowd to see us." While, on the other hand, as S. Augustine remarks[206]: "To be seen by men is not wrong, but to do things to be seen by men."

Cajetan: Note carefully, ye who murmur at the Church's services, these three points: the different kinds of vocal prayer, its necessity, and the conditions attaching to it. For vocal prayer is divided into that which is in common and that which is private or individual.

The general necessity of vocal prayer arises from the fact that it is offered in the person of the Church. For since the Church is composed of created beings dependent on the senses, prayer made through the medium of the senses—i.e., vocal prayer—must needs be offered by its ministers; else we should not know whether the worship of prayer was being offered by God's ministers, nor should we be conscious of the gift to God which was being offered by them in prayer; for the Church only judges from the things that appear externally.

Our individual need of vocal prayer arises from the necessity of stirring up our own devotion, and preserving it.

The conditions of prayer in common are twofold: it must be vocal, and it must be out loud. Hence those who say private Masses in such a low tone—and that consciously—as to be unintelligible to their hearers, appear to act unreasonably and are inexcusable, unless it should happen by accident that no one is present; in this case it is sufficient if they can be heard by the server who is close at hand. This will also show us what use we are to make of chant, or of recitation without chant, in prayer in common: it must be governed by our common devotion. And in whatever fashion such prayer may be made this rule must always be observed: it must be said so intelligibly that the meaning of the words may be distinctly perceived both by the reciters and by others, that so the Church's devotion may be aroused.

And reason tells us what conditions attach to our private prayer: viz., our own private devotion. This shews, too, the error of those who, in order to complete the tale of a large number of private vocal prayers each day, lay aside meditation and mental prayer. They neglect the end for the means (on 2. 2. 83. 12).

S. Augustine: Oh! How I lifted up my voice to Thee, O Lord, when I sang the Psalms of David, those songs full of faith, those strains full of piety which soothed my swelling spirit! And I was then but uninstructed in

Thy true love; a catechumen spending my leisure with Alypius, another catechumen. And my mother stayed with us: clad indeed in woman's garb, but with a man's faith, with a matron's calm, with a mother's love, with a Christian's piety. Oh! How I lifted up my voice in those Psalms! How they inflamed my heart! How I yearned to recite them, if I could, to the whole world—as an answer to the pride of the human race! Though, indeed, they are sung throughout the world, and none can hide himself from Thy heat! (Confess., IX. iv. 8).

S. Augustine: Sometimes, indeed, through immoderate fear of this mistake I err by excessive severity; nay, sometimes, though it is but rarely, I could almost wish to shut out from my ears and even from the Church itself all those sweet-sounding melodies used in the accompaniment of David's Psalms. Sometimes it seems to me as though it would be safer to do as I have often heard that Athanasius, the Bishop of Alexandria, did, for he made the reader of the Psalms so modulate his voice that he came to be rather speaking than singing. Yet, on the other hand, when I remember the tears which I shed when I heard the Church's chant in the early days of my regaining the faith, and when I notice that even now I am stirred—not so much by the chant as by the things that are chanted—when, that is, they are chanted with clear intonation and suitable modulation, then once more I recognize the great value of this appointed fashion (Confess., X. xxxiii. 50).

S. Augustine: I have cried with my whole heart, hear me, O Lord![207] Who can question but that when men pray their cry to the Lord is vain if it be nought but the sound of the corporeal voice and their heart be not intent upon God? But if their prayer come from the heart, then, even though the voice of the body be silent, it may be hidden from all men, yet not from God. Whether, then, we pray to God with our voice—at times when such prayer is necessary—or whether we pray in silence, it is our heart that must send forth the cry. But the heart's cry is the earnest application of our minds. And when this accompanies our prayer it expresses the deep affections of him who yearns and asks and so despairs not of his request. And further, a man cries with his whole heart when he has no other thought. Such prayers with many are rare; with few are they frequent; I know not whether anyone's prayers are always so (Enarr. in Ps. cxviii., Sermon, xxix. 1).

"Incline Thy ear, O Lord, and hear me; for I am needy and poor. Preserve my soul, for I am holy: save Thy servant, O my God, that trusteth in Thee. Have mercy on me, O Lord, for I have cried to Thee all the day. Give joy to the soul of Thy servant, for to Thee, O Lord, I have lifted up my soul. For Thou, O Lord, art sweet and mild; and plenteous in mercy to all that call upon Thee."[208]

XIII

Must Prayer necessarily be Attentive?

That even holy men sometimes suffer distraction of mind when at prayer is clear from the words: My heart hath forsaken me![209]

This question particularly concerns vocal prayer. And for its solution we must know that a thing is said to be necessary in two senses: firstly, in the sense that by it a certain end is more readily attained, and in this sense attention is absolutely requisite in prayer. But a thing is said to be necessary also because without it a certain thing cannot attain its object at all. Now the effect or object of prayer is threefold. Its first effect—an effect, indeed, which is common to all acts springing from charity—is merit; but to secure this effect it is not necessarily required that attention should be kept up throughout the prayer, but the initial intention with which a man comes to prayer renders the whole prayer meritorious, as, indeed, is the case in all other meritorious acts.

The second effect of prayer is peculiar to it, and that is to obtain favours; and for this, too, the primary intention suffices, and to it God principally looks. But if the primary intention is wanting, prayer is not meritorious, neither can it win favours; for, as S. Gregory says, God hears not the prayer of a man who when he prays does not give heed to God.[210]

The third effect of prayer is that which it immediately and actually brings about, namely, the spiritual refreshment of the soul; and to attain this end attention is necessarily required in prayer. Whence it is said, If I pray in a tongue my understanding is without fruit.[211]

At the same time, we must remember that there is a threefold species of attention which may find place in our vocal prayer: one by which a man attends to the words he recites, and is careful to make no mistake in them; another by which he attends to the meaning of the words; and a third by which he attends to the end of all prayer—namely, God Himself—and to the object for which he is praying. And this species of attention is the most necessary of all, and one which even uninstructed folk can have; sometimes, indeed, the intensity with which the mind is borne towards God is, as says Hugh of S. Victor, so overwhelming that the mind is oblivious of all else.[212]

Some, however, argue that prayer must of necessity be attentive, thus:

1. It is said in S. John's Gospel[213]: God is a spirit, and they that adore Him must adore Him in spirit and truth. But inattentive prayer is not in spirit.

But he prays in spirit and in truth who comes to pray moved by the impulse of the Spirit, even though, owing to human infirmity, his mind afterwards wanders.

2. But again, prayer is "the ascent of the mind towards God." But when prayer is inattentive the mind does not ascend towards God.

But the human mind cannot, owing to Nature's weakness, long remain on high, for the soul is dragged down to lower things by the weight of human infirmity; and hence it happens that when the mind of one who prays ascends towards God in contemplation it suddenly wanders away from Him owing to his infirmity.

3. Lastly, prayer must needs be without sin. But not without sin does a man suffer distraction of mind when he prays, for he seems to mock God, just as if one were to speak with his fellow-man and not attend to what he said. Consequently S. Basil says[214]: "The Divine assistance is to be implored, not remissly, nor with a mind that wanders here and there; for such a one not only will not obtain what he asks, but will rather be mocking God."

Of course, if a man purposely allowed his mind to wander in prayer, he would commit a sin and hinder the fruit of his prayer. Against such S. Augustine says in his Rule[215]: "When you pray to God in Psalms and hymns, entertain your heart with what your lips are reciting." But that distraction of mind which is unintentional does not destroy the fruit of prayer.

Hence S. Basil also says: "But if through the weakness of sinful nature you cannot pray with attention, restrain your imagination as far as you can, and God will pardon you, inasmuch as it is not from negligence but from weakness that you are unable to occupy yourself with Him as you should."

Cajetan: Does a man satisfy the precept of the Church if, being bound to the recitation of the Divine Office, he sets out with the intention of meditating upon the Divine Goodness or upon the Passion of Christ, and thus keeping his mind firmly fixed upon God? Clearly a man who strives to keep his mind occupied during the whole of the Divine Office with contemplation of and devout affections towards God and Divine things fully satisfies his obligation. So, too, a man who aims at meditation on the Passion of Christ and devout affections on it during the whole Office, undoubtedly satisfies his obligation, for he is making use of a better means for keeping in touch with the Divinity than if he merely dwelt upon the meaning of the words. At the same time, he must be ready to lay this aside if in the course of the Office he finds himself uplifted to Divine things, for at this he must primarily aim. One who so prays, then, must make the Passion of Christ a means and not an end; he must, that is, be prepared to ascend thereby, if God grants it, to Divine things. In short, we may make use of any one of the species of attention enumerated above provided we do not exclude the higher forms. Thus, for example, if a man feels that it is more suited to his small capacity to aim simply at making no mistakes, and habitually makes use of this form of attention, he must still use it as a means only; he must, that is, be at God's disposition, for God may have mercy upon him and grant him, by reason of his dispositions, some better form of attention.

Again, when a person prays for things needful for his support in life he must not be so occupied with the thought of these things as to appear to subordinate Divine things to human, as though prayer was but a means and his daily living the end. We must bear in mind the doctrine laid down above[216]—viz., that all our prayers should tend to the attainment of grace and glory. We must occupy ourselves with the thought of eternal glory, or of the glory of the adoption of sons during this life, or with the virtues as means to arriving at our eternal home, and as the adornment of the inhabitants of heaven, and the commencement here of heavenly "conversation"; such things as these must be counted as the highest forms of attention (on 2. 2. 83. 13).

S. Augustine: Give joy to the soul of Thy servant, for to Thee, O Lord, I have lifted up my soul. For Thou, O Lord, art sweet and mild.[217] It seems to me that he calls God "mild" because He endures all our vagaries, and only awaits our prayers that He may perfect us. And when we offer Him our prayers He accepts them gratefully and hears them. Neither does He reflect on the careless way in which we pour them out, He even accepts prayers of which we are hardly conscious! For, Brethren, what man is there who would put up with it if a friend of his began a conversation with him, and yet, just when he was ready to reply to what his friend said, should discover that he was paying no attention to him but was saying something to someone else? Or supposing you were to appeal to a judge and were to appoint a place for him to hear your appeal, and then suddenly, while you were talking with him, were to put him aside and begin to gossip with a friend! How long would he put up with you? And yet God puts up with the hearts of so many who pray to Him and who yet are thinking of other things, even evil things, even wicked things, things hateful to God; for even to think of unnecessary things is an insult to Him with Whom you have begun to talk. For your prayer is a conversation with God. When you read, God speaks to you; when you pray, you speak to God.... And you may picture God saying to you: "You forget how often you have stood before Me and have thought of such idle and superfluous things and have so rarely poured out to Me an attentive and definite prayer!" But Thou, O Lord, art sweet and mild! Thou art sweet, bearing with me! It is from weakness that I slip away! Heal me and I shall stand; strengthen me and I shall be firm! But until Thou dost so, bear with me, for Thou, O Lord, art sweet and mild (Enarr. in Ps. lxxxv. 7).

S. Augustine: Praise the Lord, O my soul![218] What mean these words, Brethren? Do we not praise the Lord? Do we not sing hymns day by day? Do not our mouths, each according to their measure, sound forth day by day the praises of God? And what is it we praise? It is a great Thing that we praise, but that wherewith we praise is weak as yet. When does the singer fill up the praises of Him Whom he sings? A man stands and sings before God, often for a long space; but oftentimes, whilst his lips move to frame the words of his song, his thoughts fly away to I know not what desires! And so, too, our mind has sometimes been fixed on praising God in a definite manner, but our soul has flitted away, led hither and thither by divers desires and anxious cares. And then our mind, as though from up above, has looked down upon the soul as it flitted to and fro, and has seemed to turn to it and address its uneasy wanderings—saying to it: Praise the Lord, O my soul! Why art thou anxious about other things than Him? Why busy thyself with the mortal things of earth? And then our soul, as though weighed down and unable to stand firm as it should, replies to our mind: I will praise the Lord in my life! Why does it say in my life? Why? Because now I am in my death!

Rouse yourself, then, and say: Praise the Lord, O my soul! And your soul will reply to you: "I praise Him as much as I can, though it is but weakly, in small measure, and with little strength." But why so? Because while we are in the body we are absent from the Lord.[219] And why do you thus praise the Lord so imperfectly and with so little fixity of attention? Ask Holy Scripture: The corruptible body weigheth down the soul, and the earthly habitation presseth down the mind that museth upon many things.[220] O take away, then, my body which weigheth down the soul, and then will I praise the Lord! Take away my earthly habitation which presseth down the mind that museth upon many things, so that, instead of many things I may be occupied with One Thing alone, and may praise the Lord! But as long as I am as I am, I cannot, for I am weighed down! What then? Wilt thou be silent? Wilt thou never perfectly praise the Lord? I will praise the Lord in my life! (Enarr in Ps. cxlv. 1).

"My spirit is in anguish within me; my heart within me is troubled. I remembered the days of old, I meditated on all Thy works; I meditated upon the works of Thy hands. I stretched forth my hands to Thee; my soul is as earth without water unto Thee. Hear me speedily, O Lord: my spirit hath fainted away."[221]

S. Thomas: The fruits of prayer are twofold. For first there is the merit which thereby accrues to a man; and, secondly, there is the spiritual consolation and devotion which is begotten of prayer. And he who does not attend to, or does not understand his prayer, loses that fruit which is spiritual consolation; but we cannot say that he loses that fruit which is merit, for then we should have to say that very many prayers were without merit since a man can hardly say the Lord's Prayer without some distraction of mind. Hence we must rather say that when a person is praying and is sometimes distracted from what he is saying, or—more generally—when a person is occupied with some meritorious work and does not continuously and at every moment reflect that he is doing it for God, his work does not cease to be meritorious. And the reason is that in meritorious acts directed to a right end it is not requisite that our intention should be referred to that end at every moment, but the influence of the intention with which we begun persists throughout even though we now and again be distracted in some particular point; and the influence of this initial intention renders the whole body of what we do meritorious unless it be broken off by reason of some contrary affection intruding itself and diverting us from the end we had first in view to some other end contrary to it.

And it must be remembered that there are three kinds of attention. The first is attention to the words we are actually saying; and sometimes this is harmful, for it may hinder devotion. The second is attention to the meaning of the words, and this, too, may be harmful, though not gravely so. The third is attention to the goal of our prayer, and this better and almost necessary (Commentary on 1 Cor. xiv. 14).

XIV

Should our Prayers be Long?

It would seem that we ought to pray continuously, for our Lord said: We ought always to pray and not to faint[222]; so also S. Paul: Pray without ceasing.[223]

But we must notice that when we speak of prayer we can mean either prayer considered in itself or the cause of prayer. Now the cause of prayer is the desire of the love of God; and all prayer ought to spring from this desire which is, indeed, continuous in us, whether actually or virtually, since this desire virtually remains in everything which we do from charity. But we ought to do all things for the glory of God: whether you eat or whether you drink, or whatsoever else you do, do all to the glory of God.[224] In this sense, then, prayer ought to be continual. Hence S. Augustine says to Proba: "Therefore by our faith, by our hope, and by our charity, we are always praying, for our desire is continued."

But prayer considered in itself cannot be so continuous; for we must needs be occupied with other things. Hence S. Augustine says in the same place: "At certain intervals, at divers hours and times, we pray to God in words so that by these outward signs of things we may admonish ourselves, and may learn what progress we have made in this same desire, and may stir ourselves up to increase it."

But the quantity of a thing has to be determined by its purpose, just as a draught has to be proportioned to the health of the man who takes it. Consequently it is fitting that prayer should only last so long as it avails to stir up in us this fervour of interior desire. And when it exceeds this measure, and its prolongation only results in weariness, it must not be prolonged further. Hence S. Augustine also says to Proba: "The Brethren in Egypt are said to have had frequent prayers; but they were exceedingly brief, hardly more than eager ejaculations; and they adopted this method lest, if they prolonged their prayer, that vigilant attention which is requisite for prayer should lose its keen edge and become dulled. And thus they clearly show that this same attention, just as it is not to be forced if it fails to last, so neither is it to be quickly broken off if it does last."

And just as we have to pay attention to this in our private prayers, and have to be guided by our powers of attention, so must we observe the same principles in public prayer where we have to be governed by the people's devotion.

Some, however, argue that our prayers ought not to be continual, thus:

1. Our Lord said[225]: And when you are praying speak not much. But it is not easy to see how a man can pray long without "speaking much"; more especially if it is a question of vocal prayer.

But S. Augustine says to Proba: "To prolong our prayer does not involve 'much-speaking.' 'Much-speaking' is one thing; the unceasing desire of the heart is another. Indeed we are told of the Lord Himself that He passed the whole night in the prayer of God[226]; and, again, that being in an agony He prayed the longer,[227] and this that He might afford us an example." And Augustine adds a little later: "Much speaking in prayer is to be avoided, but not much petition, if fervent attention lasts. For 'much-speaking' in prayer means the use of superfluous words when we pray for something necessary; but much petition means that with unceasing and devout stirrings of the heart we knock at His door to Whom we pray; and this is often a matter rather of groans than of words, of weeping than of speaking."

2. Further, prayer is but the unfolding of our desires. But our desires are holy in proportion as they are confined to one thing, in accordance with those words of the Psalmist[228]: One thing I have asked of the Lord, this will I seek after. Whence it would seem to follow that our prayers are acceptable to God just in proportion to their brevity.

But to prolong our prayer does not mean that we ask for many things, but that our hearts are continuously set upon one object for which we yearn.

3. Once more, it is unlawful for a man to transgress the limits which God Himself has fixed, especially in matters which touch the Divine worship, according to the words: Charge the people lest they should have a mind to pass the limits to see the Lord, and a very great multitude of them should perish.[229] But God Himself has assigned limits to our prayer by instituting the Lord's Prayer, as is evident from the words: Thus shalt thou pray.[230] Hence we ought not to extend our prayer beyond these limits.

But our Lord did not institute this prayer with a view to tying us down exclusively to these words when we pray, but to show us that the scope of our prayer should be limited to asking only for the things contained in it, whatever form of words we may use or whatever may be our thoughts.

4. And lastly, with regard to the words of our Lord that we ought always to pray and not to faint,[231] and those of S. Paul, Pray without ceasing,[232] we must remark that a man prays without ceasing, either because of the unceasing nature of his desire, as we have above explained; or because he does not fail to pray at the appointed times; or because of the effect which his prayer has, whether upon himself—since even when he has finished praying he still remains devout—or upon others, as, for instance, when a man by some kind action induces another to pray for him whereas he himself desists from his prayer.

"Our soul waiteth for the Lord; for He is our helper and protector. For in Him our hearts shall rejoice; and in His Holy Name we have trusted. Let Thy mercy, O Lord, be upon us, as we have hoped in Thee."[233]

XV

Is Prayer Meritorious?

On the words of the Psalmist, My prayer shall be turned into my bosom,[234] the interlinear Gloss has: "And if it is of no profit to them (for whom it is offered), at least I myself shall not lose my reward." A reward, however, can only be due to merit. Prayer, then, is meritorious.

As we have said above, prayer has, besides the effect of spiritual consolation which it brings with it, a twofold power regarding the future: the power, namely, of meriting, and that of winning favours. But prayer, as indeed every other virtuous act, derives its power of meriting from that root which is charity, and the true and proper object of charity is that Eternal Good, the enjoyment of Which we merit. Now prayer proceeds from charity by means of the virtue of religion whose proper act is prayer; there accompany it, however, certain other virtues which are requisite for a good prayer—namely, faith and humility. For it belongs to the virtue of religion to offer our prayers to God; while to charity belongs the desire of that the attainment of which we seek in prayer. And faith is necessary as regards God to Whom we pray; for we must, of course, believe that from Him we can obtain what we ask. Humility, too, is called for on the part of the petitioner, for he must acknowledge his own needs. And devotion also is necessary; though this comes under religion of which it is the first act, it conditions all subsequent effects.

And its power of obtaining favours prayer owes to the grace of God to Whom we pray, and Who, indeed, induces us to pray. Hence S. Augustine says[235]: "He would not urge us to ask unless He were ready to give"; and S. Chrysostom says: "He never refuses His mercies to them who pray, since it is He Who in His loving-kindness stirs them up so that they weary not in prayer."

But some say that prayer cannot be meritorious, thus:

1. Merit proceeds from grace, but prayer precedes grace, since it is precisely by prayer that we win grace: Your Father from Heaven will give the Good Spirit to them that ask Him.[236]

But prayer, like any other virtuous act, cannot be meritorious without that grace which makes us pleasing to God. Yet even that prayer which wins for us the grace which renders us pleasing to God must proceed from some grace—that is, from some gratuitous gift; for, as S. Augustine says, to pray at all is a gift of God.[237]

2. Again, prayer cannot be meritorious, for if it were so it would seem natural that prayer should especially merit that for which we actually pray. Yet this is not always the case, for even the prayers of the Saints are often

not heard; S. Paul, for example, was not heard when he prayed that the sting of the flesh might be taken away from him.[238]

But we must notice that the merit of our prayers sometimes lies in something quite different from what we beg for. For whereas merit is to be especially referred to the possession of God, our petitions in our prayers at times refer directly to other things, as we have pointed out above. Consequently, if what a man asks for will not tend to his ultimate attainment of God, he does not merit it by his prayer; sometimes, indeed, by asking and desiring such a thing he may lose all merit, as, for example, if a man were to ask of God something which was sinful and which he could not reverently ask for. Sometimes, however, what he asks for is not necessary for his salvation, nor yet is it clearly opposed to his salvation; and when a man so prays he may by his prayer merit eternal life, but he does not merit to obtain what he actually asks for. Hence S. Augustine says[239]: "He who asks of God in faith things needful for this life is sometimes mercifully heard and sometimes mercifully not heard. For the physician knows better than the patient what will avail for the sick man." It was for this reason that Paul was not heard when he asked that the sting of the flesh might be taken away—it was not expedient. But if what a man asks for will help him to the attainment of God, as being something conducive to his salvation, he will merit it, and that not only by praying for it but also by doing other good works; hence, too, he undoubtedly will obtain what he asks for, but when it is fitting that he should obtain it: "for some things are not refused to us but are deferred, to be given at a fitting time," as S. Augustine says.[240] Yet even here hindrance may arise if a man does not persevere in asking; hence S. Basil says[241]: "When then you ask and do not receive, this is either because you asked for what you ought not, or because you asked without lively faith, or carelessly, or for what would not profit you, or because you ceased to ask." And since a man cannot, absolutely speaking, merit eternal life for another, nor, in consequence, those things which belong to eternal life, it follows that a man is not always heard when he prays for another. For a man, then, always to obtain what he asks, four conditions must concur: he must ask for himself, for things necessary for salvation; he must ask piously and perseveringly.

3. Lastly, prayer essentially reposes upon faith, as S. James says: But let him ask in faith, nothing wavering.[242] But faith is not sufficient for

merit, as is evident in the case of those who have faith without charity. Therefore prayer is not meritorious.

But while it is true that prayer rests principally upon faith, this is not for its power of meriting—for as regards this it rests principally on charity—but for its power of winning favours; for through faith man knows of the Divine Omnipotence and Mercy whence prayer obtains what it asks.

S. Augustine: Men, then, love different things, and when each one seemeth to have what he loves, he is called happy. But a man is truly happy, not if he has what he loves, but if he loves what ought to be loved. For many become more wretched through having what they love than they were when they lacked it. Miserable enough through loving harmful things, more miserable through having them. And our Merciful God, when we love amiss, denies us what we love; but sometimes in His anger He grants a man what he loves amiss!... But when we love what God wishes us to love, then, doubtless, He will give it us. This is That One Thing Which ought to be loved: that we may dwell in the House of the Lord all the days of our life! (Enarr. in Ps. xxvi.).

S. Augustine: In those tribulations, then, which can both profit us and harm us, we know not what we should pray for as we ought. Yet none the less since they are hard, since they are vexatious, since, too, they are opposed to our sense of our own weakness, mankind with one consent prays that they may be removed from us. But we owe this much devotion to the Lord our God that, if He refuses to remove them, we should not therefore fancy that we are neglected by Him, but, while bearing these woes with devout patience, we should hope for some greater good, for thus is power perfected in infirmity. Yet to some in their impatience the Lord God grants in anger what they ask, just as in His mercy He refused it to the Apostle (Ep. cxxx. ad Probam).

"Hear my prayer, O Lord, and my supplication; give ear to my tears. Be not silent: for I am a stranger with Thee, and a sojourner as all my fathers were. O forgive me, that I may be refreshed; before I go hence, and be no more."[243]

XVI

Do Sinners gain Anything From God by their Prayers?

S. Augustine says[244]: "If God did not hear sinners, in vain would the publican have said, God be merciful to me a sinner"; and S. Chrysostom says[245]: "Every one that asketh receiveth—that is, whether he be just man or sinner." Hence the prayers of sinners do win something from God.

In a sinner we have to consider two things: his nature, which God loves; his fault, which God hates. If, then, a sinner asks something of God formally as a sinner—that is, according to his sinful desires—God, out of His mercy, does not hear him, though sometimes He does hear him in His vengeance, as when He permits a sinner to fall still farther into sin. For God "in mercy refuses some things which in anger He concedes," as S. Augustine says.[246] But that prayer of a sinner which proceeds from the good desire of his nature God hears, not, indeed, as bound in justice to do so, for that the sinner cannot merit, but out of His pure mercy, and on condition, too, that the four above-mentioned conditions are observed—namely, that he prays for himself, for things needful for his salvation, that he prays devoutly and perseveringly.

Some, however, maintain that sinners do not by their prayers win anything from God, thus:

1. It is said in the Gospel,[247] Now we know that God doth not hear sinners; and this accords with those words of Proverbs[248]; He that turneth away his ears from hearing the law, his prayer shall be an abomination. But a prayer which is "an abomination" cannot win anything from God.

But, as S. Augustine remarks,[249] the words first quoted are due to the blind man as yet unanointed—viz., not yet perfectly illumined—and hence they are not valid; though they might be true if understood of a sinner precisely as such, and in this sense, too, his prayer is said to be "an abomination."

2. Again, just men obtain from God what they merit, as we have said above. Sinners, however, can merit nothing, since they are without grace, and even without charity which, according to the Gloss[250] on the words, Having an appearance of piety, but denying the power thereof, is "the power of piety." And hence they cannot pray piously, which, as we have said above, is requisite if prayer is to gain what it asks for.

But though a sinner cannot pray piously in the sense that his prayer springs from the habit of virtue, yet his prayer can be pious in the sense that he asks for something conducive to piety, just as a man who has not got the habit of justice can yet wish for some just thing, as we have pointed out above. And though such a man's prayer is not meritorious, it may yet have the power of winning favours; for while merit reposes upon justice, the power of winning favours reposes upon grace.

3. Lastly, S. Chrysostom says[251]: "The Father does not readily hear prayers not dictated by the Son." But in the prayer which Christ dictated it is said: Forgive us our debts as we also forgive our debtors, which sinners do not. Hence sinners either lie when they say this prayer, and so do not deserve to be heard, or, if they do not say it, then they are not heard because they do not make use of the form of prayer instituted by Christ.

But, as we have explained above, the Lord's Prayer is spoken in the name of the whole Church. Consequently, if a man—while unwilling to forgive his neighbour his debts—yet says this prayer, he does not lie; for while what he says is not true as regards himself, it yet remains true as regards the Person of the Church outside of which he deservedly is, and he loses, in consequence, the fruit of his prayer. Sometimes, however, sinners are ready to forgive their debtors, and consequently their prayers are heard, in accordance with those words of Ecclesiasticus[252]: Forgive thy neighbour if he hath hurt thee, and then shall thy sins be forgiven to thee when thou prayest.

"With the Lord shall the steps of a man be directed, and he shall like well his way. When he shall fall, he shall not be bruised, for the Lord putteth His hand under him. I have been young, and now am old; and I have not seen the just forsaken, nor his seed seeking bread."[253]

XVII

Can We rightly term Supplications," "Prayers," "Intercessions," and "Thanksgivings," parts of Prayer?

The Apostle says to Timothy[254]: I desire therefore first of all that supplications, prayers, intercessions, and thanksgivings be made by all men.

For prayer three things are required: first of all, that he who prays come nigh to God; and this is signified by the name prayer, for prayer is "the uplifting of the mind towards God." Secondly, petition is required, and is signified by the word postulation; now a petition may be set forth in definite terms—and this some term postulation, properly so called; or it may be set forth in no express terms, as when a man asks for God's help, and this some call supplication; or, again, the fact in question may be simply narrated, as in S. John[255]: He whom Thou lovest is sick, and this some call insinuation. And thirdly, there is required a reason for asking for what we pray for, and this reason may be either on the part of God or on the part of the petitioner. The reason for asking on the part of God is His holiness, by reason of which we ask to be heard: Incline Thine ear and hear ... for Thine own sake, O my God;[256] to this belongs obsecration—namely, an appeal to sacred things, as when we say: By Thy Nativity, deliver us, O Lord! But the reason for asking on the part of the petitioner is thankfulness, for by giving thanks for benefits already received we merit to receive still greater ones, as is set forth in the Church's Collect.[257] Hence the Gloss[258] says that in the Mass "Obsecrations are the prayers which precede the Consecration," for in them we commemorate certain sacred things; "in the Consecration itself we have prayers," for then the mind is especially uplifted towards God; "but in the subsequent petitions we have postulations, and at the close thanksgivings." These four parts of prayer may be noticed in many of the Church's Collects: thus in the Collect for Trinity Sunday, the words Almighty and Everlasting God signify the uplifting of the soul in prayer to God; the words: Who hast granted to Thy servants to acknowledge in their profession of the true faith the glory of the Eternal Trinity, and in the Power of Its Majesty to adore Its Unity, signify giving of thanks; the words: Grant, we beseech Thee, that by perseverance in this same faith we may be ever defended from all adversities, signify postulation; while the closing words: Through our Lord Jesus Christ, etc., signify obsecration.

In the Conferences of the Fathers, however,[259] we read: "Obsecration is imploring pardon for sin; prayer is when we make vows to God; postulation is when we make petition for others; giving of thanks, those ineffable outpourings by which the mind renders thanks to God." But the former explanation is preferable.

Some, however, object to these divisions of prayer, thus:

1. Obsecration is apparently to swear by someone, whereas Origen remarks[260]: "A man who desires to live in accordance with the Gospel must not swear by anyone, for if it is not allowed to swear, neither is it allowed to swear by anyone."

But it is sufficient to remark that obsecration is not a swearing by, or adjuring of God, as though to compel Him, for this is forbidden, but to implore His mercy.

2. Again, S. John Damascene says[261] that prayer is "the asking God for things that are fitting." Hence it is not exact to distinguish prayers from postulations.

But prayer, generally considered, embraces all the above-mentioned parts; when, however, we distinguish one part against another, prayer, properly speaking, means the uplifting of the mind to God.

3. Lastly, giving of thanks refers to the past, whereas the other parts of prayer refer to the future. Hence giving of thanks should not be placed after the rest.

But whereas in things which are different from one another the past precedes the future, in one and the same thing the future precedes the past. Hence giving of thanks for benefits already received precedes petition; yet those same benefits were first asked for, and then, when they had been received, thanks were offered for them. Prayer, however, precedes petition, for by it we draw nigh to God to Whom we make petition. And obsecration precedes prayer, for it is from dwelling upon the Divine Goodness that we venture to approach to Him.

Cajetan: We might be asked how the mind can be especially elevated to God at the moment of consecration. For in the consecration the priest has to express distinctly the words of consecration, and consequently cannot have his mind uplifted towards God at that moment. Indeed, the more his mind is uplifted to God, the less he thinks of inferior things, words, and so forth.

But in the consecration of the Holy Eucharist—in which the priest in a sense brings God down upon earth—the very greatness of our uplifting of mind towards the Divine Goodness Which has thus deigned to come amongst us is the very reason for our attention to the words in the act of consecration, and makes the priest pronounce them distinctly and reverently. Some scrupulous folk, however, concentrate their whole attention on being intent and attentive; but this is really a distraction, and not attention, for its object is precisely the being attentive. The uplifting, then, of our minds to God in the consecration has indeed to be the very greatest, not, indeed, intensively and by abstraction from the things of sense, but objectively and concentrated—though always within the limits compatible with attention—on the endeavour to say the words as they should be said (on 2. 2. 83. 17.)

S. Augustine: And David went in and sat before the Lord[262]; and Elias, casting himself down upon the earth, put his face between his knees.[263] By examples such as these we are taught that there is no prescribed position of the body in prayer provided the soul states its intention in the presence of God. For we pray standing, as it is written: The Publican standing afar off. We pray, too, on our knees, as we read in the Acts of the Apostles;[264] and we pray sitting, as in the case of David and Elias. And unless it were lawful to pray lying down, it would not be said in the Psalms[265]: Every night I will wash my bed, I will water my couch with my tears. When, then, a man desires to pray, he settles himself in any position that serves at the time for the stirring up of his soul. When, on the other hand, we have no definite intention of praying, but the wish to pray suddenly occurs to us—when, that is, there comes of a sudden into our mind something which rouses the desire to pray "with unspeakable groanings"—then, in whatsoever position such a feeling may find us, we are not to put off our prayer; we are not to look about for some place whither we can withdraw, for some place in which to stand or in which to make prostration. For the very intention of the mind begets a solitude, and we often forget to which quarter of the heavens we were looking, or in what bodily position the occasion found us (Of Divers Questions, iv.).

"Hear, O God, my prayer, and despise not my supplication; be attentive to me and hear me. I am grieved in my exercise; and am troubled at the voice of the enemy, and at the tribulation of the sinner. For they have cast iniquities upon me, and in wrath they were troublesome to me. My heart is troubled within me, and the fear of death is fallen upon me. Fear and trembling are come upon me, and darkness hath covered me. And I said: Who will give me wings like a dove, and I will fly and be at rest?"[266]

FOOTNOTES 4

[98] Etymologies, x., sub litt. O.
[99] Ps. xxxviii. 13.
[100] Ethics, I. xiii. 15.
[101] Rabanus Maurus, De Universis, vi. 14.
[102] On the Orthodox Faith, iii. 24.
[103] Ps. x. 17.
[104] Isa. lxv. 24.
[105] Of the Divine Names, vi. 1.
[106] Ps. xxvi. 4.
[107] Art. XV.
[108] Isa. lxiv. 8, 9.
[109] xviii. 1.
[110] Mal. iii. 14.
[111] Dialogue, i. 8.
[112] S. Matt. vi. 32.
[113] 1 Kings xv. 29.
[114] Of Good Deeds, ii. 1.
[115] Hom. II., On Prayer; also Hom. XXX., On Genesis.
[116] Eph. i. 4.
[117] Ps. lxx. 17, 18.
[118] S. Matt. vii. 7.
[119] Ps. cxx. 4.
[120] S. Matt. vi. 8.
[121] Ps. ciii. 33, 34.
[122] Ps. lxxxiii. 12.
[123] viii. 4.
[124] 1 Cor. xiv. 15.
[125] On Care for the Dead, chaps, xiii., xv., xvi.
[126] Moralia in Job, xii. 14.
[127] Ps. lxvi.
[128] S. Matt. vi. 9-13; S. Luke xi. 2-4.
[129] Of Socrates the Philosopher, vii. 21.
[130] Ps. lxxix. 4.
[131] Ps. cxviii. 35.

[132] On the Orthodox Faith, iii. 24.
[133] iv. 3.
[134] Rom. viii. 26.
[135] S. John iv. 24.
[136] 1 Tim. ii. 4.
[137] Isa. lxiii. 15, 16.
[138] xxx. 8.
[139] Ep., CXXX., chap. xii.
[140] Ethics, I. vii. 15.
[141] Ep., CXXX., chap. vi.
[142] S. Matt. vi. 33.
[143] On the Sermon on the Mount, II. x. 1.
[144] S. Matt. vi. 25.
[145] 2 Cor. iv. 18.
[146] Ps. xxxvii. 10.
[147] 1 Thess. v. 17.
[148] Heb. iv. 3.
[149] Ps. liv. 23.
[150] v. 16.
[151] Opus Imperf. in Matthæum, Hom. XIV.
[152] On the Lord's Prayer.
[153] S. John xvi. 23.
[154] Tractatus in Joannem, 102.
[155] xv. 1.
[156] Ps. xxxiv. 13.
[157] Jer. vii. 16.
[158] Eccles. vii. 14.
[159] 1 John v. 16.
[160] De Correptionibus et Gratia, cap. xv.
[161] Rom. xv. 30.
[162] 1 Cor. i. 11.
[163] S. John xxii. 24.
[164] S. Matt. v. 44.
[165] xv. 4.
[166] Ps. vi. 11.
[167] On the Sermon on the Mount, i. 21.

[168] Apoc. vi. 10.
[169] Ps. lvii. 11.
[170] On the Sermon on the Mount, i. 22, and Questions on the Gospels, II., xlv.
[171] Questions on the Old and New Testament, Qu. lxviii.
[172] Ecclus. xxxvi. 1-3.
[173] Ep. cxxx. 12.
[174] Ep. cxxx. 11.
[175] Comment. on S. Matthew, vi.
[176] 1 Cor. vi. 9, 10.
[177] S. Luke i. 49.
[178] Ps. cxliv. 13.
[179] Isa. xlvi. 10.
[180] On the Sermon on the Mount, ii. 5.
[181] Ep. cxxx. 11.
[182] Enchiridion, 115.
[183] On the Sermon on the Mount, ii. 11.
[184] xi. 2-4.
[185] Enchiridion, 116.
[186] 1 John iv. 19.
[187] S. John xvii. 1-3.
[188] See Touron, O.P., Vie de S. Thomas d'Aquin, p. 254; Paris, 1740.
[189] S. John xiv. 16.
[190] Rom. viii. 26.
[191] xcvi. 7.
[192] Ps. cxlvi. 9.
[193] Ecclus. xxxvi. 18, 19.
[194] 2 Macc. xv. 14.
[195] Contra Vigilantium, vi.
[196] Heb. vii. 25. S. Thomas is quoting from memory.
[197] Exod. iii. 6.
[198] Ps. cxli. 1.
[199] Ep. cxxx. 9.
[200] Ps. xxvi. 8.
[201] 1 Kings i. 13.
[202] Osee xiv. 3.

[203] Ps. xv. 9.
[204] S. Matt. vi. 6.
[205] Opus Imperf. Hom. XIII. in Matt.
[206] On the Sermon on the Mount, ii. 3.
[207] Ps. cxviii. 145.
[208] Ps. lxxxv. 1-5.
[209] Ps. xxxix. 13.
[210] Implicitly, Moralia in Job, xxii. 13; but see Hugh of S. Victor, Exposition of the Rule of S. Augustine, iii.
[211] 1 Cor. xiv. 14.
[212] Of the Manner of Prayer, ii.
[213] iv. 24.
[214] On the Monastic Constitutions, chap. i.
[215] Ep. cxxi.
[216] Art. IV.
[217] Ps. lxxv. 4, 5.
[218] Ps. cxlv. 1.
[219] 2 Cor. v. 6.
[220] Wisd. ix. 15.
[221] Ps. cxlii. 4-7.
[222] S. Luke xviii. 1.
[223] 1 Thess. v. 17.
[224] 1 Cor. x. 31.
[225] S. Matt. vi. 7.
[226] S. Luke vi. 12.
[227] S. Luke xxii. 43.
[228] Ps. xxvi. 4.
[229] Exod. xix. 21.
[230] S. Matt. vi. 9.
[231] S. Luke xviii. 1.
[232] 1 Thess. v. 17.
[233] Ps. xxxii. 20-22.
[234] Ps. xxxiv. 13.
[235] On the Sermon on the Mount, Sermon CV. i.
[236] St. Luke vi. 13.
[237] On Perseverance, chap. xxiii.

[238] 2 Cor. xii. 7-9.

[239] S. Prosper, The Book of Sentences gleaned from S. Augustine, Sent. 212.

[240] Tractatus in Joannem, 102.

[241] Monastic Constitutions, chap, i.

[242] i. 6.

[243] Ps. xxxviii. 13, 14.

[244] Tractatus in Joannem, 44.

[245] Opus Imperf. in Matt., Hom. XVIII.

[246] Tractatus in Joannem, 73; and De Verbis Domini, Sermon cccliv. 7.

[247] S. John ix. 31.

[248] xxviii. 8.

[249] Tractatus in Joannem, 44.

[250] Implicitly in the old interlinear Gloss on 2 Tim. iii. 5.

[251] Opus Imperf. in Matt., Hom. XIV.

[252] xxviii. 2.

[253] Ps. xxxvi. 23-25.

[254] 1 Tim. ii. 1.

[255] xi. 3.

[256] Dan. ix. 18, 19.

[257] Friday in the September Ember days.

[258] The Ordinary Gloss on the words obsecrations, prayers, etc., in 1 Tim. ii. 1.

[259] Collat., IX., chaps. xi-xiii.

[260] Tractatus xxxv. in Matt.

[261] De Orthodoxa Fide, iii. 24.

[262] 2 Kings vii. 18.

[263] 3 Kings xviii. 42.

[264] vii. 59; xx. 36.

[265] vi. 7.

[266] Ps. liv. 1-7.

FROM THE SUPPLEMENT TO THE SUMMA—QUESTION 4

OF THE PRAYERS OF THE SAINTS WHO ARE IN HEAVEN

I. Are the Saints cognizant of our Prayers?

II. Ought we to appeal to the Saints to intercede for us?

III. Are the Saints' Prayers to God for us always heard?

I

Are the Saints cognizant of our Prayers?

On those words of Job,[267] Whether his children come to honour or dishonour, he shall not understand, S. Gregory says: "This is not to be understood of the souls of the Saints, for they see from within the glory of Almighty God, it is in nowise credible that there should be anything without of which they are ignorant."[268]

And he says also: "To the soul that sees its Creator all created things are but trifling; for, however little of the Creator's light he sees, all that is created becomes of small import to him."[269] Yet the greatest difficulty in saying that the souls of the Saints know our prayers and other things which concern us, is their distance from us. But since, according to the authority just quoted, this distance does not preclude such knowledge, it appears that the souls of the Saints do know our prayers and other things which concern us.

Further, if they did not know what concerned us, neither would they pray for us, since they would not know our deficiencies. But this was the error of Vigilantius, as S. Jerome says in his Epistle against him.[270] The Saints, then, know what concerns us.

The Divine Essence, then, is a sufficient medium for knowing all things, as, indeed, is evident from the fact that God in seeing His own essence sees all things. Yet it does not follow that whoever sees the Essence of God therefore sees all things, but those only who comprehend the Essence of God; just in the same way as it does not follow that because we know a principle we therefore know all that that principle contains, for that would only be the case if we comprehended the whole power of the principle. Since, then, the souls of the Saints do not comprehend the Divine Essence, it does not follow that they know everything which could be known through the medium of that Divine Essence. Hence the inferior Angels are taught certain things by the higher Angels, though all see the Divine Essence. But each person in possession of the Beatific Vision only sees in the Divine Essence as much of other things as is necessitated by the degree of perfection of his beatitude; and for the perfection of beatitude it is required that a man "should have whatever he wants, and should desire nothing in an inordinate fashion."[271] Each one, however, rightly desires to know those things which concern himself. Hence, since no rectitude is lacking to the Saints, they wish to know those things which concern themselves, and consequently they must know them in the Word. But it belongs to their glory that they should be able to help on the salvation of those who need it, for it is thus that they are made co-workers with God—"than which there is nought more Divine," as Denis says.[272] It is clear, then, that the Saints have a knowledge of those things which are requisite for this end. And so, too, it is manifest that they know in the Word the desires, the devout acts and the prayers, of men who fly to them for help.

Some, however, maintain that the Saints do not know our prayers, thus:

1. On the words of Isaias,[273] Thou art our Father, and Abraham hath not known us, and Israel hath been ignorant of us, the Interlinear Gloss has: "For the Saints who are dead know not what the living do, even their own children." This is taken from S. Augustine's treatise On Care for the Dead, xiii., where he quotes these words, and adds: "If these great Patriarchs were ignorant of what concerned those whom they had begotten, how can the dead be concerned with knowing and assisting the affairs and the deeds of the living?" Hence it would seem that the Saints are not cognizant of our prayers.

But these words of S. Augustine are to be understood of the natural knowledge of the souls separated (from this world); and this knowledge is not obscured in holy men as it is in sinners. Moreover, S. Augustine is not talking of that knowledge which is in the Word, a knowledge which it is clear that Abraham had not at the time that Isaias said these things; for anterior to Christ's Passion no one had attained to the Vision of God.

2. In 4 Kings xxii. 20, it is said to Josias the king: Therefore—because, that is, thou didst weep before Me—I will gather thee to thy fathers ... that thy eyes may not see all the evils which I will bring upon this place. But the

death of Josias would have been no relief to him if he was to know after death what was going to happen to his nation. The Saints, then, who are dead, do not know our acts, and consequently cannot understand our prayers.

But although after this life the Saints know the things which are done here below, we are not therefore to suppose that they are filled with grief at the knowledge of the afflictions of those whom they loved in the world. For they are so filled with the joy of their beatitude that sorrow finds no place in them. Hence, if they know after death the evil plight of those dear to them, it is none the less a relief to their sorrow if they are withdrawn from this world before those woes come on.

At the same time it is possible that souls not yet in glory would feel a certain grief if they were made aware of the sorrows of those dear to them. And since the soul of Josias was not immediately glorified on its quitting the body, S. Augustine endeavours to argue that the souls of the dead have no knowledge of the deeds of the living.[274]

3. Again, the more a person is perfected in charity the more ready he is to succour his neighbour in peril. But the Saints while still in the flesh had a care for their neighbours, and especially for their relatives, when in peril. Since, then, they are after death far more perfected in charity, if they were cognizant of our deeds, they would have now a much greater care for those dear to them or related to them, and would help them much more in their necessities; but this does not seem to be the case. Whence it would seem that they are not cognizant of our actions nor of our prayers.

But the souls of the Saints have their will perfectly conformed to the Will of God, even in what they would will. Consequently, while retaining their feelings of charity towards their neighbour, they afford them no other assistance than that which they see is arranged for them in accordance with Divine Justice. Yet at the same time we must believe that they help their neighbours very much indeed by interceding for them with God.

4. Further, just as the Saints after death see the Word, so also do the Angels, for of them it is said: Their Angels in Heaven always see the face of My Father Who is in Heaven.[275] But the Angels, though seeing the Word, do not therefore know all things, for the inferior Angels are purified of their ignorance by the superior Angels, as is evident from Denis.[276]

Consequently, neither do the Saints, although they see the Word, know in It our prayers and other things which concern us.

But although it is not necessary that those who see the Word should see all things in the Word, they none the less see those things which belong to the perfection of their beatitude, as we have said above.

5. Lastly, God alone is the Searcher of hearts. But prayer is essentially an affair of the heart. Consequently God alone knows our prayers.

But God alone knows of Himself the thoughts of the heart; others know them according as they are revealed to them either in their vision of the Word or in any other way.

II

Ought we to appeal to the Saints to intercede for us?

In the Book of Job,[277] it is said: Call now, if there be any that will answer thee; and turn to some of the Saints. And on this S. Gregory says: "It is our business to call, and to beseech God in humble prayer."[278] When, then, we desire to pray to God, we ought to turn to the Saints that they may pray for us.

Further, the Saints who are in the Fatherland are more acceptable in the sight of God than they were when upon earth. But we ought to ask the Saints even when on earth to be our intercessors with God, as the Apostle shows us by his example when he says: I beseech you, therefore, brethren, through our Lord Jesus Christ, and by the charity of the Holy Ghost, that you help me in your prayers for me to God.[279] Much more, then, should we ask the Saints who are in our Fatherland to help us by their prayers to God.

Moreover, the common custom of the Church confirms this, since in her Litanies she asks the prayers of the Saints.

In the words of Denis,[280] "there is this Divinely established harmony in things—that they which hold the lowest place should be brought to God through them that come between them and God." Since, then, the Saints who are in our Fatherland are most nigh to God, the harmony of the Divine Government demands that we who, abiding in the body, are "absent from the Lord," should be led to Him by the Saints who stand midway; and this is secured when through their means the Divine Goodness pours out Its effects upon us. And since our return to God ought to correspond to the orderly way in which His goodnesses flow upon us—for His benefits flow out upon us through the intervention of the Saints' suffrages for us—so also ought we to be brought back to God through the intervention of the Saints, and thus once more receive His benefits. Whence it is that we make them our intercessors for us with God—and, as it were, mediators—by begging them to pray for us.

But some say that we should not ask the Saints to pray for us, thus:

1. No one asks a man's friends to intercede for him except in so far as he thinks that he can obtain a favour more easily through them. But God is infinitely more merciful than any Saint, and consequently His Will is more readily inclined to hear us than is the will of any Saint. Whence it would seem superfluous to make the Saints mediators between ourselves and God, and so ask them to intercede for us.

But just as it is not by reason of any deficiency on the part of the Divine Power that It works through the mediumship of secondary causes, whereas it rather tends to the fulfilment of the harmony of the universe that His Goodness should be more copiously diffused upon things, so that things not only receive from Him their own peculiar goodness, but themselves become a source of goodness to other things as well; so in the same way it is not by reason of any lack of mercy on His part that appeal to His mercy by means of the prayers of the Saints is fitting; but this is done in order that the aforesaid harmony may be preserved.

2. If we ought to ask the Saints to pray for us, it can only be because we know that their prayers are acceptable to God. But the more saintly is a Saint, the more acceptable is his prayer to God. Consequently we ought always to make the greater Saints our intercessors with God, and never the lesser ones.

Yet although the greater Saints are more acceptable to God than are the lesser ones, it is still useful to pray sometimes to the lesser Saints. And this for five reasons: Firstly, because a man sometimes has a greater devotion to some lesser Saint than to one who is greater; and the efficacy of our prayers depends very much on our devotion. Secondly, in order to avoid weariness; for unremitting application to one thing begets distaste; but when we pray to various Saints fresh devotional fervour is stirred up in practically each case. Thirdly, because certain Saints are appointed the patrons of certain particular cases, so S. Antony for the avoidance of hell-fire. Fourthly, that so we may show due honour to them all. Fifthly, because sometimes a favour may be gained at the prayer of many which would not be gained at the prayer of one alone.

3. Christ, even as man, is termed the Saint of Saints;[281] and it belongs to Him, as man, to pray. Yet we never ask Christ to pray for us. Hence it is superfluous to make the Saints our intercessors with God.

But prayer is an act. And acts belong to individual beings. Consequently, if we were to say, Christ, pray for us, we should appear, unless we added something, to be referring this to Christ's Person, and thus we might seem to fall into the error of Nestorius who regarded the Person of the Son of Man as distinct in Christ from the Person of the Son of God; or perhaps, too, into the error of Arius who regarded the Person of the Son as less than the Father. In order, then, to avoid these errors, the Church does not say, Christ, pray for us, but Christ, hear us, or Christ, have mercy on us.

4. Once more, when one is asked to intercede for another, he presents the latter's prayers to him with whom he has to intercede. But it is superfluous to present anything to Him to Whom all things are present. Hence it is superfluous to make the Saints our intercessors with God.

But the Saints are not said to present our prayers to God as though they were manifesting to Him something which He did not know, but in the sense that they ask that these prayers may be heard by God, or that they consult the Divine Truth concerning them, so as to know what, according to His providence, ought to be done.

5. Lastly, that must be held superfluous which is done for the sake of something which, whether the former were done or not, would yet take place—or not take place—all the same. But similarly, the Saints would pray for us or not pray for us whether we asked them to do so or not. For if we deserve that they should pray for us, they would pray for us, even though we did not ask them to do so; if, on the other hand, we are not deserving that they should pray for us, then they do not pray for us—even though we ask them to do so. Hence to ask them to pray for us seems altogether superfluous.

But a man becomes deserving that some Saint should pray for him from the very fact that with pure-hearted devotion he has recourse to him in his needs. Hence it is not superfluous to pray to the Saints.

III

Are the Saints' Prayers to God for us always heard?

In 2 Maccabees xv. 14 it is said: This is he that prayeth much for the people, and for all the Holy City, Jeremias the prophet of God; and that his prayer was heard is evident from what follows, for Jeremias stretched forth his right hand and gave to Judas a sword of gold, saying: Take this holy sword, a gift from God, etc.

Further, S. Jerome says[282]: "You say in your book that while we live we can pray for one another, but that after we are dead no one's prayer for others will be heard"; and S. Jerome condemns this statement thus: "If the Apostles and Martyrs while still in the body could pray for others while as yet solicitous for themselves, how much more when they have won their crown, completed the victory, and gained their triumph?"

Moreover, the Church's custom confirms this, for she frequently asks to be helped by the prayers of the Saints.

The Saints are said to pray for us in two ways: firstly, by express prayer, when they by their ardent desires appeal to the ears of the Divine Mercy for us; secondly, by interpretative prayer—namely, by their merits which, standing as the Saints do in the sight of God, not only tend to their own glory but are, as it were, suffrages—and even prayers—for us; just as the Blood of Christ, shed for us, is said to ask pardon for us. And in both ways the prayers of the Saints are, as far as in them lies, efficacious in obtaining what they ask for. But that we do not obtain the fruit of their prayers may be due to defects on our part, according, that is, as they are said to pray for us in the sense that their merits avail for us. But according as they actually do pray for us—that is, ask something for us by their desires—they are always heard. For the Saints only wish what God wishes, and they only ask for what they wish should be done; what God, however, wishes is always done—unless, indeed, we are speaking of the antecedent will of God, according to which He wills all men to be saved: this will is not always fulfilled. Hence it is not to be wondered at if what the Saints also will according to this kind of will is not always fulfilled.

But some maintain that the Saints' prayers for us are not always heard, thus:

1. If the Saints' prayers were always heard, they would be especially heard when they pray for those things which affect themselves. Yet they are not always heard as regards these things, for to the Martyrs who prayed for vengeance upon the inhabitants of the earth it was said that they should rest for a little time till the number of their brethren should be filled up.[283] Much less, then, are their prayers heard for things that do not concern them.

But this prayer of the Martyrs is nothing more than their desire to obtain the garment of the body and the society of the Saints who are to be saved; it expresses their agreement with the Divine Justice which punishes the wicked. Hence on those words of the Apocalypse,[284] How long, O Lord, the Ordinary Gloss says: "They yearn for a greater joy, and for the companionship of the Saints, and they agree with the justice of God."

2. It is said in Jeremias[285]: If Moses and Samuel shall stand before Me, My soul is not towards this people. The Saints, then, are not always heard when they pray for us to God.

But God here speaks of Moses and Samuel according as they were in this life, for they are said to have prayed for the people and thus withstood the wrath of God. Yet none the less, had they lived in Jeremias' time they would not have been able to appease by their prayers God's wrath upon the people, so great was the latter's wickedness. This is the meaning of that passage.

3. The Saints in our Fatherland are said to be the equals of the Angels.[286] But the Angels are not always heard in their prayers to God, as is evident from Daniel[287]: I am come for thy words. But the Prince of the kingdom of the Persians resisted me one and twenty days. But the Angel who spoke had not come to Daniel's assistance without asking his freedom from God; yet none the less the fulfilment of his prayer was hindered. In the same way, then, neither are the prayers of other Saints to God for us always heard.

But this contest of the good Angels is not to be understood in the sense that they put forth contrary prayers before God, but that they set before the Divine scrutiny conflicting merits on either hand, and awaited the Divine decision. Thus S. Gregory, expounding the above words of Daniel, says: "These sublime Spirits who rule over the nations in no sense strive for those who do evil, but they scrutinize their deeds and judge justly; hence, when the faults or the merits of any nation are submitted to the Council of the Supreme Court, he who is set over that particular nation is described as either losing or failing in the contest. But the sole victory for all of them is the supreme will of his Creator above him; and since they ever look towards that Will, they never desire what they cannot obtain,"[288] and hence never ask for it. Whence it is clear that their prayers are always heard.

4. Whoever obtains something by prayer in a certain sense merits it. But the Saints who are in our Fatherland are no longer capable of meriting. Therefore they cannot obtain anything for us from God by their prayers.

But although the Saints when once they are in our Fatherland are not capable of meriting for themselves, they are still capable of meriting for others, or rather of helping others by reason of their own previous merits. For when alive they merited from God that their prayers should be heard after death. Or we might say that in prayer merit and the power to obtain what we ask do not rest on the same basis. For merit consists in a certain correspondence between an act and the end towards which it is directed and which is given to it as its reward; but the impetratory power of prayer rests upon the generosity of him from whom we ask something. Consequently prayer sometimes wins from the generosity of him to whom it is made what perhaps was not merited either by him who asked nor by him for whom he asked. And thus, though the Saints are no longer capable of meriting, it does not follow that they are incapable of winning things from God.

5. Again, the Saints conform their will in all things to the Divine Will. Therefore they can only will what they know God wills. But no one prays save for what he wishes. Consequently they only pray for what they know God wills. But what God wills would take place whether they prayed or not. Consequently their prayers have no power to obtain things.

But, as is evident from the passage of S. Gregory quoted above in reply to the third difficulty, neither the Saints nor the Angels will anything save what they see in the Divine Will. And consequently they ask for nothing else save this. But it does not follow that their prayers are without fruit, for, as S. Augustine says in his treatise, On the Predestination of the Saints,[289] and S. Gregory in his Dialogues,[290] the prayers of the Saints avail for the predestinate, because perhaps it was pre-ordained that they should be saved by the prayers of those who interceded for them. And so, too, God wills that by the prayers of the Saints should be fulfilled what the Saints see that He wills.

6. Lastly, the prayers of the entire Court of Heaven should, if they can gain anything at all, be far more efficacious than all the suffrages of the Church on earth. But if all the suffrages of the Church on earth were to be accumulated upon one soul in Purgatory, it would be entirely freed from punishment. Since, then, the Saints who are in our Fatherland have the same reason for praying for the souls in Purgatory as they have for praying for us, they would by their prayers, if they could obtain anything for us, wholly deliver from suffering those who are in Purgatory. But this is false, for if it were true, then the suffrages of the Church for the dead would be superfluous.

But the suffrages of the Church for the dead are, as it were, satisfactions offered by the living in place of the dead, and thus they free the dead from that debt of punishment which they have not paid. But the Saints who are in our Fatherland are not capable of making satisfaction. And thus there is no parity between their prayers and the Church's suffrages.

FOOTNOTES 5

[267] xiv. 21.
[268] Moralia in Job, xii. 14.
[269] Dialogue, li. 35.
[270] Contra Vigilant., vi.
[271] S. Augustine: Of the Trinity, xiii. 5.
[272] Of the Heavenly Hierarchy, iii.
[273] lxiii. 16.
[274] De Cura Mortuorum, 13, 14, 15.
[275] S. Matt, xviii. 10.
[276] Of the Heavenly Hierarchy, vii.; and Of the Ecclesiastical Hierarchy, vi.
[277] v. 1.
[278] Moralia in Job, v. 30.
[279] Rom. xv. 30.
[280] Of the Ecclesiastical Hierarchy, v.
[281] Dan. ix. 14.
[282] Ep. contra Vigilantium, vi.
[283] Apoc. vi. 11.
[284] vi. 10.
[285] xv. 1.
[286] S. Matt. xxii. 30.
[287] x. 12-13.
[288] Moralia on Job, xvii. 12.
[289] De Dono Perseverantiæ, xxii.
[290] i. 8.

QUESTION 5

OF THE DIVISION OF LIFE INTO THE ACTIVE AND THE CONTEMPLATIVE

I. May Life be fittingly divided into the Active and the Contemplative?

S. Augustine, De Consensu Evangelistarum, I., iv. 8

Tractatus, cxxiv. 5, in Joannem

II. Is this division of Life into the Active and the Contemplative a sufficient one?

S. Augustine, Of the Trinity, I., viii. 17

I

May Life be fittingly divided into the Active and the Contemplative?

S. Gregory the Great says[291]: "There are two kinds of lives in which Almighty God instructs us by His Sacred Word—namely, the active and the contemplative."

Those things are properly said to live which move or work from within themselves. But what especially accords with the innermost nature of a thing is that which is proper to it and towards which it is especially inclined; consequently every living thing shows that it is living by those very acts which are especially befitting it and towards which it is especially inclined. Thus the life of plants is said to consist in their growing and in their producing seed; the life of animals in their feeling and moving; while that of man consists in his understanding and in his acting according to reason.

Hence among men themselves each man's life appears to be that in which he takes special pleasure, that with which he is particularly occupied, that, in fine, in which each one wishes to live with a friend, as is said in the Ethics of Aristotle.[292]

Since, then, some men are especially occupied with the contemplation of the truth while others are especially-occupied with external things, man's life may be conveniently divided into the active and the contemplative.

Some, however, repudiate this division, thus:

1. The soul is by its essence the principle of life; thus the Philosopher says[293]: "For living things, to live is to be." But the same soul with its

faculties is the principle both of action and of contemplation. Hence it would seem that life cannot be suitably divided into the active and the contemplative.

But the peculiar nature of every individual thing—that which makes it actually be—is the principle of its own proper action; consequently to live is said to be the very being of living things, and this because living things—by the very fact that they exist through such a nature—act in such a way.

2. Again, when one thing precedes another it is unfitting to divide the former by differences which find place in the latter. But action and contemplation, like speculation and practice, are distinctions in the intellect, as is laid down by the Philosopher.[294] But we live before we understand; for life is primarily in living things by their vegetative soul, as also the Philosopher says.[295] Therefore life is not fittingly divided according to contemplation and action.

But we do not say that life universally considered is divided into the active and the contemplative, but that man's life is so divided. For man derives his species from his intellect, hence the same divisions hold good for human life as hold good for the intellect.

3. Lastly, the word "life" implies motion, as is clear from Denis the Areopagite.[296] But contemplation more especially consists in repose, according to the words: When I go into my house I shall repose myself with her (Wisdom).[297]

But while contemplation implies a certain repose from external occupations, it is still a certain motion of the intellect in the sense that every operation is a motion; in this sense the Philosopher says that to feel and to understand are certain motions in the sense that motion is said to be the act of a perfect thing.[298] It is in this sense, too, that Denis[299] assigns three movements to the soul in contemplation: the direct, the circular, and the oblique.[300]

S. Augustine: Two virtues are set before the human soul, the one active, the other contemplative; the former shows the path, the latter shows the goal; in the one we toil that so the heart may be purified for the Vision of God, in the other we repose and we see God; the one is spent in the practice of the precepts of this temporal life, the other is occupied with the teachings of the life that is eternal. Hence it is that the one is a life of toil and the other a life of rest; for the former is engaged in purging away its sins, the latter already stands in the light of the purified. Hence, too, during this mortal life the former is occupied with the works of a good life, whereas the latter rather stands in faith, and, in the case of some few, sees through a mirror in a dark manner, and enjoys in part a certain glimpse of the Unchangeable Truth (De Consensu Evangelistarum, I., iv. 8).

"The Lord is the portion of my inheritance and of my cup; it is Thou that wilt restore my inheritance to me. The lines are fallen unto me in goodly places; for my inheritance is goodly to me."[301]

S. Augustine: There is another life, the life of immortality, and in it there are no ills; there we shall see face to face what we now see through a glass and in a dark manner even when we have made great advance in our study of the Truth. The Church, then, knows of two kinds of life Divinely set before Her and commended to Her; in the one we walk by faith, in the other by sight; the one is the pilgrimage of time, the other is the mansion of eternity; the one is a life of toil, the other of repose; in the one we are on the way, in the other in Our Father's Home; the one is spent in the toil of action, the other in the reward of contemplation; the one turneth away from evil and doth good, the other hath no evil from which to turn away, but rather a Great Good Which it enjoys; the one is in conflict with the foe, the other reigns—conscious that there is no foe; the one is strong in adversity, the other knows of no adversity; the one bridles the lusts of the flesh, the other is given up to the joys of the Spirit; the one is anxious to overcome, the other is tranquil in the peace of victory; the one is helped in temptations, the other, without temptation, rejoices in its Helper; the one succours the needy, the other dwells where none are needy; the one condones the sins of others that thereby its own sins may be condoned, the other suffers naught that it can pardon nor does ought that calls for pardon; the one is afflicted in sufferings lest it should be uplifted in good things, the other is steeped in such fulness of grace as to be free from all evil that so, without temptation to pride, it may cling to the Supreme Good; the one distinguishes between good and evil, the other sees naught save what is good; the one therefore is good—yet still in miseries, the other is better—and in Blessedness (Tractatus, cxxiv. 5, in Joannem).

"Jesu nostra Redemptio

Amor et Desiderium!
Deus Creator omnium,
Homo in fine temporum!"

II

Is this division of Life into the Active and the Contemplative a sufficient one?

These two kinds of life are signified by the two wives of Jacob—namely, the active life by Lia, the contemplative by Rachel. They are also signified by those two women who afforded hospitality to the Lord: the contemplative, namely, by Mary, the active by Martha, as S. Gregory says.[302] But if there were more than two kinds of life, these significations would not be fitting.

As we have said above, the division in question concerns human life regarded as intellectual. And the intellect itself is divided into the contemplative and the active, for the aim of intellectual knowledge is either the actual knowledge of the truth—and this belongs to the contemplative intellect, or it is some external action—and this concerns the practical or active intellect. Hence life is quite sufficiently divided into the active and the contemplative.

But some argue that this division is not a sufficient one, thus:

1. The Philosopher[303] says that there are three specially excellent kinds of life: the pleasurable, the civil—which seems to be identified with the active—and the contemplative.

But the pleasurable life makes its end consist in the pleasures of that body which we have in common with the brute creation. Hence, as the Philosopher says in the same place, this is a bestial life. Consequently it is not comprised in our division of life into the active and the contemplative.

2. Again, S. Augustine[304] speaks of three different kinds of life: the life of leisure, which is referred to the contemplative; the busy life, which is referred to the active life; and he adds a third composed of these two.

But things which hold a middle course are compounded of the extremes, and hence are virtually contained in them, as the tepid in the hot and the cold, the pallid in the white and the black. And similarly, under the active and the contemplative lives is comprised that kind of life which is compounded of them both. But just as in every mixture one of the simple elements predominates, so in this mixed kind of life now the contemplative, now the active predominates.

3. Lastly, men's lives are diversified according to their various occupations. But there are more than two classes of human occupations.

But all classes of human occupations are, if they are concerned with the necessities of this present life, and in accordance with right reason, comprised under the active life which, by properly regulated acts, takes heed for the needs of the present life. But if these actions minister to our concupiscences, then they fall under the voluptuous life which is not comprised in the active life. But human occupations which are directed to the consideration of the truth are comprised under the contemplative life.

S. Augustine: Your life is hid with Christ in God. When Christ shall appear, Who is your life, then you also shall appear with Him in glory;[305] but until that shall come to pass we see now through a glass in a dark manner—that is, in images as it were—but then face to face.[306] This, indeed, is the contemplation that is promised to us, the goal of all our actions, the eternal perfection of all our joys. For we are the sons of God, and it hath not yet appeared what we shall be; we know that when He shall appear we shall be like Him, for we shall see Him as He is.[307] And as He said to His servant Moses: I am Who am ... thus shalt thou say to the children of Israel: He Who is hath sent me to you,[308] even that shall we contemplate when we live in eternity. Thus, too, He says: This is eternal life, that they may know Thee, the only True God, and Jesus Christ Whom Thou hast sent.[309] And this shall be when the Lord shall come and bring to light the hidden things of darkness,[310] when the gloom of our mortal corruption shall have passed away. Then will be our "morning," that "morning" of which the Psalmist says: In the morning I will stand before Thee and I will see.[311] ... Then, too, will come to pass that which is written: Thou shall fill me with joy with Thy countenance.[312] Beyond that joy we shall seek for nothing, for there is naught further to be sought. The Father will be shown to us, and that will suffice for us. Well did Philip understand this when he said to the Lord: Show us the Father, and it is enough for us![313] ... Such contemplation, indeed, is the reward of faith, and for this reward's sake are our hearts purified by faith, as it is written: Purifying their hearts by faith[314] (De Trinitate, I., viii. 17).

"Remember, O Lord, Thy bowels of compassion; and Thy mercies that are from the beginning of the world. The sins of my youth and my ignorances do not remember. According to Thy mercy remember Thou me; for Thy goodness' sake, O Lord. The Lord is sweet and righteous; therefore He will give a law to sinners in the way. He will guide the mild in judgment; He will teach the meek His ways. All the ways of the Lord are mercy and truth to them that seek after His covenant and His testimonies. For Thy Name's sake, O Lord, Thou wilt pardon my sin; for it is great."[315]

FOOTNOTES 6

[291] Hom. XIV., On Ezechiel.
[292] IX., xii. 21.
[293] De Anima, II., iv. 4.
[294] De Anima, III., x. 2.
[295] Ibid., II., iv. 2.
[296] Of the Divine Names, vi.
[297] Wisd. viii. 16.
[298] De Anima, III., vii. 1.
[299] Of the Divine Names, IV., i. 7.
[300] For a commentary on this passage of S. Denis, see Qu. CLXXX., Art. 6, pp. 203-210.
[301] Ps. xv. 5-6.
[302] Moralia in Job, vi. 18; and Hom. XIV., On Ezechiel.
[303] Ethics, I., v. 21.
[304] Of the City of God, xix. 2 and 19.
[305] Col. iii. 3-4.
[306] 1 Cor. xiii. 12.
[307] 1 John iii. 2.
[308] Exod. iii. 14.
[309] S. John xvii. 3.
[310] 1 Cor. iv. 5.
[311] Ps. v. 5.
[312] Ps. xv. 11.
[313] S. John xiv. 8.
[314] Acts xv. 9.
[315] Ps. xxiv. 6-11.

QUESTION 6

OF THE CONTEMPLATIVE LIFE

I. Is the Contemplative Life wholly confined to the Intellect, or does the Will enter into it?
S. Thomas, On the Beatific Vision, I., xii.
ad 3m

II. Do the Moral Virtues pertain to the Contemplative Life?
S. Augustine, Of the City of God, xix. 19

III. Does the Contemplative Life comprise many Acts?
S. Augustine, Of the Perfection of Human Righteousness, viii. 18
Ep., cxxx. ad probam

IV. Does the Contemplative Life consist solely in the Contemplation of God, or in the Consideration of other Truths as well?
S. Augustine, Sermon, CLXIX., xiv. 17
Ep., cxxx. ad probam

V. Can the Contemplative Life attain, according to the State of this Present Life, to the Contemplation of the Divine Essence?
S. Augustine, Of the Sermon on the Mount, II., ix. 35

VI. Is the Act of Contemplation rightly distinguished according to the three kinds of Motion—Circular, Direct, and Oblique?

VII. Has Contemplation its Joys?

VIII. Is the Contemplative Life lasting?
S. Augustine, Sermon, cclix., On Low Sunday

I

Is the Contemplative Life wholly confined to the Intellect, or does the Will enter into it?

S. Gregory the Great says[316]: "The contemplative life means keeping of charity towards God and our neighbour, and fixing all our desires on our Creator." But desire and love belong to the affective or appetitive powers; consequently the contemplative life is not confined to the intellect.

When men's thoughts are principally directed towards the contemplation of the truth, their life is said to be "contemplative." But to "intend" or direct is an act of the will, since "intention" or direction is concerned with the end in view, and the end is the proper object of the will. Hence contemplation, having regard to the actual essence of it, is an act of the intellect; but if we consider that which moves us to the exercise of such an act, then contemplation is an act of the will; for it is the will which moves all the other faculties, including the intellect, to the exercise of their appropriate acts.

But the appetitive faculty—the will, that is—moves us to consider some point either sensibly or intellectually, that is, sometimes out of love for the thing itself—for *Where thy treasure is there is thy heart also*,—and sometimes out of love of that very knowledge which follows from its consideration. For this reason S. Gregory[317] makes the contemplative life consist in the love of God, since from love of God a man yearns to look upon His beauty. And since we are delighted when we obtain what we love, the contemplative life consequently results in delight, and this resides in the affective powers, from which, too, love took its rise.

Some, however, urge that the contemplative life lies wholly in the intellect, thus:

1. The Philosopher says[318]: "The end of contemplation is truth." But truth belongs wholly to the intellect.

But from the very fact that truth is the goal of contemplation it derives its character of a desirable and lovable and pleasing good, and in this sense it comes under the appetitive powers.

2. Again, S. Gregory says[319]: "Rachel, whose name is interpreted 'the Beginning seen,' signifies the contemplative life." But the vision of a principle, or beginning, belongs to the intellect.

But it is love of God which excites in us desire of the vision of the First Principle of all—viz., God Himself—and hence S. Gregory says[320]: "The contemplative life, trampling underfoot all cares, ardently yearns to look upon the face of the Creator."

3. S. Gregory says[321]: "It belongs to the contemplative life to rest from all exterior action." But the affective or appetitive powers tend towards external action. Hence it would seem that the contemplative life does not come under them.

But the appetitive powers not only move the bodily members to the performance of external acts, but the intellect, too, is moved by them to the exercise of contemplation.

"Hear, you that are far off, what I have done, and you that are near, know My strength. The sinners in Sion are afraid, trembling hath seized upon the hypocrites. Which of you can dwell with devouring fire? which of you shall dwell with everlasting burnings? He that walketh in justices, and speaketh truth, that casteth away avarice by oppression, and shaketh his hands from all bribes, that stoppeth his ears lest he hear blood, and shutteth his eyes that he may see no evil. He shall dwell on high, the fortifications of rocks shall be his highness: bread is given him, his waters are sure. His eyes shall see THE KING IN HIS BEAUTY, they shall see the land far off."[322]

S. Thomas: We do not enjoy all the things that we have; and this is either because they do not afford us delight, or because they are not the ultimate goal of our desires, and so are incapable of satisfying our yearnings or affording us repose. But these three things the Blessed have in God: for they see Him, and seeing Him they hold Him ever present to them, for they have it in their power always to see Him; and holding Him, they enjoy Him, satisfying their yearnings with That Which is The Ultimate End (Summa Theologica, I., xii. 7, ad 3m).

"As the hart panteth after the fountains of water: so my soul panteth after Thee, O God. My soul hath thirsted after the strong living God; when shall I come and appear before the face of God? My tears have been my bread day and night, whilst it is said to me daily: Where is thy God? These things I remembered, and poured out my soul in me; for I shall go over into the place of the wonderful tabernacle, even to the house of God. With the voice of joy and praise; the noise of one feasting. Why art thou sad, O my soul? and why dost thou trouble me? Hope in God, for I will still give praise to Him: the salvation of my countenance, and my God."[323]

II

Do the Moral Virtues pertain to the Contemplative Life?

The moral virtues are directed towards external actions, and S. Gregory says[324]: "It belongs to the contemplative life to abstain from all external action." Hence the moral virtues do not pertain to the contemplative life.

A thing may pertain to the contemplative life either essentially or by way of disposition towards it. Essentially, then, the moral virtues do not pertain to the contemplative life; for the goal of the contemplative life is the consideration of truth. "Knowledge," says the Philosopher, "which pertains to the consideration of truth, has little to do with the moral virtues."[325] Hence he also says[326] that moral virtues pertain to active, not to contemplative happiness.

But dispositively the moral virtues do belong to the contemplative life. For actual contemplation, in which the contemplative life essentially consists, is impeded both by the vehemence of the passions which distract the soul from occupation with the things of the intellect, and divert it to the things of sense, and also by external disturbances. The moral virtues, however, keep down the vehemence of the passions, and check the disturbance that might arise from external occupations.

Consequently the moral virtues do pertain to the contemplative life, but by way of disposition thereto.

But some maintain that the moral virtues do pertain to the contemplative life, thus:

1. S. Gregory says[327]: "The contemplative life means keeping charity towards God and our neighbour with our whole soul." But all the moral virtues—acts of which fall under precept—are reduced to love of God and of our neighbour; for Love is the fulfilling of the Law.[328] Consequently it would seem that the moral virtues do pertain to the contemplative life.

But, as we have already said, the contemplative life is motived by the affective faculties, and consequently love of God and of our neighbour are required for the contemplative life. Impelling causes, however, do not enter into the essence of a thing, but prepare for it and perfect it. Hence it does not follow that the moral virtues essentially pertain to the contemplative life.

2. Again; the contemplative life is especially directed towards the contemplation of God, as S. Gregory says: "The soul, trampling all cares underfoot, ardently yearns to see its Creator's face." But no one can attain to this without that cleanness of heart which the moral virtues procure: Blessed are the clean of heart, for they shall see God,[329] and again:

Follow peace with all men with holiness, without which no man shall see God.[330]

But holiness—that is, cleanness of heart—is produced by those virtues which have to do with those passions which hinder the purity of the reason. And peace is produced by justice—the moral virtue which is concerned with our works: The work of justice shall be peace[331] inasmuch, that is, as a man, by refraining from injuring others, removes occasions of strife and disturbance.

3. Lastly, S. Gregory says[332]: "The contemplative life is something beautiful in the soul," and it is for this reason that it is said to be typified by Rachel, for She was well-favoured and of a beautiful countenance.[333] But the beauty of the soul, as S. Ambrose remarks, depends upon the moral virtues and especially on that of temperance.[334]

But beauty consists in a certain splendour combined with a becoming harmony. Both of these points are radically to be referred to the reason, for to it belongs both the light which manifests beauty, and the establishment of due proportion in others. Consequently in the contemplative life—which consists in the act of the reason—beauty is necessarily and essentially to be found; thus of the contemplation of Wisdom it is said: And I became a lover of her beauty.[335] But in the moral virtues beauty is only found by a certain participation—in proportion, namely, as they share in the harmony of reason; and this is especially the case with the virtue of temperance whose function it is to repress those desires which particularly obscure the light of reason. Hence it is, too, that the virtue of chastity especially renders a man fit for contemplation, for venereal pleasures are precisely those which, as S. Augustine points out, most drag down the mind to the things of sense.[336]

S. Augustine: While it is true that any one of these three kinds of life—the leisurely, the busy, and the life commingled of them both—may be embraced by anybody without prejudice to his faith, and may be the means of leading him to his eternal reward, it is yet important that a man should take note of what it is that he holds to through love of the truth, and should reflect on the nature of the work to which he devotes himself at the demand of charity. For no man should be so addicted to leisure as for its sake to neglect his neighbour's profit; neither should any man be so devoted to the active life as to forget the thought of God. For in our leisured life we are not to find delight in mere idle repose, but the seeking and finding of the truth must be our aim; each must strive to advance in that, to hold fast what he finds, and yet not to grudge it to his neighbour. Similarly, in the life of action: we must not love honour in this life, nor power; for all things are vain under the sun. But we must love the toil itself which comes to us together with such honour or power if it be rightly and profitably used—as tending, that is, to the salvation under God of those under us.... Love of truth, then, seeks for a holy leisure; the calls of charity compel us to undertake the labours of justice. If no one lays on us this burden, then must we devote our leisure to the search after and the study of the truth; but if such burden be imposed upon us, we must shoulder it at the call of charity; yet withal we must not wholly abandon the delights of the truth, lest while the latter's sweetness is withdrawn from us, the burden we have taken up overwhelm us (Of the City of God, xix. 19).

"O expectation of Israel, the Saviour thereof in time of trouble: why wilt Thou be as a stranger in the land, and as a wayfaring man turning in to lodge? Why wilt Thou be as a wandering man, as a mighty man that cannot save? but Thou, O Lord, art among us, and Thy Name is called upon us, forsake us not."[337]

III

Does the Contemplative Life comprise many Acts?

By "life" is here meant any work to which a man principally devotes himself. Hence if there were many acts or works in the contemplative life, it would not be one life, but several.

It must be understood that we are speaking of the contemplative life as it concerns man. And between men and Angels there is, as S. Denis says,[338] this difference—that whereas an Angel knows the truth by one simple act of intelligence, man, on the contrary, only arrives at a knowledge of the simple truth by arguing from many premises. Hence the contemplative life has only a single act in which it finds its final perfection—namely, the contemplation of the truth—and from this one act it derives its oneness. But at the same time it has many acts by means of which it arrives at this final act. Of these various acts, some are concerned with the establishment of principles from which the mind proceeds to the contemplation of truth; others, again, are concerned with deducing from these principles that truth the knowledge of which is sought. But the ultimate act, the complement of the foregoing, is the contemplation of truth.

Some, however, maintain that many acts pertain to the contemplative life, thus:

1. Richard of S. Victor[339] distinguishes between contemplation, meditation, and thought. But these all seem to belong to the contemplative life.

But thought, according to Richard of S. Victor, seems to signify the consideration of many things from which a man intends to gather some single truth. Consequently, under the term thought may be comprised perceptions by the senses, whereby we know certain effects—imaginations, too, as well as investigation of different phenomena by the reason; in a word, all those things which conduce to a knowledge of the truth we are in search of. At the same time, according to S. Augustine,[340] every operation of the intellect may be termed thought. Meditation, again, seems to refer to the process of reasoning from principles which have to do with the truth we desire to contemplate. And contemplation, according to S. Bernard,[341] means the same thing, although, according to the Philosopher,[342] every operation of the intellect may be termed "consideration." But contemplation is concerned with the simple dwelling upon the truth itself. Hence Richard of S. Victor says[343]: "Contemplation is the soul's clear, free, and attentive dwelling upon the truth to be perceived; meditation is the outlook of the soul occupied in searching for the truth; thought is the soul's glance, ever prone to distraction."

2. Further, the Apostle says: But we all, beholding the glory of the Lord with open face, are transformed into the same image from glory to glory.[344] But this refers to the contemplative life; therefore, besides the three things already mentioned—namely, contemplation, meditation and thought,—speculation, too, enters into the contemplative life.

But speculation, as S. Augustine's Gloss has it,[345] "is derived from speculum, a 'mirror,' not from specula, a 'watch-tower.'" To see a thing in a mirror, however, is to see a cause by an effect in which its likeness is shown; thus speculation seems reducible to meditation.

3. Again, S. Bernard says[346]: "The first and chiefest contemplation is the marvelling at God's Majesty." But to "marvel" is, according to S. John Damascene,[347] a species of fear. Consequently it seems that many acts belong to contemplation.

But wonderment is a species of fear arising from our learning something which it is beyond our powers to understand. Hence wonderment is an act subsequent to the contemplation of sublime truth, whereas contemplation reaches its goal in the affective powers.

4. Lastly, prayer, reading, and meditation seem to belong to the contemplative life. Devout hearing, too, belongs to it, for it is said of Mary, who is the type of the contemplative life, that sitting at the Lord's feet, she heard His word.[348]

Man, however, arrives at the knowledge of truth in two ways: first of all, by receiving things from others; as regards, then, the things a man receives from God: prayer is necessary, according to the words: I called upon God, and the spirit of Wisdom came upon me.[349] And as for the things he receives from men: hearing is necessary if he receive them from one who speaks, reading is necessary if it be question of what is handed down in Holy Scripture. And secondly, a man arrives at the knowledge of truth by his own personal study, and for this is required meditation.

"Uni trinoque Domino
Sit sempiterna gloria!
Qui vitam sine termino
Nobis donet in Patria!"

S. Augustine: As long, then, as we are absent from the Lord, we walk by faith and not by sight,[350] whence it is said: The just man shall live in his faith.[351] And this is our justice as long as we are on our pilgrimage—namely, that here now by the uprightness and perfection with which we walk we strive after that perfection and fulness of justice where, in all the glory of its beauty, will be full and perfect charity. Here we chastise our body and bring it into subjection; here we give alms by conferring benefits and forgiving offences against ourselves; and we do this with joy and from the heart, and are ever instant in prayer; and all this we do in the light of that sound doctrine by which is built up right faith, solid hope, and pure charity. This, then, is our present justice whereby we run hungering and thirsting after the perfection and fulness of justice, so that hereafter we may be filled therewith (De Perfectione justitiæ Hominis, viii. 18).

S. Augustine: You know, then, I think, not only how you ought to pray, but what you ought to pray for; and this not because I teach you, but because He teaches you Who has deigned to teach us all. The Life of Beatitude is what we have to seek; this we have to ask for from the Lord God. And what Beatitude means is, with many, a source of much dispute. But why should we appeal to the many and their many opinions? For pithily and truly it is said in God's Scripture: Happy is that people whose God is the Lord![352] Oh, that we may be counted amongst that people! Oh, that we may be enabled to contemplate Him, and may come one day to live with Him unendingly! The end of the commandment is charity from a pure heart and a good conscience, and an unfeigned faith.[353] And among these three, hope stands for a good conscience. Faith, therefore, with hope and charity, leads to God the man who prays—that is, the man who believes, who hopes, and who desires, and who in the Lord's Prayer meditates what he should ask from the Lord (Ep. cxxx. ad probam).

"For my heart hath been inflamed, and my reins have been changed: and I am brought to nothing, and I knew not. I am become as a beast before Thee; and I am always with Thee. Thou hast held me by my right hand; and by Thy will Thou hast conducted me; and with glory Thou hast received me. For what have I in Heaven? and besides Thee what do I desire upon earth? For Thee my flesh and my heart hath fainted away; Thou art the God of my heart; and the God that is my portion for ever. For behold they that go far from Thee shall perish; Thou hast destroyed all them that are disloyal to Thee. But it is good for me to adhere to my God, to put my hope in the Lord God: that I may declare all Thy praises, in the gates of the daughter of Sion."[354]

IV

Does the Contemplative Life consist solely in the Contemplation of God, or in the Consideration of other Truths as well?

S. Gregory says[355]: "In contemplation it is the Principle—namely, God—which is sought."

A thing may come under the contemplative life in two ways: either primarily, or secondarily—that is, dispositively. Now primarily the contemplation of Divine Truth belongs to the contemplative life, since such contemplation is the goal of all human life. Hence S. Augustine says[356]: "The contemplation of God is promised to us as the goal of all our acts and the eternal consummation of all our joys." And this will be perfect in the future life when we shall see God face to face—when, consequently, it will render us perfectly blessed. But in our present state the contemplation of Divine Truth belongs to us only imperfectly—namely, through a glass and in a dark manner; it causes in us now a certain commencement of beatitude, which begins here, to be continued in the future. Hence even the Philosopher[357] makes the ultimate happiness of man consist in the contemplation of the highest intelligible truths.

But since we are led to a contemplation of God by the consideration of His Divine works—The invisible things of God ... are clearly seen, being understood by the things that are made[358]—it follows also that the contemplation of the Divine works belongs in a secondary sense to the contemplative life—according, namely, as by it we are led to the knowledge of God. For this reason S. Augustine says[359]: "In the study of created things we must not exercise a mere idle and passing curiosity, but must make them a stepping-stone to things that are immortal and that abide for ever."

Thus from what we have said it is clear that four things belong, and that in a certain sequence, to the contemplative life: firstly, the moral virtues; secondly, other acts apart from that of contemplation; thirdly, the contemplation of the Divine works; and fourthly—and this is the crown of them all—the actual contemplation of the Divine Truth.

Some, however, say that the contemplative life is not merely confined to the contemplation of God but is extended to the consideration of any truth whatsoever, thus:

1. In Ps. cxxxviii. 14 we read: Wonderful are Thy works! My soul knoweth right well! But the knowledge of the works of God is derived from a certain contemplation of the truth. Whence it would seem that it belongs to the contemplative life to contemplate not only the Divine Truth, but also any other truth we please.

But David sought the knowledge of God's works that he might thereby be led to God Himself, as he says elsewhere: I meditated on all Thy works, I mused upon the works of Thy hands; I stretched forth my hands to Thee.[360]

2. Again, S. Bernard says[361]: "The first point in contemplation is to marvel at God's majesty; the second, at His judgments; the third, at His benefits; the fourth, at His promises." But of these only the first comes under the Divine Truth—the rest are effects of it.

But from the consideration of the Divine judgments a man is led to the contemplation of the Divine justice; and from a consideration of the Divine benefits and promises a man is led to a knowledge of the Divine mercy and goodness, as it were by effects either already shown or to be shown.

3. Once more, Richard of S. Victor[362] distinguishes six kinds of contemplation; the first is according to the imagination simply, when, namely, we consider corporeal things; the second is in the imagination directed by the reason, as when we consider the harmony and arrangement of the things of the senses; the third is in the reason, but based on the imagination, as when by the consideration of visible things we are uplifted to the invisible; the fourth is in the reason working on the things of the reason, as when the soul occupies itself with invisible things unknown to the imagination; the fifth is above the reason, but not beyond its grasp, when, for instance, we know by Divine Revelation things which cannot be comprehended by the human reason; and the sixth is above the reason and beyond its grasp, as when by Divine illumination we know things which are apparently repugnant to human reason—for example, the things we are told concerning the mystery of the Holy Trinity.

And only the last named of these seems to come under Divine Truth; consequently contemplation of the truth is not limited to Divine Truth, but extends also to those truths which we consider in created things.

But by these six are signified the steps by which we ascend through created things to the contemplation of God. For in the first we have the perception of the things of sense; in the second, the progress from the things of sense to the things of the intellect; in the third judgment upon the things of sense according to intellectual principles; in the fourth, the simple consideration of intellectual truths at which we have arrived by means of the things of sense; in the fifth, the contemplation of intellectual truths to which we could not attain by the things of sense, but which can be grasped by reason; in the sixth, the contemplation of intellectual truths such as the reason can neither find nor grasp—truths, namely, which belong to the sublime contemplation of the Divine Truth, in which contemplation is finally perfected.

4. Lastly, in the contemplative life the contemplation of truth is sought as being man's perfection. But any truth whatsoever is a perfection of the human intellect. Consequently the contemplative life consists in the contemplation of any kind of truth whatsoever.

But the ultimate perfection of the human intellect is the Divine Truth; other truths perfect the intellect by way of preparation for the Divine Truth.

S. Augustine: Martha, Martha, thou hast chosen a good part, but Mary hath chosen the better. Yours is good—for it is good to busy oneself with waiting on the Saints—but hers is better. What you have chosen will pass away at length. You minister to the hungry, you minister to the thirsty, you make the beds for them that would sleep, you find house-room for them that need it—but all these things will pass away! For there will come a time when none will hunger, when none will thirst, when none will sleep. And then thy care will be taken from thee. But Mary hath chosen the better part, which shall never be taken from her! It shall not be taken away, for she chose to live the life of contemplation, she chose to live by the Word. What kind of life will that be that flows from the Word without spoken word? Here on earth she drew life from the Word, but through the medium of the spoken word. Then will be life, from the Word indeed, but with no spoken word. For the Word Himself is life. We shall be like Him, for we shall see Him as He is[363] (Sermon, CLXIX., xiv. 17).

S. Augustine: One thing I have asked of the Lord, this will I seek after: that I may dwell in the house of the Lord all the days of my life![364]

Whosoever asks for This One Thing and seeks after It prays with sure and certain confidence; nor need he fear lest, when he shall have obtained It, he shall find It disagreeable to him, for without It naught that he prays for as he ought, and obtains, is of any avail. For this is the one, true, and only Blessed Life—to contemplate the delights of the Lord for eternity, in immortality and incorruptibility of body as well as soul. For the sake of

This One Thing are all other things to be sought after, and only thus our petitions for them are rendered not unbecoming. Whosoever hath this One Thing will have all that he wishes for, nor indeed will he be able to wish there for anything which is unfitting. For there is the Fountain of Life, for which we must now thirst in prayer as long as we live by hope—as long, too, as we see not What we hope for. For we dwell 'neath the shadow of His wings before Whom is all our desire, that so we may be inebriated with the plenty of His house, and may drink of the torrent of His pleasure: for with Him is the Fountain of Life, and in His light we shall see light.[365] Then shall our desire be sated with all good things, then will there be naught for us to seek for with groanings, but only What we shall cling to with joy. Yet none the less, since this is the peace that surpasseth all understanding, even when praying for it we know not what we should pray for as we ought[366] (Ep. cxxx. ad probam).

"He shall cast death down headlong for ever: and the Lord God shall wipe away tears from every face, and the reproach of His people He shall take away from off the whole earth: for the Lord hath spoken it. And they shall say in that day: Lo, this is our God, we have waited for Him, and He will save us: this is the Lord, we have patiently waited for Him, we shall rejoice and be joyful in His salvation."[367]

V

Can the Contemplative Life attain, according to the State of this Present Life, to the Contemplation of the Divine Essence?

S. Gregory says[368]: "As long as we live in this mortal flesh none of us can make such progress in the virtue of contemplation as to fix his mind's gaze on that Infinite Light."

S. Augustine also says[369]: "No one who looks on God lives with that life with which we mortals live in the bodily senses; but unless he be in some sort dead to this life, whether as having wholly departed from the body, or as rapt away from the bodily senses, he is not uplifted to that vision."

A man, then, can be "in this life" in two ways: he can be in it actually—that is, as actually using his bodily senses—and when he is thus "in the body" no contemplation such as belongs to this present life can attain to the vision of the Essence of God; or a man may be "in this life" potentially, and not actually; that is, his soul may be joined to his body as its informing principle, but in such fashion that it neither makes use of the bodily senses nor even of the imagination, and this is what takes place when a man is rapt in ecstasy: in this sense contemplation such as belongs to this life can attain to the vision of the Divine Essence.

Consequently the highest degree of contemplation which is compatible with the present life is that which S. Paul had when he was rapt in ecstasy and stood midway between the state of this present life and the next.

Some, however, say that the contemplative life can, even according to our present state of life, attain to the vision of the Divine Essence, thus:

1. Jacob said: I have seen God face to face, and my soul hath been saved.[370] But the vision of the face of God is the vision of the Divine Essence. Whence it would seem that a man may by contemplation actually reach, even during this present life, to the vision of the Essence of God.

But S. Denis says[371]: "If anyone saw God and understood what he saw, then it was not God he saw, but something belonging to Him." And similarly S. Gregory says[372]: "Almighty God is never seen in His Glory, but the soul gazes at something derived from It, and thus refreshed, makes advance, and so ultimately arrives at the glory of vision." Hence when Jacob said, I saw God face to face, we are not to understand that he saw the Essence of God, but that he saw some appearance—that is, some imaginary appearance—in which God spoke to him; or, as the Gloss of S. Gregory[373] has it, "Since we know people by the face, Jacob called knowledge of God His face."

2. Further, S. Gregory says[374]: "Contemplative men turn back within upon themselves in that they search into spiritual things, and do not carry with them the shadows of things corporeal; or if perchance they touch them, they drive them away with discreet hands. But when they would look upon the Infinite Light, they put aside all images which limit It, and in striving to arrive at a height superior to themselves, they become conquerors of their nature." But a man is only withheld from the vision of the Divine Essence, which is Infinite Light, by the necessity he is under of turning to corporeal images. From this it would seem that contemplation can, even in this present life, arrive at the sight of the Infinite Essential Light.

But human contemplation according to this present state cannot exist without recourse to the imagination, for it is in accordance with man's nature that he should see intelligible forms through the medium of pictures in the imagination, as also the Philosopher teaches.[375] Yet intellectual knowledge does not consist in such images, rather does the intellect contemplate in them the purity of intelligible truth; and this is not merely the case in natural knowledge, but also in those things which we know by revelation. For S. Denis says: "The Divine Light manifests to us the Angelic hierarchies by means of symbolical figures by force of which we are restored to the simple ray," that is, to the simple knowledge of intelligible truth. It is thus that we ought to understand S. Gregory's words when he says: "In contemplation men do not carry with them the shadows of things corporeal," for their contemplation does not abide in these things but rather in the consideration of intelligible truth.

3. Lastly, S. Gregory says[376]: "To the soul that looks upon its Creator all created things are but narrow. Consequently the man of God—namely, the Blessed Benedict—who saw in a tower a fiery globe and the Angels mounting up to Heaven, was doubtless only able to see these things by the light of God." But the Blessed Benedict was then still in this life. Consequently contemplation, even in this present life, can attain to the vision of the Essence of God.

But we are not to understand from S. Gregory's words that the Blessed Benedict saw the Essence of God in that vision; S. Gregory wishes to show that since "to him who looks upon his Creator all created things are but as nothing," it follows that certain things can easily be seen by the illumination afforded by the Divine Light. Hence he adds: "For, however little of the Creator's Light he sees, all created things become of small account."

Veni Sancte Spiritus
Et emitte coelitus
Lucis Tuæ radium!
O Lux Beatissima
Reple cordis intima
Tuorum fidelium!

S. Augustine: And thus, the remaining burden of this mortal life being laid aside at death, man's happiness will, in God's own time, be perfected from every point of view—that happiness which is begun in this life, and to the attainment and securing of which at some future time our every effort must now tend (Of the Sermon on the Mount, II., ix. 35).

"The old error is passed away; Thou wilt keep peace: peace, because we have hoped in Thee. You have hoped in the Lord for evermore, in the Lord God mighty for ever. And in the way of Thy judgments, O Lord, we have patiently waited for Thee: Thy Name, and Thy remembrance are the desire of the soul. My soul hath desired Thee in the night: yea, and with my spirit within me in the morning early I will watch to Thee."[377]

VI

Is the Act of Contemplation Rightly Distinguished According to the Three Kinds of Motion—Circular, Direct, and Oblique?

S. Denis the Areopagite[378] does so distinguish the acts of contemplation.

The operation of the intellect in which contemplation essentially consists is termed "motion" in the sense that motion is the act of a perfect thing, according to the Philosopher.[379] And since we arrive at a knowledge of intelligible things through the medium of the things of sense, and the operations of the senses do not take place without motion, it follows that the operations also of the intellect are correctly described as a species of motion, and are differentiated according to the analogy of divers motions. But the more perfect and the chiefest of bodily motions are local motions, as is proved by the Philosopher.[380] Consequently the chief intellectual motions are described according to the analogy of these latter.

Now, there are three species of local motion: one is circular, according as a thing is moved uniformly about the same centre; another is direct, according as a thing proceeds from one point to another; and a third is oblique, compounded as it were from the two foregoing.

Hence in intelligible operations, that which simply has uniformity is attributed to circular motion; that intellectual motion by which a man proceeds from one thing to another is attributed to direct motion; while that intellectual operation which has a certain uniformity combined with progress towards different points, is attributed to oblique motion.

All, however, do not agree with this division, thus:

1. Contemplation means a state of repose, as is said in Wisdom[381]: When I go into my house I shall repose myself with Her. And motion is opposed to repose. Consequently the operations of the contemplative life cannot be designated according to these different species of motion.

But whereas external bodily movements are opposed to that repose of contemplation which is understood to be rest from external occupations, the motion of intellectual operations belongs precisely to the repose of contemplation.

2. Again, the action of the contemplative life pertains to the intellect wherein man is at one with the Angels. But S. Denis does not apply these motions to the Angels in the same way as he does to the soul; for he says that the circular motion of the Angels "corresponds to the illumination of the beautiful and the good." But of the circular motion of the soul he gives several definitions, of which the first is "the return of the soul upon itself as opposed to external things"; the second is "a certain wrapping together of the powers of the soul whereby it is freed from error and from external occupation"; and the third is "the union of the soul with things superior to it." Similarly, he speaks in different terms of the direct motion of the soul as compared with that of the Angels. For he says that the direct motion of an Angel is "according as he proceeds to the care of the things subject to him"; while the direct motion of the soul is made to consist in two things: first of all "that it proceeds to those things which are around it"; secondly, that "from external things it is uplifted to simple contemplation." And lastly, he explains the oblique motion differently in each case. For he makes the oblique motion of the Angels consist in this that, "while providing for those that have less than themselves, they remain in the same attitude towards God"; but the oblique motion of the soul he explains as meaning that "the soul is illumined by Divine knowledge rationally and diffusely."

Consequently it does not appear that the operations of contemplation are fittingly distinguished according to the aforesaid species of motion.

But while man's intellect is generally the same with that of the Angels, the intellectual powers of the latter are far higher than in man. It was therefore necessary to assign the aforesaid motions to human souls and to the Angels in different fashion in proportion as their intellectual powers are not uniform. For the Angelic intellect has uniform knowledge in two respects: firstly, because the Angels do not acquire intelligible truth from the variety of compound things; and secondly, because they do not understand intelligible truth discursively, but by simple intuition. Whereas the intellect of the human soul, on the contrary, acquires intelligible truth from the things of sense, and understands it by the discursive action of the reason.

Hence S. Denis assigns to the Angels circular motion in that they uniformly and unceasingly, without beginning or end, gaze upon God; just as circular motion, which has neither beginning nor end, is uniformly maintained round the same central point. But in the case of the human soul, its twofold lack of uniformity must be removed before it can attain to the above-mentioned uniformity. For there must first be removed that lack of uniformity which arises from the diversity of external things: that is, the soul must quit external things. And this S. Denis expresses first of all in his definition of the circular motion of the soul when he speaks of "the return of the soul upon itself as opposed to external things." And there must be removed in the second place that second lack of uniformity which arises from the discursive action of the reason. And this takes place when all the operations of the soul are reduced to the simple contemplation of intelligible truth. This forms the second part of S. Denis's definition of this circular motion—namely, when he speaks of the necessity of "a certain wrapping together of the powers of the soul," with the result that, when discursive action thus ceases, the soul's gaze is fixed on the contemplation of the one simple truth. And in this operation of the soul there is no room for error, just as there is no room for error in our understanding of first principles which we know by simple intuition.

Then, when these first two steps have been taken, S. Denis puts in the third place that uniformity, like to that of the Angels, by which the soul, laying aside all else, persists in the simple contemplation of God. And this he expresses when he says: "Then, as now made uniform, it, as a whole"—that is, as conformed (to God)—"is, with all its powers unified, led by the hand to the Beautiful and the Good."

But the direct motion in the Angels cannot be understood in the sense that, by considering, they proceed from one point to another; but solely according to the order of their providential care for others—according, namely, as the superior Angels illumine the inferior through those who stand between. And this is what S. Denis means when he says that the direct motion of an Angel is "according as he proceeds to the care of the things subject to him, taking in his course all things that are direct" following—that is, those things which are disposed in direct order. But to the human soul S. Denis assigns direct motion in the sense that it proceeds from the exterior things of sense to the knowledge of intelligible things.

And he assigns oblique motion to the Angels—a motion, that is, compounded of the direct and the circular—inasmuch as an Angel, according to his contemplation of God, provides for those inferior to him. To the human soul, on the contrary, he assigns this same oblique motion, similarly compounded of the direct and the circular motions, inasmuch as in its reasonings it makes use of the Divine illuminations.

3. Lastly, Richard of S. Victor[382] gives many other and different kinds of motion. For, following the analogy of the birds of the air, he says of these latter that "some at one time ascend on high, at another swoop down to earth, and they do this again and again; others turn now to the right, now to the left, and this repeatedly; others go in advance, others fall behind; some sail round and round in circles, now narrower and now wider; while others again remain almost immovably suspended in one place." From all which it would seem that there are not merely three movements in contemplation.

But all these diversities of motion which are expressed by, up and down, to right and left, backwards and forwards, and in varying circles, are reducible either to direct or to oblique motion, for they all signify the discursive action of the reason. For if this discursive action be from the genus to the species or from the whole to the part, it will be, as Richard of S. Victor himself explains, motion upwards and downwards. If, again, it means argumentation from one thing to its opposite, it will come under motion to right and left. Or if it be deduction from cause to effect, then it will be motion backwards and forwards. And finally, if it mean arguing from the accidents which surround a thing, whether nearly or remotely, it will be circuitous motion. But the discursive action of the reason arguing from the things of sense to intelligible things according to the orderly progress of the natural reason, belongs to direct motion. When, however, it arises from Divine illuminations, it comes under oblique motion, as we have already said (in the reply to the second argument). Lastly, only the immobility which he mentions will come under circular motion.

Whence it appears that S. Denis has quite sufficiently, and with exceeding subtlety, described the movements of contemplation.

"For behold my witness is in Heaven, and He that knoweth my conscience is on high. For behold short years pass away, and I am walking in a path by which I shall not return."[383]

VII

Has Contemplation its Joys?

In Wisdom viii. 16 we read: Her conversation hath no bitterness, nor Her company any tediousness, but joy and gladness. And S. Gregory says[384]: "The contemplative life means a truly lovable sweetness."

There are two sources of pleasure in contemplation; for, firstly, there is the very act of contemplating, and everyone finds a certain pleasure in the performance of acts which are appropriate to his nature or to his habits. And the contemplation of truth is natural to man as a rational animal; hence it is that "all men naturally desire to know," and consequently find a pleasure in the knowledge of truth. And this pleasure is enhanced according as a man has habits of wisdom and knowledge which enable him to indulge in contemplation without difficulty.

Secondly, contemplation is pleasurable owing to the object which we contemplate, as when a man looks at something which he loves. And this holds good of even bodily vision, for not only is the mere exercise of the visual faculties pleasurable, but the seeing people whom we love is pleasurable.

Since, then, the contemplative life especially consists in the contemplation of God, to which contemplation we are moved by charity, it follows that the contemplative life is not merely pleasurable by reason of the simple act of contemplating, but also by reason of Divine Love Itself. And in both these respects the delights of contemplation exceed all other human delights. For on the one hand spiritual delights are superior to carnal delights; and on the other hand, the love of Divine charity wherewith we love God exceeds all other love; whence it is said in the Psalm: Taste and see that the Lord is sweet.[385]

Some maintain, however, that contemplation is not pleasurable, thus:

1. Pleasure belongs to the appetitive powers, whereas contemplation is mainly in the intellect.

But while the contemplative life mainly consists in the intellect, it derives its principle from the affective powers, since a man is moved to contemplation by love of God. And since the end corresponds to the principle, it follows that the goal and term of the contemplative life is in the affective powers, in the sense, namely, that a man finds a pleasure in the sight of a thing which he loves, and this very pleasure stirs up in him a yet greater love. Hence S. Gregory says[386]: "When a man sees one whom he loves his love is yet more enkindled." And in this lies the full perfection of the contemplative life: that the Divine Truth should not only be seen but loved.

2. Again, strife and contention hinder delight. But in contemplation there is strife and contention, for S. Gregory says[387]: "The soul, when it strives after the contemplation of God, finds itself engaged in a species of combat; at one time it seems to prevail, for by understanding and by feeling it tastes somewhat of the Infinite Light; at other times it is overwhelmed, for when it has tasted it faints."

It is true indeed that contest and strife arising from the opposition presented by external things prevent us from finding pleasure in those same things. For no man finds a pleasure in the things against which he fights. But he does find a pleasure, other things being equal, in the actual attainment of a thing for which he has striven; thus S. Augustine says[388]: "The greater the danger in the battle, the greater the joy in the triumph." And in contemplation the strife and the combat do not arise from any opposition on the part of the truth which we contemplate, but from our deficient understanding and from the corruptible nature of our bodies which ever draw us down to things beneath us: The corruptible body is a load upon the soul, and the earthly habitation presseth down the mind that museth upon many things.[389] Hence it is that when a man attains to the contemplation of truth he loves it still more ardently; but at the same time he more than ever hates his own defects and the sluggishness of his corruptible body, so that with the Apostle he cries out: Unhappy man that I am! Who shall deliver me from the body of this death?[390] Hence, too, S. Gregory says: "When God is known by our desires and our understanding, He causes all pleasures of the flesh to wither up within us."[391]

3. But again, delight follows upon a perfect work.[392] But contemplation on this earth is imperfect, according to the words of the Apostle: We see now through a glass in a dark manner.[393] Hence it would seem that the contemplative life does not afford delight.

It is indeed true that the contemplation of God during this life is imperfect compared with our contemplation of Him in our eternal home; and in the same way it is true that the delights of contemplation here on earth are imperfect compared with the delights of contemplation in that home, of which latter joys the Psalmist says: Thou shalt make them drink of the torrent of Thy pleasure.[394] Yet, none the less, the contemplation of Divine things here on earth is, although imperfect, far more perfect than any other subject of contemplation howsoever perfect it may be, and this by reason of the excellence of what we contemplate. Whence the Philosopher says[395]: "It may indeed be the case that with regard to such noble existences and Divine substances we have to be content with insignificant theories, yet even though we but barely touch upon them, none the less so ennobling is such knowledge that it affords us greater delight than any other which is accessible to us." Hence, too, S. Gregory says: "The contemplative life has its most desirable sweetness which uplifts the soul above itself, opens the way to heavenly things, and makes spiritual things plain to the eyes of the soul."

4. Lastly, bodily injuries are a hindrance to delight. But contemplation is productive of bodily injuries, for we read in Genesis[396] that Jacob, after saying I have seen God face to face, ... halted on his foot ... because He touched the sinew of his thigh and it shrank. Whence it would seem that the contemplative life is not pleasurable.

But after that contemplation Jacob halted on one foot because, as S. Gregory says, "it must needs be that as the love of this world grows weaker, so a man grows stronger in his love of God," and consequently, "when once we have known the sweetness of God, one of our feet remains sound while the other halts; for a man who halts with one foot leans only on the one that is sound."[397]

"Tu esto nostrum gaudium
Qui es futurus Præmium.
Sit nostra in Te gloria
Per cuncta semper sæcula!"

S. Gregory: Between the delights of the body and those of the heart there is ever this difference that the delights of the body are wont, when we have them not, to beget a keen yearning for them; but when we have them and eat our fill, they straightway beget disgust for them, for we are sated therewith. Spiritual joys, on the contrary, when we have them not are a weariness, but when we have them we desire them still more, and the more we feed upon them the more we hunger after them. In the case of the former, the yearning for them was a pleasure, trial of them brought disgust. In the case of the latter, in desire we held them cheap, trial of them proved a source of pleasure. For spiritual joys increase the soul's desire of them even while they sate us, for the more their savour is perceived, the more we know what it is we ought eagerly to love. Whence it comes to pass that when we have them not we cannot love them, for their savour is unknown to us. For how can a man love what he is ignorant of? Wherefore the Psalmist admonishes us, saying: O taste and see that the Lord is sweet![398] As though he would say to us in plain terms: You know not His sweetness if ye have never tasted it; touch, then, the Food of Life with the palate of your soul that so, making proof of Its sweetness, ye may be able to love It.

These joys man lost when he sinned in Paradise; he went out when he closed his mouth to the Food of Eternal Sweetness. Whence we too, who are born amidst the toils of this pilgrimage, come without relish to this Food; we know not what we ought to desire, and the sickness of our disgust grows the more the further our souls keep away from feeding upon that Sweetness; and less and less does our soul desire those interior joys the longer it has grown accustomed to do without them. We sicken, then, by reason of our very disgust, and we are wearied by the long-drawn sickness of our hunger (Hom. XXXVI., On the Gospels).

VIII

Is the Contemplative Life lasting?

The Lord said Mary hath chosen the best part which shall not be taken away from her[399] because, as S. Gregory says: "Contemplation begins here below that it may be perfected in our heavenly home."

A thing may be termed "lasting" in two ways: from its very nature, or as far as we are concerned. As far as its nature is concerned, the contemplative life is lasting in two ways: for first of all it is concerned with incorruptible and unchangeable things, and in the second place there is nothing which is its contrary: for, as Aristotle says[400]: "To the pleasure which is derived from thought there is no contrary."

And also as far as we are concerned the contemplative life is lasting; and this both because it comes under the action of the incorruptible portion of our soul—namely, our intellect—and so can last after this life; and also because in the work of the contemplative life there is no bodily toil, and we can consequently apply ourselves more continuously to such work, as also the Philosopher remarks.[401]

Some, however, argue that the contemplative life is not lasting, thus:

1. The contemplative life essentially concerns the intellect. But all the intellectual perfections of this life will be made void, as we read: Whether prophecies shall be made void, or tongues shall cease, or knowledge shall be destroyed.[402]

But the fashion of contemplation here and in our Father's home is not the same; and the contemplative life is said "to last" by reason of charity, which is both its principle and its end; wherefore S. Gregory says: "The contemplative life begins here below that it may be perfected in our heavenly home, for the fire of love which begins to burn here below, when it sees Him Whom it loves, burns yet more strongly with love of Him."

2. Again, men but taste the sweetness of contemplation here, snatching at it, as it were, and in passing: whence S. Augustine says: "Thou introducest me to a most unwonted affection within me, to an unspeakable sweetness; yet I fall back again as though dragged down by a grievous weight!"[403] And S. Gregory, expounding those words of Job, When a spirit passed before me, says: "The mind does not long remain steadfastly occupied with the sweetness of intimate contemplation, for it is recalled to itself, stricken back by the immensity of that Light." The contemplative life, then, is not lasting.

It is true indeed that no action can remain long at the pitch of its intensity. And the goal of contemplation is to attain to the uniformity of Divine contemplation, as Denis the Areopagite says.[404] Hence, although in this sense contemplation cannot last long, yet it can last long as regards its other acts.

3. Lastly, what is not natural to a man cannot be lasting. "But the contemplative life," as the Philosopher says, "is beyond man."[405]

But the Philosopher says that the contemplative life is "beyond man" in the sense that it belongs to us according to what is Divine in us—namely, our intellect; for our intellect is incorruptible and impassible in itself, and consequently its action can be more lasting.

S. Augustine: This day sets before us the great mystery of our eternal beatitude. For that life which this day signifies will not pass away as to-day is to pass away. Wherefore, brethren, we exhort and beseech you by the Name of our Lord Jesus Christ by Whom our sins are forgiven, by Him Who willed that His Blood should be our ransom, by Him Who has deigned that we who are not deserving to be called His slaves should yet be called His brethren—we beseech you that your entire aim, that which gives you your very name of "Christian," and by reason of which you bear His Name upon your foreheads and in your hearts, may be directed solely to that life which we are to share with the Angels; that life where is to be unending repose, everlasting joy, unfailing happiness, rest without disturbance, joy without sadness, no death. What that life is none can know save those who have made trial of it; and none can make trial of it save those who have faith (Sermon, CCLIX., On Low Sunday).

"And thou shalt say in that day: I will give thanks to Thee, O Lord, for Thou wast angry with me: Thy wrath is turned away, and Thou hast comforted me. Behold, God is my Saviour. I will deal confidently, and will not fear: because the Lord is my strength, and my praise, and He is become my salvation. You shall draw waters with joy out of the Saviour's fountains: And you shall say in that day: Praise ye the Lord, and call upon His Name: make His works known among the people: remember that His Name is high. Sing ye to the Lord, for He hath done great things: shew this forth in all the earth. Rejoice, and praise, O thou habitation of Sion: for great is He that is in the midst of thee, the holy One of Israel."[406]

FOOTNOTES 7

[316] Moralia in Job, vi. 18.
[317] Hom. XIV., On Ezechiel.
[318] Metaphysics, ii. 3.
[319] Moralia in Job, vi. 18; and Hom. XIV., On Ezechiel.
[320] On Ezechiel, loc. cit.
[321] Hom. XIV., On Ezechiel.
[322] Isa. xxxiii. 13-17.
[323] Ps. xli. 1-6.
[324] Moralia in Job, vi. 18.
[325] Ethics, II., iv. 3.
[326] Ibid., X., viii. 1.
[327] Hom. XIV., On Ezechiel.
[328] Rom. xiii. 10.
[329] S. Matt. v. 8.
[330] Heb. xii. 14.
[331] Isa. xxxii. 17.
[332] Hom. XIV., On Ezechiel.
[333] Gen. xxix. 17.
[334] De Officiis, i. 43, 45, 46.
[335] Wisd. viii. 2.
[336] Soliloquies, i. 10.
[337] Jer. xiv. 8, 9.
[338] Of the Divine Names, vii. 2.
[339] On Contemplation, i. 3 and 4.
[340] De Trinitate, xiv. 7.
[341] De Consideratione, ii. 2.
[342] De Anima, II., i. 2.
[343] Loc. cit., i. 4.
[344] 2 Cor. iii. 18.
[345] De Trinitate, xv. 8.
[346] De Consideratione, v. 14.
[347] De Fide Orthodoxa, ii. 15.
[348] S. Luke x. 39.
[349] Wisd. vii. 7.

[350] 2 Cor. v. 6-7.
[351] Hab. ii. 4.
[352] Ps. cxliii. 15.
[353] 1 Tim. i. 5.
[354] Ps. lxxii. 21-28.
[355] Moralia in Job, vi. 28.
[356] On the Trinity, i. 8.
[357] Ethics, X., vii. 2.
[358] Rom. i. 20.
[359] De Vera Religione, xxix.
[360] Ps. cxlii. 5, 6.
[361] De Consideratione, v. 14.
[362] Of Contemplation, i. 6.
[363] 1 John iii. 2.
[364] Ps. xxvi. 4.
[365] Ps. xxxv. 9, 10.
[366] Phil. iv. 7; Rom. viii. 26.
[367] Isa. xxv. 8, 9.
[368] Hom. XIV., On Ezechiel.
[369] De Genesi ad Litt., xii. 27.
[370] Gen. xxxii. 30.
[371] Epistola I., to Caius the Monk.
[372] Hom. XIV., On Ezechiel.
[373] The Glossa Ordinaria, taken from S. Gregory's Moralia in Job, xxiv. 5.
[374] Moralia, vi. 27.
[375] De Anima, III., vii. 3.
[376] Dialogues, ii. 35.
[377] Isa. xxvi. 3, 4, 8, 9.
[378] Of the Divine Names, IV., i. 7.
[379] De Anima, III., vii. 1 and 2.
[380] Physica, VIII., vii. 2.
[381] viii. 16.
[382] Of Contemplation, i. 5.
[383] Job xvi. 20, 23.
[384] Hom. XIV., On Ezechiel.

[385] Ps. xxxiii. 9.
[386] Hom. XIV., On Ezechiel.
[387] Ibid.
[388] Conf., viii. 3.
[389] Wisd. ix. 15.
[390] Rom. vii. 24.
[391] Hom. XIV., On Ezechiel.
[392] Ethics, X., iv. 6.
[393] 1 Cor. xiii, 12.
[394] Ps. xxxv. 9.
[395] De Partibus Animalium, i. 5.
[396] xxxii. 30-32.
[397] Hom. XIV., On Ezechiel.
[398] Ps. xxxiii. 9.
[399] S. Luke x. 42.
[400] Topics, I., xiii. 5.
[401] Ethics, X., vii. 2.
[402] 1 Cor. xiii. 8.
[403] Conf., x. 40.
[404] Of the Divine Names, IV., i. 7; and Of the Heavenly Hierarchy, iii.
[405] Ethics, X., vii. 8.
[406] Isa. xii. 1-6.

QUESTION 7

OF THE ACTIVE LIFE

I. Do all Acts of the Moral Virtues come under the Active Life?
II. Does Prudence pertain to the Active Life?
III. Does Teaching belong to the Active or to the Contemplative Life?
IV. Does the Active Life continue after this Life?

I

Do all Acts of the Moral Virtues come under the Active Life?

S. Isidore says[407]: "In the active life all the vices are first of all to be removed by the practice of good works, so that in the contemplative life a man may, with now purified mental gaze, pass to the contemplation of the Divine Light." But all the vices can only be removed by the acts of the moral virtues. Consequently the acts of the moral virtues belong to the active life.

As we have said already,[408] the active and the contemplative lives are distinguished by the different occupations of men who are aiming at different ends, one being the consideration of Truth—the goal of the contemplative life; the other external works with which the active life is occupied. But it is clear that the moral virtues are not especially concerned with the contemplation of truth but with action; thus the Philosopher says[409]: "For virtue, knowledge is of little or no avail." It is therefore manifest that the moral virtues essentially belong to the active life; and in accordance with this the Philosopher[410] refers the moral virtues to active happiness.

Some, however, maintain that all the acts of the moral virtues do not belong to the active life, thus:

1. The active life seems to consist solely in those things which have to do with our neighbour; for S. Gregory says[411]: "The active life means breaking bread to the hungry;" and at the close, after enumerating many things which have to do with our neighbour, he adds: "And to provide for each according as they have need." But not by all the acts of the moral virtues are we brought into contact with others, but only by justice and its divisions. Consequently all the acts of the moral virtues do not belong to the active life.

But the chief of the moral virtues is justice, and by it a man is brought into contact with his neighbour, as the Philosopher proves.[412] We describe, then, the active life by those things by means of which we are brought into contact with our neighbour; yet we do not thereby mean that the active life consists solely in these things, but chiefly in them.

2. Again, S. Gregory says[413]: "By Lia, who was blear-eyed but fruitful, is signified the active life which sees less clearly, since occupied with works; but when, now by word, now by example, it arouses its neighbour to imitation, it brings forth many children in good works." But all this seems rather to come under charity, by which we love our neighbour, than under the moral virtues. Consequently the acts of the moral virtues seem not to belong to the active life.

But a man can, by acts of all the moral virtues, lead his neighbour to good works by his example; and this S. Gregory here attributes to the active life.

3. Lastly, the moral virtues dispose us to the contemplative life. But disposition to a thing and the perfect attainment of that thing come under the same head. Consequently the moral virtues do not belong to the active life.

But just as a virtue which is directed towards the end of another virtue passes over, in some sort, into the species of that latter virtue, so also when a man uses those things which belong to the active life precisely as disposing him to contemplation, then those things which he so uses are comprised under the contemplative life. But for those who devote themselves to the works of the moral virtues as being good in themselves and not as dispositive towards the contemplative life, the moral virtues belong to the active life. Although at the same time it might be said that the active life is a disposition to the contemplative life.

"O death, how bitter is the remembrance of thee to a man that hath peace in his possessions, to a man that is at rest, and whose ways are prosperous in all things, and that is yet able to take meat! O death, thy sentence is welcome to the man that is in need, and to him whose strength faileth, who is in a decrepit age, and that is in care about all things, and to the distrustful that loseth patience! Fear not the sentence of death. Remember what things have been before thee, and what shall come after thee: this sentence is from the Lord upon all flesh. And what shall come upon thee by the good pleasure of the Most High whether ten, or a hundred, or a thousand years."[414]

II

Does Prudence pertain to the Active Life?

The Philosopher says[415] that prudence pertains to active happiness, and to this pertain the moral virtues.

As we have said above, when one thing is directed towards the attainment of another thing as its end, it—and this especially holds good in morals—is, so to speak, drawn into the species of that towards which it is thus directed, thus: "He who commits adultery in order to steal" says the Philosopher,[416] "is rather a thief than an adulterer." Now it is clear that that knowledge which is prudence is directed to the acts of the moral virtues as its end, for prudence is "the right mode of procedure in our actions;"[417] hence, too, the ends of the moral virtues are the principles of prudence, as the Philosopher also says in the same work.[418] In the same way, then, as we said above that in the case of a man who directs them to the repose of contemplation, the moral virtues pertain to the contemplative life, so also the knowledge which is prudence, and which is by its very nature directed to the operations of the moral virtues, directly pertains to the active life—that is, of course, on the supposition that prudence is understood in the strict sense in which the Philosopher speaks of it.

If, however, prudence be understood in a broad sense—namely, as embracing all kinds of human knowledge—then prudence pertains, at least in certain of its aspects, to the contemplative life; thus Cicero says[419]: "The man who can see a truth the most clearly and quickly, and explain the reason of it, is rightly regarded as most prudent and most wise."

But some maintain that prudence does not pertain to the active life, thus:

1. Just as the contemplative life pertains to the cognoscitive powers, so does the active life pertain to the appetitive powers. But prudence does not pertain to the appetitive powers but rather to the cognoscitive. Consequently it does not pertain to the active life.

But moral acts derive their character from the end towards which they are directed; consequently to the contemplative life belongs that kind of knowledge which makes its end consist in the very knowledge of truth. But the knowledge which is prudence, and which is rather directed to the acts of the appetitive powers, pertains to the active life.

2. Again, S. Gregory says[420] "The active life, occupied as it is with works, sees less clearly," and hence is typified by Lia, who was blear-eyed. But prudence demands clear vision, so that a man may judge what is to be done. Whence it would seem that prudence does not pertain to the active life.

But occupation with external things only makes a man see less clearly those intelligible truths which are not connected with the things of sense; the external occupations of the active life, however, make a man see more clearly in his judgment on a course of action—and this is a question of prudence—for he has experience, and his mind is attentive: "When you are attentive," says Sallust,[421] "then mental acumen avails."

3. Lastly, prudence comes midway betwixt the moral and the intellectual virtues. But just as the moral virtues pertain to the active life, so do the intellectual virtues pertain to the contemplative. Hence it would seem that prudence belongs neither to the active nor to the contemplative life, but, as S. Augustine says, to a kind of life which is betwixt and between.[422]

But prudence is said to come betwixt the intellectual and the moral virtues in the sense that, whereas it has the same subject as the intellectual virtues, it yet coincides as regards its object with the moral virtues. And that third species of life comes betwixt and between the active and the contemplative life as regards the things with which it is concerned, for at one time it is occupied with the contemplation of truth, at another time with external matters.

"For what shall I do when God shall rise to judge? and when He shall examine, what shall I answer Him? For I have always feared God as waves swelling over me, and His weight I was not able to bear."[423]

III

Does Teaching Belong to the Active or to the Contemplative Life?

S. Gregory says[424]: "The active life means breaking bread to the hungry; teaching words of wisdom to them that know them not."

The act of teaching has a twofold object: for teaching is by speaking, and speaking is the audible sign of an interior mental concept. One object, therefore, of our teaching is the matter to be taught, the object, that is, of our interior concepts; and in this sense teaching sometimes belongs to the active, sometimes to the contemplative life. It belongs to the active life if a man forms interiorly some concept of a truth with a view to thus directing his external acts; but it belongs to the contemplative life if a man interiorly conceives some intelligible truth and delights in the thought of it and the love of it. Whence S. Augustine says[425]: "Let them choose for themselves the better part—that, namely, of the contemplative life; let them devote themselves to the Word of God; let them yearn for the sweetness of teaching; let them occupy themselves with the knowledge that leads to salvation"—where he clearly says that teaching belongs to the contemplative life.

The second object of teaching arises from the fact that teaching is given through the medium of audible speech and thus the hearer himself is the object of the teaching; and from this point of view all teaching belongs to the active life to which pertain all external actions.

Some, however, regard teaching as rather belonging to the contemplative than to the active life, thus:

1. S. Gregory says[426]: "Perfect men declare to their brethren those good things of Heaven which they themselves have been able to contemplate at least 'through a glass,' and they thus kindle in their hearts the love of that hidden beauty." Yet what is this but teaching? To teach, therefore, is an act of the contemplative life.

But S. Gregory expressly speaks here of teaching from the point of view of the matter that is presented—that is, of teaching as it is concerned with the consideration of and love of the truth.

2. Again, acts and habits seem to belong to the same kind of life. But to teach is an act of wisdom, for the Philosopher says: "The proof that a man knows is that he is able to teach."[427] Since, then, wisdom—that is, knowledge—pertains to the contemplative life, it would seem that teaching also must pertain to the contemplative life.

But habits and acts agree in their object, and consequently the argument just given is based upon the material of the interior concept. For the capacity for teaching is possessed by a wise or learned man just in proportion as he can express in outward words the concepts of his mind and so be able to bring home a truth to someone else.

3. Lastly, prayer is an act of the contemplative life just in the same way as is contemplation itself. But prayer, even when one man prays for another, belongs to the contemplative life. Hence it would seem that when

one man brings to the knowledge of another some truth upon which he has meditated, such an act pertains to the contemplative life.

But he who prays for another in no way acts upon him for whom he prays; his acts are directed towards God alone, the Intelligible Truth. But he who teaches another does act upon him by some external action. Hence there is no parallel between the two cases.

IV

Does the Active Life continue after this Life?

S. Gregory says[428]: "The active life passes away with this present world; the contemplative life begins here so as to be perfected in our heavenly home."

As already said, the active life makes its end consist in external actions, and these, if they are directed towards the repose of contemplation, already belong to the contemplative life. But in the future life of the blessed all occupation with external things will cease; or if there are any external acts they will be directed towards that end which is contemplation. Hence S. Augustine says, at the close of his Of the City of God: "There we shall be at rest from toil, we shall gaze, we shall love, we shall praise." And he had just previously said: "There will God be seen unendingly, be loved without wearying, be praised without fatigue; this duty, this disposition of soul, this act, will be the lot of all."[429]

Some, however, maintain that the active life will be continued after this life, thus:

1. To the active life belong the acts of the moral virtues. But the moral virtues remain after death, as S. Augustine says.[430]

But the acts of the moral virtues which are concerned with the means to the end will not remain after death, but only those which have to do with the end itself. Yet it is precisely these latter which go to form the repose of contemplation to which S. Augustine alludes in the above-quoted passage where he speaks of being "at rest from toil"; and this "rest" is not to be understood of freedom from merely external disturbances, but also from the internal conflict of the passions.

2. Again, to teach others pertains to the active life. But in the next life—where we shall be as the Angels—there can be teaching; for we see it in the case of the Angels of whom one illumines, clarifies, and perfects another, all of which refer to their reception of knowledge, as is clear from Denis the

Areopagite.[431] Hence it seems that the active life is to be continued after this life.

But the contemplative life especially consists in the contemplation of God; and as regards this no Angel teaches another, for it is said of the Angels of the little ones[432]—Angels who are of an inferior choir—that they always see the face of the Father. And similarly in the future life: there no man will teach another about God, for we shall all see Him as He is.[433] And this agrees with the words of Jeremias[434]: *And they shall teach no more every man his neighbour ... saying: Know the Lord; for all shall know Me from the least of them even to the greatest.*

But when it is question of dispensing the mysteries of God, then one Angel can teach another by clarifying, illumining, and perfecting. And in this sense the Angels do in some sort share in the active life as long as this world lasts, for they are occupied with ministering to the inferior creation. This is what was signified by Jacob's vision of the Angels ascending the ladder—whereby was meant the contemplative life—and descending the ladder—whereby was meant the active life. At the same time, as S. Gregory says[435]: "Not that they so went out from the Divine Vision as to be deprived of the joys of contemplation." And thus in their case the active life is not distinguished from the contemplative as it is in us who find the works of the active life an impediment to the contemplative life. Moreover, we are not promised a likeness to the Angels in their work of administering to the inferior creation, for this does not belong to us according to our nature, as is the case with the Angels, but according to our vision of God.

3. Lastly, the more durable a thing is the more capable it seems of lasting after this life. But the active life is more durable than the contemplative, for S. Gregory says[436]: "We can remain steadfast in the active life, but in nowise can we maintain the mind's fixed gaze in the contemplative life." Consequently the active life is much more capable of continuing after death than is the contemplative life.

But in our present state the durability of the active life as compared with the contemplative life does not arise from any feature of either of these kinds of life considered in themselves, but from a defect on our part; for we are dragged down from the heights of contemplation by the body's burden. And thus S. Gregory goes on to say that, "thrust back by its very weakness from those vast heights, the soul relapses into itself."

"O bless our God, ye Gentiles: and make the voice of His praise to be heard. Who hath set my soul to live: and hath not suffered my feet to be moved. For Thou, O God, hast proved us; Thou hast tried us by fire, as silver is tried. Thou hast brought us into a net, Thou hast laid afflictions on our back; Thou hast set men over our heads. We have passed through fire and water, and Thou hast brought us out into a refreshment."[437]

FOOTNOTES 8

[407] Of the Supreme Good, III., xv.
[408] Qu. CLXXIX. 1.
[409] Ethics, II., iv. 3.
[410] Ibid., X., viii. 1.
[411] Hom. XIV., On Ezechiel.
[412] Ethics, V., i. 15.
[413] Hom. XIV., On Ezechiel.
[414] Ecclus. xli. 1-6.
[415] Ethics., X., viii. 2.
[416] Ibid., V., ii. 4.
[417] Ethics, VI., v. 4.
[418] Ibid., X., viii. 2.
[419] De Officiis, I., v.
[420] Hom. XIV., On Ezechiel.
[421] Conjuratio Catilinæ, li.
[422] Of the City of God, xix. 2, 3, and 19.
[423] Job xxxi. 14, 23.
[424] Hom. XIV., On Ezechiel.
[425] On the Words of the Lord, Sermon civ., alias xxvii. 1.
[426] Hom. V., On Ezechiel.
[427] Metaphysics, I., i. 9.
[428] Hom. XIV., On Ezechiel.
[429] xxii. 30.
[430] On the Trinity, xiv. 9.
[431] Of the Heavenly Hierarchy, vii.
[432] S. Matt. xviii. 10.
[433] 1 John iii. 2.
[434] xxxi. 34.
[435] Moralia in Job, ii. 2.
[436] Hom. V., On Ezechiel.
[437] Ps. lxv. 8-12.

QUESTION 8

OF THE COMPARISON BETWEEN THE ACTIVE AND THE CONTEMPLATIVE LIFE

I. Is the Active Life preferable to the Contemplative?
   Cardinal Cajetan, On Preparation for the Contemplative Life
   S. Augustine, Confessions, X., xliii. 70
   On Psalm xxvi.
II. Is the Active Life more Meritorious than the Contemplative?
III. Is the Active Life a Hindrance to the Contemplative Life?
   Cardinal Cajetan, On the True Interior Life
   S. Augustine, Sermon, CCLVI., v. 6
IV. Does the Active Life precede the Contemplative?

I

Is the Active Life preferable to the Contemplative?

The Lord said: Mary hath chosen the best part, which shall not be taken away from her.[438] And by Mary is signified the contemplative life, which is consequently to be preferred to the active.

There is no reason why one thing should not be in itself more excellent than another while yet this latter is, for certain reasons, preferable to it. Absolutely speaking, then, the contemplative life is better than the active. And the Philosopher[439] alleges eight proofs of this. Firstly, that the contemplative life pertains to that which is best in a man, namely his intellect and its proper objects, i.e. intelligible truths, whereas the active life is concerned with external things. Hence Rachel, who typifies the contemplative life, is interpreted as meaning "the Beginning seen"; while Lia, who was blear-eyed, typifies, according to S. Gregory, the active life.[440]

Secondly, because the contemplative life can be more continuous, even though we cannot maintain our contemplation at its highest pitch; thus Mary, who is typical of the contemplative life, is depicted as sitting ever at the Lord's feet.

Thirdly, because the delights of the contemplative life surpass those of the active life; whence S. Augustine says[441]: "Martha was troubled, but Mary feasted."

Fourthly, because in the contemplative life a man is more independent, since for this kind of life he needs less; whence we read: Martha, Martha, thou art careful, and art troubled about many things.[442]

Fifthly, because the contemplative life is loved rather for its own sake, whereas the active life is directed towards an end other than itself; whence it is said in Ps. xxvi. 4: One thing I have asked of the Lord, this will I seek after, that I may dwell in the house of the Lord all the days of my life.

Sixthly, because the contemplative life consists in a certain stillness and repose, as is said in Ps. xlv. 11: Be still, and see that I am God.

Seventhly, because the contemplative life is occupied with Divine things whereas the active life is occupied with human things; whence S. Augustine says[443]: "In the beginning was the Word: see What Mary heard! The Word was made Flesh; see to What Martha ministered!"

Eighthly, because the contemplative life pertains to that which is more peculiar to man—namely, his intellect—whereas in the works of the active life our inferior powers—those, namely, which we share with the brute creation—have a part; whence, in Ps. xxxv. 7, after saying: Beasts and men Thou wilt preserve, O Lord, the Psalmist adds what belongs to men alone: In Thy light we shall see light.

And the Lord Himself gives a ninth reason when He says: Mary hath chosen the best part which shall not be taken away from her,[444] words which S. Augustine thus expounds: "Not that thou, Martha, hast chosen badly, but that Mary hath chosen better; and see in what sense she hath chosen better: because it shall not be taken away from her; for from thee shall one day be taken away the burden of necessity; but eternal is the sweetness of truth."[445]

But in a certain sense, and in certain cases, the active life is to be chosen in preference to the contemplative, and this by reason of the needs of this present life; as also the Philosopher says: "To practise philosophy is better than to become rich; but to become rich is better for one who suffers need."[446]

Some, however, think that the active life is preferable to the contemplative, thus:

1. "The lot which falls to the better people seems to be the more honourable and better," as the Philosopher says.[447] But the active life is the lot of those who are in the higher position—of prelates, for instance,

who are placed in honourable and powerful positions; thus S. Augustine says[448]: "In the life of action we must not love the honour which belongs to this life, nor its power." Whence it would seem that the active life is preferable to the contemplative.

But it is not the active life only which belongs to prelates, they must needs excel in the contemplative life; whence S. Gregory says in his Pastoral Rule[449]: "Let the superior be foremost in action, but before all let him be uplifted in contemplation."

2. Again, in all acts and habits the control belongs to the more important: the soldier, for instance—as being higher placed—directs the saddle-maker. But it is the active life which directs and controls the contemplative, as is clear from the words addressed to Moses: Go down and charge the people, lest they should have a mind to pass the limits to see the Lord.[450] The active life is therefore more important than the contemplative.

But the contemplative life consists in a certain liberty of spirit; for S. Gregory says[451]: "The contemplative life means passing over to a certain liberty of spirit since in it a man thinks not of temporal but of eternal things." Similarly Boëthius says[452]: "The human soul must needs be free when occupied with the thought of the Divine Mind; not so when distracted with the things of the body." From all this it is clear that the active life does not directly guide the contemplative, but by preparing the way for it it does direct certain works pertaining to the contemplative life, and in this sense the active life is rather the servant than the master of the contemplative. And this S. Gregory expresses when he says: "The active life is termed a service, the contemplative life freedom."[453]

3. Lastly, no one should be withdrawn from what is greater in order to apply himself to what is less; thus the Apostle says: Be zealous for the better gifts.[454] But some are withdrawn from the contemplative state of life and are made to busy themselves with the affairs of the active life; this is the case, for instance, with those who are placed in positions of authority. Whence it seems that the active life is of more importance than the contemplative.

But though a man may happen to be called away from contemplation to the works of the active life owing to the needs of the present life, yet he is not thereby compelled completely to relinquish his contemplation. Hence S.

Augustine says:[455] "The love of truth asks for a holy leisure; the demands of charity undertake honest toil—that, namely, of the active life. And if no one imposes this latter burden on us, then we must devote ourselves to the study and contemplation of the truth; if, however, such a burden is imposed upon us, then must we undertake it because of the demands of charity. Yet not even then are we altogether to resign the joys flowing from the contemplation of truth, lest the sweetness of such contemplation be withdrawn from us and the burden we have assumed crush us."

Whence it appears that when a man is called from the contemplative to the active life it is not so much that something is withdrawn from him, but that an additional burden is imposed upon him.

"As we have heard, so have we seen, in the city of the Lord of Hosts, in the city of our God: God hath founded it for ever. We have received Thy mercy, O God, in the midst of Thy temple. For this is God, our God unto eternity, and for ever and ever: He shall rule us for evermore."[456]

Cajetan: Those whose duty it is to instruct others in spiritual progress should note that they are bound to take great pains to exercise them in the active life before they urge them to ascend the heights of contemplation. For they must learn to subdue their passions by acquiring habits of meekness, patience, generosity, humility, and tranquillity of soul, before they ascend to the contemplative life. Through lack of this, many, not so much walking in the way of God as leaping along it, find themselves—after they have spent the greater portion of their life in contemplation—devoid of virtue, impatient, irascible, and proud, if one but so much as touch them on this point! Such people have neither the active nor the contemplative life, nor even a mixture of the two; they have built upon sand! And would that such cases were rare! (on 2. 182. 1 2.).

S. Augustine: Terrified by my sins and my weight of misery I was disturbed within my soul and meditated flight into solitude. But Thou didst forbid it and didst strengthen me and say: Christ died for all, that they also who live may not now live to themselves, but unto Him Who died for them and rose again.[457] Behold, O Lord, I cast my care upon Thee so that I may live, and I will meditate on the wondrous things of Thy law. Thou knowest my lack of skill and my weakness; teach me and heal me! He—

Thine Only-Begotten Son—in Whom lie hid all the treasures of wisdom and knowledge, He redeemed me with His blood. Let not the proud calumniate me! When I think of my Ransom then I eat and I drink, and I pray, and in my poverty I yearn to be filled with Him, to be among those who eat and are filled and they praise the Lord who seek Him (Conf., X., xliii. 70).

S. Augustine: He hath hid me in His tabernacle in the day of evils.[458]

Wherefore without any arrogance have I sought for That One Thing, neither doth my soul reproach me, saying: Why do you seek after It? From whom do you seek It? Do you, a sinner, wickedly dare to ask something of God? Do you, weak man, of unclean heart, dare to hope that you will one day attain to the contemplation of God? I dare! Not indeed of myself, but because of His pleasure in me; not out of presumptuous trust in myself, but from confidence in His promise. For will He Who gave such a pledge to the pilgrim desert him when he comes to Him? For He hath hid me in His tabernacle in the day of evils (Enarr. in Ps. xxvi.).

II

Is the Active Life more Meritorious than the Contemplative?

S. Gregory says[459]: "Great are the merits of the active life, but they are surpassed by those of the contemplative life."

The source of merit is charity. Charity, however, consists in the love of God and of our neighbour; and to love God is, in itself, more meritorious than to love our neighbour. Consequently that which more directly pertains to the love of God is more meritorious in its nature than something that directly pertains to the love of our neighbour for God's sake. The contemplative life, however, directly and immediately pertains to the love of God, as S. Augustine says[460]: "The love of truth asks for a holy leisure; that is the contemplative life," and this truth is the Divine Truth on Which the contemplative life is centred. The active life, on the other hand, is more immediately concerned with the love of our neighbour, it is busy about much serving.[461] Hence of its very nature the contemplative life is more meritorious than the active, as is well expressed by S. Gregory[462] when he says: "The contemplative life is more meritorious than the active, for the latter toils in the wear and tear of present work by which it must needs help its neighbour; whereas the former, by a certain inward savour, already has a foretaste of the repose to come"—that is, in the contemplation of God.

It may, however, chance that one man derives greater merit from the works of the active life than another does from his contemplative life; as, for example, when, from the superabundance of the Divine love, in order to fulfil God's will, and for His greater glory, a man is content to be separated for a space from the sweetness of Divine contemplation, as the Apostle says: I wished myself to be an anathema from Christ for my brethren.[463] On these words S. Chrysostom[464] comments thus: "The love of Christ had so completely taken possession of his heart that he could even despise that which he desired beyond all things—namely, to be with Christ—and that because it was pleasing to Christ."

Yet some maintain that the active life is more meritorious than the contemplative, thus:

1. A thing is said to be meritorious because of the reward. But reward is due to work, as S. Paul says: And every man shall receive his own reward according to his own labour.[465] Labour, however, belongs to the active life, repose to the contemplative, as S. Gregory says[466]: "Everyone who is converted to God must needs first labour in toil; he must take Lia—that is, that so he may arrive at 'the vision of the Beginning'—that is, the embraces of Rachel." Whence it seems as though the active life was more meritorious than the contemplative.

But while external toil makes for an increase of accidental reward, the increase of merit as regards essential reward consists mainly in charity, one proof of which is external toil undertaken for Christ's sake; but a much greater proof of this is given when a man puts aside all that pertains to this life and delights in giving himself up solely to Divine contemplation.

2. Again, contemplative life is in some sort the commencement of future bliss; and consequently the words of S. John: So will I have him to remain till I come, S. Augustine comments as follows: "This might be more fully expressed thus: May perfect actions, modelled on the example of My Passion, follow Me; but may contemplation begun here on earth remain till I come, to be perfected when I come"[467]; and similarly S. Gregory says[468]: "The contemplative life begins here below to be perfected in our heavenly home." But in that future life we shall not merit, but shall receive the reward of our merits. Consequently the contemplative life seems to

have less of the ratio of merit than has the active life; but it has more of the ratio of reward.

But in the state of future bliss a man has arrived at his perfection and consequently there is no room left for merit; but if there were room left his merits would be more efficacious owing to the pre-eminence of his charity. The contemplation of this present life, however, has some accompanying imperfection, and consequently there is room for improvement; hence such contemplation does not destroy the idea of meriting but makes increase of merit in proportion as Divine charity is more and more exercised.

3. Lastly, S. Gregory says[469]: "No sacrifice is more acceptable to God than zeal for souls." But zeal for souls means that a man gives himself up to the works of the active life. Whence it seems that the contemplative life is not more meritorious than the active.

But a sacrifice is spiritually offered to God when anything is presented to Him; and of all man's good things God specially accepts that of the human soul when offered to Him in sacrifice. But a man ought to offer to God first of all his own soul, according to the words of Ecclesiasticus[470]: Have pity on thine own soul, pleasing God; secondly, the souls of others, according to the words: And he that heareth let him say: Come.[471] But the more closely a man knits his own soul, or his neighbour's soul, to God, the more acceptable to God is his sacrifice; consequently it is more pleasing to God that a man should give his soul, and the souls of others, to contemplation than to action. When, then, S. Gregory says: "No sacrifice is more acceptable to God than zeal for souls," he does not mean that the merit of the active life is greater than that of the contemplative, but that it is more meritorious that a man should offer to God his own soul and the soul of others than that he should offer any other external gift whatsoever.

"But thou, our God, art gracious and true, patient, and ordering all things in mercy. For if we sin, we are Thine, knowing Thy greatness: and if we sin not, we know that we are counted with Thee. For to know Thee is perfect justice: and to know Thy justice, and Thy power, is the root of immortality."[472]

III

Is the Active Life a Hindrance to the Contemplative Life?

S. Gregory says[473]: "They who would hold the citadel of contemplation must first needs exercise themselves on the battle-field of toil."

We may consider the active life from two points of view. For we may first of all consider the actual occupation with, and practice of, external works; and from this point of view it is clear that the active life is a hindrance to the contemplative, for it is impossible for a man to be simultaneously occupied with external works, and yet at leisure for Divine contemplation.

But we may also consider the active life from the standpoint of the harmony and order which it introduces into the interior passions of the soul; and from this point of view the active life is an assistance to contemplation since this latter is hindered by the disturbance arising from the passions. Thus S. Gregory says[474]: "They who would hold the citadel of contemplation must first needs exercise themselves on the battle-field of toil; they must learn, forsooth, whether they still do harm to their neighbours, whether they bear with equanimity the harm their neighbours may do them; whether, when temporal good things are set before them, their minds are overwhelmed with joy; whether when such things are withdrawn they are over much grieved. And lastly, they must ask themselves whether, when they withdraw within upon themselves and search into the things of the spirit, they do not carry with them the shadows of things corporeal, or whether, if perchance they have touched upon them, they discreetly repel them."

Thus, then, the exercises of the active life are conducive to contemplation, for they still those interior passions whence arise those imaginations which serve as a hindrance to contemplation.

Some, however, maintain that the active life is a hindrance to the contemplative, thus:

1. A certain stillness of mind is needful for contemplation, as the Psalmist says: Be still and see that I am God.[475] But the active life implies anxiety: Martha, Martha, thou art careful, and art troubled about many things.[476]

2. Again, a certain clearness of vision is called for in the contemplative life. But the active life hinders this clearness of vision, for S. Gregory

says[477]: "Lia was blear-eyed and fruitful, for the active life, since occupied with toil, sees less clearly."

3. And lastly, things that are contrary hinder one another. But the active and the contemplative life are contrary to one another; for the active life is occupied with many things, whereas the contemplative life dwells upon one object of contemplation; they are, then, in opposite camps.

But all these arguments insist upon the occupation with external affairs which is but one feature in the active life, not upon its other feature—namely, its power to repress the passions.

Cajetan: But the five foolish virgins, having taken their lamps, did not take oil with them. But the wise took oil in their vessels with the lamps.[478]

By this oil is signified testimony to a man's goodness or love of God. For there is this difference between people who perform good works, that the only testimony which some men have to their goodness is without—namely, in the works themselves; within, however, they do not feel that they love God with their whole heart, that they repent of their sins because they are hateful to God, or that they love their neighbour for God's sake. But there are others who so perform good works that both their works that shine before men bear witness without to the good soul within, and also within their own conscience the Holy Spirit Himself testifies to their spirit that they are the sons of God; for such men feel that they love God with their whole heart, that they repent of their sins for God's sake, and that they love their neighbour and themselves for God's sake: in brief, they feel that God is the sole reason why they love, why they hope, fear, rejoice, or are sad: in a word, why they work both within and without: this is to have oil in one's own vessels (On S. Matt. xxv. 3, 4).

S. Augustine: See the life that Mary chose! Yet was she but a type of that life, she as yet possessed it not. For there are two kinds of life: one means delight; the other means a burden. And the burdensome one is toilsome, while the delightsome one is pleasurable. But enter thou within; seek not that delight without, lest ye swell with it and find yourself unable to enter by the narrow gate! See how Mary saw the Lord in the Flesh and heard the Lord by the voice of the Flesh—as ye have heard when the Epistle to the Hebrews has been read—as it were through a veil. (A new and living way which He hath dedicated to us through the veil, that is to say, His Flesh.[479]) But when we shall see Him face to Face there will be no "veil." Mary, then, sat—that is, she rested from toil—and she listened and she praised; but Martha was anxious about much serving. And the Lord said to her: Martha, Martha, thou art careful and art troubled about many things; but one thing is necessary[480] (Sermon, CCLVI., v. 6).

"Bless the Lord, O my soul: and let all that is within me bless His holy Name. Bless the Lord, O my soul, and never forget all He hath done for thee. Who forgiveth all thy iniquities: Who healeth all thy diseases. Who redeemeth thy life from destruction: Who crowneth thee with mercy and compassion. Who satisfieth thy desire with good things: thy youth shall be renewed like the eagle's. The Lord doth mercies, and judgment for all that suffer wrong. He hath made His ways known to Moses: His wills to the children of Israel. The Lord is compassionate and merciful: long suffering and plenteous in mercy. He will not always be angry: nor will He threaten for ever. He hath not dealt with us according to our sins: nor rewarded us according to our iniquities. For according to the height of the Heaven above the earth: He hath strengthened His mercy towards them that fear Him. As far as the east is from the west, so far hath He removed our iniquities from us. As a father hath compassion on his children, so hath the Lord compassion on them that fear Him: for He knoweth our frame. He remembereth that we are dust: man's days are as grass, as the flower of the field so shall he flourish."[481]

IV

Does the Active Life precede the Contemplative?

S. Gregory says[482]: "The active life precedes the contemplative in the order of time, for from good works a man passes to contemplation."

One thing may precede another in two ways: firstly by its very nature; and in this sense the contemplative life precedes the active in that it is occupied with chiefer and better things, and hence it both moves and directs the active life. For, as S. Augustine says,[483] the higher reason, which is destined for contemplation, is compared to the lower reason, which is destined for action, as man is compared to woman—she is to be governed by him.

But secondly, one thing may be prior to another as far as we are concerned, it may, that is, precede it in the way of generation. And in this sense the active life precedes the contemplative, for it conduces to it, as we have already said. In the order of generation disposition to a nature precedes that nature, though that nature is, simply speaking and considered in itself, prior to the disposition to it.

But some maintain that the active life does not precede the contemplative, thus:

1. The contemplative life is directly concerned with the love of God, the active life with the love of our neighbour. But love of God precedes love of our neighbour, for we have to love our neighbour for God's sake.

But the contemplative life is not concerned with merely any kind of love of God, but with the perfect love of Him; the active life, on the contrary, is necessary for any kind of love of our neighbour, for S. Gregory says[484]: "Without the contemplative life men can gain admittance to their heavenly home if they have not neglected the good works they could have done; but they cannot enter without the active life, if they neglect the good works they could do." Whence it appears that the active life precedes the contemplative in the sense that that which is common to everybody precedes in the order of generation that which is peculiar to the perfect.

2. Again, S. Gregory says[485]: "You must know that just as the right procedure is for a man to pass from the active to the contemplative life; so, too, it is often profitable to the soul to return to the active life." Consequently the active life is not absolutely speaking prior to the contemplative.

But while we proceed from the active life to the contemplative by way of generation, we return from the contemplative to the active by way of direction, in order, that is, that our active life may be directed by the contemplative; just in the same way as habits are generated by acts and then, as is said in the Ethics, when the habit is formed we act still more perfectly.[486]

3. Lastly, things which accord with different characters do not seem to be necessarily related. But the active and contemplative life are suited to different characters; thus S. Gregory says[487]: "It often happens that men who could have given themselves to peaceful contemplation of God have been burdened with external occupations and so have made shipwreck; while, on the contrary, men who could have lived well had they been occupied with human concerns, have been slain by the sword of their life of

repose." Consequently the active life does not seem to precede the contemplative.

But those who are subject to the influx of their passions because of their natural eagerness in action, are for that very reason more suited for the active life, and this because of the restlessness of their temperament. Hence S. Gregory says[488]: "Some are so restless that if they desist from work they suffer grievously, for the more free they are to think the worse interior tumults they have to endure." Some, on the contrary, have a natural purity of soul and a reposefulness which renders them fit for the contemplative life; if such men were to be applied wholly to the active life they would incur great loss. Hence S. Gregory says[489]: "Some men are of so slothful a disposition that if they undertake any work they succumb at the very outset." But he adds: "Yet often love stirs up even slothful souls to work, and fear exercises a restraining influence on souls which suffer a disturbing influence in their contemplation." Hence even those who are more suited for the active life, may, by the exercise of it, be prepared for the contemplative; and, on the contrary, those who are more suited for the contemplative life may profitably undertake the labours proper to the active life, that so they may be rendered still more fit for contemplation.

"I have cried to Thee, for Thou, O God, hast heard me: O incline Thy ear unto me, and hear my words. Show forth Thy wonderful mercies; Thou Who savest them that trust in Thee. From them that resist Thy right hand keep me, as the apple of Thy eye. Protect me under the shadow of Thy wings."[490]

FOOTNOTES 9

[438] S. Luke x. 42.
[439] Ethics, x. 7 and 8.
[440] Moralia in Job, vi. 18.
[441] Of the Words of the Lord, Sermon ciii., alias xxvi. 2.
[442] S. Luke x. 41.
[443] Of the Words of the Lord, Sermon civ., alias xxvii. 2.
[444] S. Luke x. 42.
[445] Sermon ciii., alias xxvi. 4.
[446] Topica, III., ii. 21.
[447] Ibid., III., i. 12.
[448] Of the City of God, xix. 19.
[449] ii. 1.
[450] Exod. xix. 21.
[451] Hom. III., On Ezechiel.
[452] Of Consolation, v. 2.
[453] Hom. III., On Ezechiel.
[454] 1 Cor. xii. 31.
[455] Of the City of God, xix. 19.
[456] Ps. xlvii. 9, 10, 15.
[457] 2 Cor. v. 15.
[458] Ps. xxvi. 5.
[459] Moralia in Job, vi. 18.
[460] Of the City of God, xix. 19.
[461] S. Luke x. 40.
[462] Hom. III., On Ezechiel.
[463] Rom. ix. 3.
[464] Of Compunction, i. 7.
[465] 1 Cor. iii. 8.
[466] Hom. XIV., On Ezechiel.
[467] Tractat., 124, On St. John, xxi. 22.
[468] Hom. XIV., On Ezechiel.
[469] Hom. XII., On Ezechiel.
[470] xxx. 24.
[471] Apoc. xxii. 17.

[472] Wisd. xv. 1-3.
[473] Moralia in Job, vi. 17.
[474] Ibid.
[475] Ps. xlv. 11.
[476] S. Luke x. 41.
[477] Hom. XIV., On Ezechiel.
[478] S. Matt. xxv. 3, 4.
[479] Heb. x. 20.
[480] S. Luke x. 41, 42.
[481] Ps. cii. 1-15.
[482] Hom. III., On Ezechiel.
[483] On the Trinity, xii. 12.
[484] Hom. III., On Ezechiel.
[485] Hom. XIV., On Ezechiel.
[486] ii. 1, 2.
[487] Moralia in Job, vi. 17.
[488] Moralia, vi. 17.
[489] Ibid., vi. 37.
[490] Ps. xvi. 6-9.

QUESTION 9

ON THE RELIGIOUS STATE

Are Contemplative Orders superior to Active Orders?

The Lord declared that Mary's was the best part, and she is the type of the contemplative life.[491]

Religious Orders differ from one another primarily according to the ends they have in view, but secondarily according to the works they practise. And since one thing cannot be said to be superior to another save by reason of the differences between them, it will follow that the superiority of one Religious Order to another must depend primarily upon their respective ends, secondarily upon the works they practise.

And these two grounds of comparison are not of equal value; for the comparison between them from the point of view of their respective ends is an absolute one, since an end is sought for its own sake; whereas the comparison arising from their respective works is a relative one, since works are not done for their own sake but for the sake of the end to be gained.

Consequently one Religious Order is superior to another if its end is absolutely a superior one, either as being in itself a greater good, or as being of wider scope. On the supposition, however, that the ends of any two Orders are the same, then the superiority of one to the other can be gauged, not by the quantity of works they undertake, but by the proportion these bear to the end in view. Thus it is that we find introduced into the Conferences of the Fathers[492] the opinion of S. Antony, who preferred that discretion by which a man moderates all things to fasts and watchings and similar observances.

The works, then, of the active life are twofold. There is one which springs from the fulness of contemplation: teaching, for example, and preaching. Whence S. Gregory says[493]: "It is said of perfect men that on their return from contemplation: They shall pour forth the memory of Thy sweetness." And this is preferable to simple contemplation. For just as it is a greater thing to shed light than to be full of light, so is it a greater thing to spread abroad the fruits of our contemplation than merely to contemplate. And the second work of the active life is that which wholly consists in external occupation, such as giving alms, receiving guests, etc. And such works are inferior to the works of contemplation, except it be in some case of necessity.

Consequently, then, those Religious Orders are in the highest rank which are devoted to teaching and preaching. And these, too, approach most nearly to the perfection of the Episcopate; just as in other things, too, the ends of those in the first place are, as S. Denis says, close knit to the principles of those in the second place.[494] The second rank is occupied by those Orders which are devoted to contemplation. And the third with those devoted to external works.

And in each of these grades there is a certain superiority according as one Order aims at acts of a higher order than does another, though of the same class. Thus in the works of the active life it is a greater thing to redeem captives than to receive guests; in the contemplative life, too, it is a greater thing to pray than to study. There may also be a certain superiority in this that one is occupied with more of such works than another; or again, that the rules of one are better adapted to the attainment of their end than are those of another.

Some, however, maintain that the contemplative Orders are not superior to the active Orders, thus:

1. In the Canon Law[495] it is said: "Since the greater good is to be preferred to the less, so, too, the common gain is to be preferred to private gain; and in this sense teaching is rightly preferred to silence, anxious care for others to contemplation, and toil to repose." But that Religious Order is the better which is directed to the attainment of the greater good. Hence it seems that Orders which are devoted to an active life are superior to those which aim solely at contemplation.

But this Decretal speaks of the active life as concerned with the salvation of souls.

2. All Religious Orders aim at the perfection of charity. But on those words in the Epistle to the Hebrews,[496] Ye have not yet resisted unto blood, the Gloss has: "There is no more perfect charity in this life than that to which the holy Martyrs attained, for they strove against sin even unto blood." But to strive unto blood belongs to the Military Religious Orders,

and they lead an active life. It would seem, then, that these latter are the highest form of Religious Order.

But these Military Orders are more concerned with shedding the blood of their enemies than with shedding their own, which is the feature of the Martyrs. At the same time, there is nothing to preclude these Religious from at times winning the crown of martyrdom and thus attaining to a greater height than other Religious; just as in some cases active works are to be preferred to contemplation.

3. Lastly, the stricter an Order the more perfect it seems to be. But there is nothing to preclude active Orders from being stricter in their observance than some contemplative Orders.

But strictness of observance is not that which is especially commendable in Religious life, as S. Antony has already told us, and as is also said in Isaias[497]: Is this such a fast as I have chosen, for a man to afflict his soul for a day? Strictness of observance is, however, made use of in Religious Orders for the subjection of the flesh; but if such strictness is carried out without discretion there is danger lest it should come to naught, as S. Antony says. Hence one Religious Order is not superior to another because its observances are stricter, but because its observances are directed to the end of that Order with greater discretion. Thus, for example, abstinence from food and drink, which means hunger and thirst, are more efficacious means for preserving chastity than wearing less clothing, which means cold and nakedness; more efficacious, too, than bodily labour.

FOOTNOTES 10

[491] S. Luke x. 42.
[492] Conf., ii. 2.
[493] Hom. V., On Ezechiel.
[494] Of the Divine Names, vii.
[495] Extrav. Of Regulars and of those who pass to the Religious Orders, cap. Licet.
[496] xii. 4.
[497] lviii. 5.

THE ONLY TEACHER

Lord, teach us how to pray

By *ANDREW MURRAY*
(Originally published in 1896)

TABLE OF CONTENTS

THE ONLY TEACHER
Prayer 1

THE TRUE WORSHIPPERS
Prayer 2

ALONE WITH GOD
Prayer 3

THE MODEL PRAYER
Prayer 4

THE ONLY TEACHER

The disciples had been with Christ, and seen Him pray. They had learnt to understand something of the connection between His wondrous life in public, and His secret life of prayer. They had learnt to believe in Him as a Master in the art of prayer—none could pray like Him. And so they came to Him with the request, 'Lord, teach us to pray.' And in after years they would have told us that there were few things more wonderful or blessed that He taught them than His lessons on prayer.

And now still it comes to pass, as He is praying in a certain place, that disciples who see Him thus engaged feel the need of repeating the same request, 'Lord, teach us to pray.' As we grow in the Christian life, the thought and the faith of the Beloved Master in His never-failing intercession becomes evermore precious, and the hope of being Like Christ in His intercession gains an attractiveness before unknown. And as we see Him pray, and remember that there is none who can pray like Him, and none who can teach like Him, we feel the petition of the disciples, 'Lord, teach us to pray,' is just what we need. And as we think how all He is and has, how He Himself is our very own, how He is Himself our life, we feel assured that we have but to ask, and He will be delighted to take us up into closer fellowship with Himself, and teach us to pray even as He prays.

Come, my brothers! Shall we not go to the Blessed Master and ask Him to enrol our names too anew in that school which He always keeps open for those who long to continue their studies in the Divine art of prayer and intercession? Yes, let us this very day say to the Master, as they did of old, 'Lord, teach us to pray.' As we meditate we shall find each word of the petition we bring to be full of meaning.

'Lord, teach us to pray.' Yes, to pray. This is what we need to be taught. Though in its beginnings prayer is so simple that the feeble child can pray, yet it is at the same time the highest and holiest work to which man can rise. It is fellowship with the Unseen and Most Holy One. The powers of the eternal world have been placed at its disposal. It is the very essence of true religion, the channel of all blessings, the secret of power and life. Not only for ourselves, but for others, for the Church, for the world, it is to prayer that God has given the right to take hold of Him and His strength. It is on prayer that the promises wait for their fulfilment, the kingdom for its coming, the glory of God for its full revelation. And for this blessed work, how slothful and unfit we are. It is only the Spirit of God can enable us to do it aright. How speedily we are deceived into a resting in the form, while the power is wanting. Our early training, the teaching of the Church, the influence of habit, the stirring of the emotions—how easily these lead to prayer which has no spiritual power, and avails but little. True prayer, that takes hold of God's strength, that availeth much, to which the gates of heaven are really opened wide—who would not cry, Oh for some one to teach me thus to pray?

Jesus has opened a school, in which He trains His redeemed ones, who specially desire it, to have power in prayer. Shall we not enter it with the petition, Lord! it is just this we need to be taught! O teach us to pray.

'Lord, teach us to pray.' Yes, us, Lord. We have read in Thy Word with what power Thy believing people of old used to pray, and what mighty wonders were done in answer to their prayers. And if this took place under the Old Covenant, in the time of preparation, how much more wilt Thou not now, in these days of fulfilment, give Thy people this sure sign of Thy presence in their midst. We have heard the promises given to Thine apostles of the power of prayer in Thy name, and have seen how gloriously they experienced their truth: we know for certain, they can become true to us too. We hear continually even in these days what glorious tokens of Thy power Thou dost still give to those who trust Thee fully. Lord! these all are men of like passions with ourselves; teach us to pray so too. The promises are for us, the powers and gifts of the heavenly world are for us. O teach us to pray so that we may receive abundantly. To us too Thou hast entrusted Thy work, on our prayer too the coming of Thy kingdom depends, in our prayer too Thou canst glorify Thy name; 'Lord, teach us to pray.' Yes, us, Lord; we offer ourselves as learners; we would indeed be taught of Thee. 'Lord, teach us to pray.'

'Lord, teach us to pray.' Yes, we feel the need now of being taught to pray. At first there is no work appears so simple; later on, none that is more difficult; and the confession is forced from us: We know not how to pray as we ought. It is true we have God's Word, with its clear and sure promises; but sin has so darkened our mind, that we know not always how to apply the Word. In spiritual things we do not always seek the most needful things, or fail in praying according to the law of the sanctuary. In temporal things we are still less able to avail ourselves of the wonderful liberty our Father has given us to ask what we need. And even when we know what to ask, how much there is still needed to make prayer acceptable. It must be to the glory of God, in full surrender to His will, in full assurance of faith, in the name of Jesus, and with a perseverance that, if need be, refuses to be denied. All this must be learned. It can only be learned in the school of much prayer, for practice makes perfect. Amid the painful consciousness of ignorance and unworthiness, in the struggle between believing and doubting, the heavenly art of effectual prayer is learnt. Because, even when we do not remember it, there is One, the Beginner and Finisher of faith and prayer, who watches over our praying, and sees to it that in all who trust Him for it their education in the school of prayer shall be carried on to perfection. Let but the deep undertone of all our prayer be the teachableness that comes from a sense of ignorance, and from faith in Him as a perfect teacher, and we may be sure we shall be taught, we shall learn to pray in power. Yes, we may depend upon it, HE teaches to pray.

'Lord, teach us to pray.' None can teach like Jesus, none but Jesus; therefore we call on Him, 'LORD, teach us to pray.' A pupil needs a teacher, who knows his work, who has the gift of teaching, who in patience and love will descend to the pupil's needs. Blessed be God! Jesus is all this and much more. He knows what prayer is. It is Jesus, praying Himself, who teaches to pray. He knows what prayer is. He learned it amid the trials and tears of His earthly life. In heaven it is still His beloved work: His life there is prayer. Nothing delights Him more than to find those whom He can take with Him into the Father's presence, whom He can clothe with power to pray down God's blessing on those around them, whom He can train to be His fellow-workers in the intercession by which the kingdom is to be revealed on earth. He knows how to teach. Now by the urgency of felt need, then by the confidence with which joy inspires. Here by the teaching of the Word, there by the testimony of another believer who knows what it is to have prayer heard. By His Holy Spirit, He has access to our heart, and teaches us to pray by showing us the sin that hinders the prayer, or giving us the assurance that we please God. He teaches, by giving not only thoughts of what to ask or how to ask, but by breathing within us the very spirit of prayer, by living within us as the Great Intercessor. We may indeed and most joyfully say, 'Who teacheth like Him?' Jesus never taught His disciples how to preach, only how to pray. He did not speak much of what was needed to preach well, but much of praying well. To know how to speak to God is more than knowing how to speak to man. Not power with men, but power with God is the first thing. Jesus loves to teach us how to pray.

What think you, my beloved fellow-disciples! would it not be just what we need, to ask the Master for a month to give us a course of special lessons on the art of prayer? As we meditate on the words He spake on earth, let us yield ourselves to His teaching in the fullest confidence that, with such a teacher, we shall make progress. Let us take time not only to meditate, but to pray, to tarry at the foot of the throne, and be trained to the work of intercession. Let us do so in the assurance that amidst our stammerings and fears He is carrying on His work most beautifully. He will breathe His own life, which is all prayer, into us. As He makes us partakers of His righteousness and His life, He will of His intercession too. As the members of His body, as a holy priesthood, we shall take part in His priestly work of pleading and prevailing with God for men. Yes, let us most joyfully say, ignorant and feeble though we be, 'Lord, teach us to pray.'

PRAYER 1

Blessed Lord! who ever livest to pray, Thou canst teach me too to pray, me to live ever to pray. In this Thou lovest to make me share Thy glory in heaven, that I should pray without ceasing, and ever stand as a priest in the presence of my God.

Lord Jesus! I ask Thee this day to enrol my name among those who confess that they know not how to pray as they ought, and especially ask Thee for a course of teaching in prayer. Lord! teach me to tarry with Thee in the school, and give Thee time to train me. May a deep sense of my ignorance, of the wonderful privilege and power of prayer, of the need of the Holy Spirit as the Spirit of prayer, lead me to cast away my thoughts of what I think I know, and make me kneel before Thee in true teachableness and poverty of spirit.

And fill me, Lord, with the confidence that with such a teacher as Thou art I shall learn to pray. In the assurance that I have as my teacher, Jesus, who is ever praying to the Father, and by His prayer rules the destinies of His Church and the world, I will not be afraid. As much as I need to know of the mysteries of the prayer-world, Thou wilt unfold for me. And when I may not know, Thou wilt teach me to be strong in faith, giving glory to God.

Blessed Lord! Thou wilt not put to shame Thy scholar who trusts Thee, nor, by Thy grace, would he Thee either. Amen.

THE TRUE WORSHIPPERS

'The hour cometh, and now is, when the true worshippers shall worship the Father in spirit and truth: for such doth the Father seek to be His worshippers. God is a Spirit: and they that worship Him must worship Him in spirit and truth.'—JOHN iv. 23, 24.

These words of Jesus to the woman of Samaria are His first recorded teaching on the subject of prayer. They give us some wonderful first glimpses into the world of prayer. The Father seeks worshippers: our worship satisfies His loving heart and is a joy to Him. He seeks true worshippers, but finds many not such as He would have them. True worship is that which is in spirit and truth. The Son has come to open the way for this worship in spirit and in truth, and teach it us. And so one of our first lessons in the school of prayer must be to understand what it is to pray in spirit and in truth, and to know how we can attain to it.

To the woman of Samaria our Lord spoke of a threefold worship. There is, first, the ignorant worship of the Samaritans: 'Ye worship that which ye know not.' The second, the intelligent worship of the Jew, having the true knowledge of God: 'We worship that which we know; for salvation is of the Jews.' And then the new, the spiritual worship which He Himself has come to introduce: 'The hour is coming, and is now, when the true worshippers shall worship the Father in spirit and truth.' From the connection it is evident that the words 'in spirit and truth' do not mean, as is often thought, earnestly, from the heart, in sincerity. The Samaritans had the five books of Moses and some knowledge of God; there was doubtless more than one among them who honestly and earnestly sought God in prayer. The Jews had the true full revelation of God in His word, as thus far given; there were among them godly men, who called upon God with their whole heart. And yet not 'in spirit and truth,' in the full meaning of the words. Jesus says, 'The hour is coming, and now is:' it is only in and through Him that the worship of God will be in spirit and truth.

Among Christians one still finds the three classes of worshippers. Some who in their ignorance hardly know what they ask: they pray earnestly, and yet receive but little. Others there are, who have more correct knowledge, who try to pray with all their mind and heart, and often pray most earnestly, and yet do not attain to the full blessedness of worship in spirit and truth. It is into this third class we must ask our Lord Jesus to take us; we must be taught of Him how to worship in spirit and truth. This alone is spiritual worship; this makes us worshippers such as the Father seeks. In prayer everything will depend on our understanding well and practising the worship in spirit and truth.

'God is a Spirit and they that worship Him must worship Him in spirit and truth.' The first thought suggested here by the Master is that there must be harmony between God and His worshippers; such as God is, must His worship be. This is according to a principle which prevails throughout the universe: we look for correspondence between an object and the organ to which it reveals or yields itself. The eye has an inner fitness for the light, the ear for sound. The man who would truly worship God, would find and know and possess and enjoy God, must be in harmony with Him, must have a capacity for receiving Him. Because God is Spirit, we must worship in spirit. As God is, so His worshipper.

And what does this mean? The woman had asked our Lord whether Samaria or Jerusalem was the true place of worship. He answers that henceforth worship is no longer to be limited to a certain place: 'Woman, believe Me, the hour cometh when neither in this mountain, nor in Jerusalem, shall ye worship the Father.' As God is Spirit, not bound by space or time, but in His infinite perfection always and everywhere the same, so His worship would henceforth no longer be confined by place or form, but spiritual as God Himself is spiritual. A lesson of deep importance. How much our Christianity suffers from this, that it is confined to certain times and places. A man who seeks to pray earnestly in the church or in the closet, spends the greater part of the week or the day in a spirit entirely at variance with that in which he prayed. His worship was the work of a fixed place or hour, not of his whole being. God is a spirit: He is the Everlasting and Unchangeable One; what He is, He is always and in truth. Our worship must even so be in spirit and truth: His worship must be the spirit of our life; our life must be worship in spirit as God is Spirit.

'God is a Spirit: and they that worship Him must worship Him in spirit and truth.' The second thought that comes to us is that this worship in the spirit must come from God Himself. God is Spirit: He alone has Spirit to give. It was for this He sent His Son, to fit us for such spiritual worship, by giving us the Holy Spirit. It is of His own work that Jesus speaks when He says twice, 'The hour cometh,' and then adds, 'and is now.' He came to baptize with the Holy Spirit; the Spirit could not stream forth till He was glorified (John i. 33, vii. 37, 38, xvi. 7). It was when He had made an end of sin, and entering into the Holiest of all with His blood, had there on our behalf received the Holy Spirit (Acts ii. 33), that He could send Him down to us as the Spirit of the Father. It was when Christ had redeemed us, and we in Him had received the position of children, that the Father sent forth the Spirit of His Son into our hearts to cry, 'Abba, Father.' The worship in spirit is the worship of the Father in the Spirit of Christ, the Spirit of Sonship.

This is the reason why Jesus here uses the name of Father. We never find one of the Old Testament saints personally appropriate the name of child or call God his Father. The worship of the Father is only possible to those to whom the Spirit of the Son has been given. The worship in spirit is only possible to those to whom the Son has revealed the Father, and who have received the spirit of Sonship. It is only Christ who opens the way and teaches the worship in spirit.

And in truth. That does not only mean, in sincerity. Nor does it only signify, in accordance with the truth of God's Word. The expression is one of deep and Divine meaning. Jesus is 'the only-begotten of the Father, full of grace and truth.' 'The law was given by Moses; grace and truth came by Jesus Christ.' Jesus says, 'I am the truth and the life.' In the Old Testament all was shadow and promise; Jesus brought and gives the reality, the substance, of things hoped for. In Him the blessings and powers of the eternal life are our actual possession and experience. Jesus is full of grace and truth; the Holy Spirit is the Spirit of truth; through Him the grace that is in Jesus is ours indeed, and truth a positive communication out of the Divine life. And so worship in spirit is worship in truth; actual living fellowship with God, a real correspondence and harmony between the Father, who is a Spirit, and the child praying in the spirit.

What Jesus said to the woman of Samaria, she could not at once understand. Pentecost was needed to reveal its full meaning. We are hardly prepared at our first entrance into the school of prayer to grasp such teaching. We shall understand it better later on. Let us only begin and take the lesson as He gives it. We are carnal and cannot bring God the worship

He seeks. But Jesus came to give the Spirit: He has given Him to us. Let the disposition in which we set ourselves to pray be what Christ's words have taught us. Let there be the deep confession of our inability to bring God the worship that is pleasing to Him; the childlike teachableness that waits on Him to instruct us; the simple faith that yields itself to the breathing of the Spirit. Above all, let us hold fast the blessed truth—we shall find that the Lord has more to say to us about it—that the knowledge of the Fatherhood of God, the revelation of His infinite Fatherliness in our hearts, the faith in the infinite love that gives us His Son and His Spirit to make us children, is indeed the secret of prayer in spirit and truth. This is the new and living way Christ opened up for us. To have Christ the Son, and The Spirit of the Son, dwelling within us, and revealing the Father, this makes us true, spiritual worshippers.

PRAYER 2

Blessed Lord! I adore the love with which Thou didst teach a woman, who had refused Thee a cup of water, what the worship of God must be. I rejoice in the assurance that Thou wilt no less now instruct Thy disciple, who comes to Thee with a heart that longs to pray in spirit and in truth. O my Holy Master! do teach me this blessed secret.

Teach me that the worship in spirit and truth is not of man, but only comes from Thee; that it is not only a thing of times and seasons, but the outflowing of a life in Thee. Teach me to draw near to God in prayer under the deep impression of my ignorance and my having nothing in myself to offer Him, and at the same time of the provision Thou, my Saviour, makest for the Spirit's breathing in my childlike stammerings. I do bless Thee that in Thee I am a child, and have a child's liberty of access; that in Thee I have the spirit of Sonship and of worship of truth. Teach me, above all, Blessed Son of the Father, how it is the revelation of the Father that gives confidence in prayer; and let the infinite Fatherliness of God's Heart be my joy and strength for a life of prayer and of worship. Amen.

ALONE WITH GOD

'But thou, when thou prayest, enter into thine inner chamber, and having shut thy door, pray to thy Father which is in secret, and thy Father which seeth in secret shall recompense thee.'—MATT. vi. 6.

After Jesus had called His first disciples He gave them their first public teaching in the Sermon on the Mount. He there expounded to them the kingdom of God, its laws and its life. In that kingdom God is not only King, but Father; He not only gives all, but is Himself all. In the knowledge and fellowship of Him alone is its blessedness. Hence it came as a matter of course that the revelation of prayer and the prayer-life was a part of His teaching concerning the New Kingdom He came to set up. Moses gave neither command nor regulation with regard to prayer: even the prophets say little directly of the duty of prayer; it is Christ who teaches to pray.

And the first thing the Lord teaches His disciples is that they must have a secret place for prayer; every one must have some solitary spot where he can be alone with his God. Every teacher must have a schoolroom. We have learnt to know and accept Jesus as our only teacher in the school of prayer. He has already taught us at Samaria that worship is no longer confined to times and places; that worship, spiritual true worship, is a thing of the spirit and the life; the whole man must in his whole life be worship in spirit and truth. And yet He wants each one to choose for himself the fixed spot where He can daily meet him. That inner chamber, that solitary place, is Jesus' schoolroom. That spot may be anywhere; that spot may change from day to day if we have to change our abode; but that secret place there must be, with the quiet time in which the pupil places himself in the Master's presence, to be by Him prepared to worship the Father. There alone, but there most surely, Jesus comes to us to teach us to pray.

A teacher is always anxious that his schoolroom should be bright and attractive, filled with the light and air of heaven, a place where pupils long to come, and love to stay. In His first words on prayer in the Sermon on the Mount, Jesus seeks to set the inner chamber before us in its most attractive light. If we listen carefully, we soon notice what the chief thing is He has to tell us of our tarrying there. Three times He uses the name of Father: 'Pray to thy Father;' 'Thy Father shall recompense thee;' Your Father knoweth what things ye have need of.' The first thing in closet-prayer is: I must meet my Father. The light that shines in the closet must be: the light of the Father's countenance. The fresh air from heaven with which Jesus would have filled the atmosphere in which I am to breathe and pray, is: God's Father-love, God's infinite Fatherliness. Thus each thought or petition we breathe out will be simple, hearty, childlike trust in the Father. This is how the Master teaches us to pray: He brings us into the Father's living presence. What we pray there must avail. Let us listen carefully to hear what the Lord has to say to us.

First, 'Pray to thy Father which is in secret.' God is a God who hides Himself to the carnal eye. As long as in our worship of God we are chiefly occupied with our own thoughts and exercises, we shall not meet Him who is a Spirit, the unseen One. But to the man who withdraws himself from all that is of the world and man, and prepares to wait upon God alone, the Father will reveal Himself. As he forsakes and gives up and shuts out the world, and the life of the world, and surrenders himself to be led of Christ into the secret of God's presence, the light of the Father's love will rise upon him. The secrecy of the inner chamber and the closed door, the entire separation from all around us, is an image of, and so a help to, that inner spiritual sanctuary, the secret of God's tabernacle, within the veil, where our spirit truly comes into contact with the Invisible One. And so we are taught, at the very outset of our search after the secret of effectual prayer, to remember that it is in the inner chamber, where we are alone with the Father, that we shall learn to pray aright. The Father is in secret: in these words Jesus teaches us where He is waiting us, where He is always to be found. Christians often complain that private prayer is not what it should be. They feel weak and sinful, the heart is cold and dark; it is as if they have so little to pray, and in that little no faith or joy. They are discouraged and kept from prayer by the thought that they cannot come to the Father as they ought or as they wish. Child of God! listen to your Teacher. He tells you that when you go to private prayer your first thought must be: The Father is in secret, the Father waits me there. Just because your heart is cold and prayerless, get you into the presence of the loving Father. As a father pitieth his children, so the Lord pitieth you. Do not be thinking of how little you have to bring God, but of how much He wants to give you. Just place yourself before, and look up into, His face; think of His love, His wonderful, tender, pitying love. Just tell Him how sinful and cold and dark all is: it is the Father's loving heart will give light and warmth to yours. O do what Jesus says: Just shut the door, and pray to thy Father, which is in secret. Is it not wonderful? to be able to go alone with God, the infinite God. And then to look up and say: My Father!

'And thy Father, which seeth in secret, will recompense thee.' Here Jesus assures us that secret prayer cannot be fruitless: its blessing will show itself in our life. We have but in secret, alone with God, to entrust our life before men to Him; He will reward us openly; He will see to it that the answer to prayer be made manifest in His blessing upon us. Our Lord would thus teach us that as infinite Fatherliness and Faithfulness is that with which God meets us in secret, so on our part there should be the childlike simplicity of faith, the confidence that our prayer does bring down a blessing. 'He that cometh to God must believe that He is a rewarder of them that seek Him.' Not on the strong or the fervent feeling with which I pray does the blessing of the closet depend, but upon the love and the power of the Father to whom I there entrust my needs. And therefore the Master has but one desire: Remember your Father is, and sees and hears in secret; go there and stay there, and go again from there in the confidence: He will recompense. Trust Him for it; depend upon Him: prayer to the Father cannot be vain; He will reward you openly.

Still further to confirm this faith in the Father-love of God, Christ speaks a third word: 'Your Father knoweth what things ye have need of before ye ask Him.' At first sight it might appear as if this thought made prayer less needful: God knows far better than we what we need. But as we get a deeper insight into what prayer really is, this truth will help much to strengthen our faith. It will teach us that we do not need, as the heathen, with the multitude and urgency of our words, to compel an unwilling God to listen to us. It will lead to a holy thoughtfulness and silence in prayer as it suggests the question: Does my Father really know that I need this? It will, when once we have been led by the Spirit to the certainty that our request is indeed something that, according to the Word, we do need for God's glory, give us wonderful confidence to say, My Father knows I need it and must have it. And if there be any delay in the answer, it will teach us in quiet perseverance to hold on: FATHER! THOU KNOWEST I need it. O the blessed liberty and simplicity of a child that Christ our Teacher would fain cultivate in us, as we draw near to God: let us look up to the Father until His Spirit works it in us. Let us sometimes in our prayers, when we are in danger of being so occupied with our fervent, urgent petitions, as to forget that the Father knows and hears, let us hold still and just quietly say: My Father sees, my Father hears, my Father knows; it will help our faith to take the answer, and to say: We know that we have the petitions we have asked of Him.

And now, all ye who have anew entered the school of Christ to be taught to pray, take these lessons, practise them, and trust Him to perfect you in them. Dwell much in the inner chamber, with the door shut—shut in from men, shut up with God; it is there the Father waits you, it is there Jesus will teach you to pray. To be alone in secret with THE FATHER: this be your highest joy. To be assured that THE FATHER will openly reward the secret prayer, so that it cannot remain unblessed: this be your strength day by day. And to know that THE FATHER knows that you need what you ask, this be your liberty to bring every need, in the assurance that your God will supply it according to His riches in glory in Christ Jesus.

PRAYER 3

Blessed Saviour! with my whole heart I do bless Thee for the appointment of the inner chamber, as the school where Thou meetest each of Thy pupils alone, and revealest to him the Father. O my Lord! strengthen my faith so in the Father's tender love and kindness, that as often as I feel sinful or troubled, the first instinctive thought may be to go where I know the Father waits me, and where prayer never can go unblessed. Let the thought that He knows my need before I ask, bring me, in great restfulness of faith, to trust that He will give what His child requires. O let the place of secret prayer become to me the most beloved spot on earth.

And, Lord! hear me as I pray that Thou wouldest everywhere bless the closets of Thy believing people. Let Thy wonderful revelation of a Father's tenderness free all young Christians from every thought of secret prayer as a duty or a burden, and lead them to regard it as the highest privilege of their life, a joy and a blessing. Bring back all who are discouraged, because they cannot find aught to bring Thee in prayer. O give them to understand that they have only to come with their emptiness to Him who has all to give, and delights to do it. Not, what they have to bring the Father, but what the Father waits to give them, be their one thought.

And bless especially the inner chamber of all Thy servants who are working for Thee, as the place where God's truth and God's grace is revealed to them, where they are daily anointed with fresh oil, where their strength is renewed, and the blessings are received in faith, with which they are to bless their fellow-men. Lord, draw us all in the closet nearer to Thyself and the Father. Amen.

THE MODEL PRAYER

'After this manner therefore pray ye: Our Father which art in heaven.'—MATT. vi. 9.

Every teacher knows the power of example. He not only tells the child what to do and how to do it, but shows him how it really can be done. In condescension to our weakness, our Heavenly Teacher has given us the very words we are to take with us as we draw near to our Father. We have in them a form of prayer in which there breathe the freshness and fulness of the Eternal Life. So simple that the child can lisp it, so divinely rich that it comprehends all that God can give. A form of prayer that becomes the model and inspiration for all other prayer, and yet always draws us back to itself as the deepest utterance of our souls before our God.

'Our Father which art in heaven!' To appreciate this word of adoration aright, I must remember that none of the saints had in Scripture ever ventured to address God as their Father. The invocation places us at once in the centre of the wonderful revelation the Son came to make of His Father as our Father too. It comprehends the mystery of redemption—Christ delivering us from the curse that we might become the children of God. The mystery of regeneration—the Spirit in the new birth giving us the new life. And the mystery of faith—ere yet the redemption is accomplished or understood, the word is given on the lips of the disciples to prepare them for the blessed experience still to come. The words are the key to the whole prayer, to all prayer. It takes time, it takes life to study them; it will take eternity to understand them fully. The knowledge of God's Father-love is the first and simplest, but also the last and highest lesson in the school of prayer. It is in the personal relation to the living God, and the personal conscious fellowship of love with Himself, that prayer begins. It is in the knowledge of God's Fatherliness, revealed by the Holy Spirit, that the power of prayer will be found to root and grow. In the infinite tenderness and pity and patience of the infinite Father, in His loving readiness to hear and to help, the life of prayer has its joy. O let us take time, until the Spirit has made these words to us spirit and truth, filling heart and life: 'Our Father which art in heaven.' Then we are indeed within the veil, in the secret place of power where prayer always prevails.

'Hallowed be Thy name.' There is something here that strikes us at once. While we ordinarily first bring our own needs to God in prayer, and then think of what belongs to God and His interests, the Master reverses the order. First, Thy name, Thy kingdom, Thy will; then, give us, forgive us, lead us, deliver us. The lesson is of more importance than we think. In true worship the Father must be first, must be all. The sooner I learn to forget myself in the desire that HE may be glorified, the richer will the blessing be that prayer will bring to myself. No one ever loses by what he sacrifices for the Father.

This must influence all our prayer. There are two sorts of prayer: personal and intercessory. The latter ordinarily occupies the lesser part of our time and energy. This may not be. Christ has opened the school of prayer specially to train intercessors for the great work of bringing down, by their faith and prayer, the blessings of His work and love on the world around. There can be no deep growth in prayer unless this be made our aim. The little child may ask of the father only what it needs for itself; and yet it soon learns to say, Give some for sister too. But the grown-up son, who only lives for the father's interest and takes charge of the father's business, asks more largely, and gets all that is asked. And Jesus would train us to the blessed life of consecration and service, in which our interests are all subordinate to the Name, and the Kingdom, and the Will of the Father. O let us live for this, and let, on each act of adoration, Our Father! there follow in the same breath, Thy Name, Thy Kingdom, Thy Will;—for this we look up and long.

'Hallowed be Thy name..' What name? This new name of Father. The word Holy is the central word of the Old Testament; the name Father of the New. In this name of Love all the holiness and glory of God are now to be revealed. And how is the name to be hallowed? By God Himself: 'I will hallow My great name which ye have profaned.' Our prayer must be that in ourselves, in all God's children, in presence of the world, God Himself would reveal the holiness, the Divine power, the hidden glory of the name of Father. The Spirit of the Father is the Holy Spirit: it is only when we yield ourselves to be led of Him, that the name will be hallowed in our prayer and our lives. Let us learn the prayer: 'Our Father, hallowed be Thy name.'

'Thy kingdom come.' The Father is a King and has a kingdom. The son and heir of a king has no higher ambition than the glory of his father's kingdom. In time of war or danger this becomes his passion; he can think of nothing else. The children of the Father are here in the enemy's territory, where the kingdom, which is in heaven, is not yet fully manifested. What more natural than that, when they learn to hallow the Father-name, they should long and cry with deep enthusiasm: 'Thy kingdom come.' The coming of the kingdom is the one great event on which the revelation of the Father's glory, the blessedness of His children, the salvation of the world depends. On our prayers too the coming of the kingdom waits. Shall we not join in the deep longing cry of the redeemed: 'Thy kingdom come'? Let us learn it in the school of Jesus.

'Thy will be done, as in heaven, so on earth.' This petition is too frequently applied alone to the suffering of the will of God. In heaven God's will is done, and the Master teaches the child to ask that the will may be done on earth just as in heaven: in the spirit of adoring submission and ready obedience. Because the will of God is the glory of heaven, the doing of it is the blessedness of heaven. As the will is done, the kingdom of heaven comes into the heart. And wherever faith has accepted the Father's love, obedience accepts the Father's will. The surrender to, and the prayer for a life of heaven-like obedience, is the spirit of childlike prayer.

'Give us this day our daily bread.' When first the child has yielded himself to the Father in the care for His Name, His Kingdom, and His Will, he has full liberty to ask for his daily bread. A master cares for the food of his servant, a general of his soldiers, a father of his child. And will not the Father in heaven care for the child who has in prayer given himself up to His interests? We may indeed in full confidence say: Father, I live for Thy honor and Thy work; I know Thou carest for me. Consecration to God and His will gives wonderful liberty in prayer for temporal things: the whole earthly life is given to the Father's loving care.

'And forgive us our debts as we also have forgiven our debtors.' As bread is the first need of the body, so forgiveness for the soul. And the provision for the one is as sure as for the other. We are children, but sinners too; our right of access to the Father's presence we owe to the precious blood and the forgiveness it has won for us. Let us beware of the prayer for forgiveness becoming a formality: only what is really confessed is really forgiven. Let us in faith accept the forgiveness as promised: as a spiritual reality, an actual transaction between God and us, it is the entrance into all the Father's love and all the privileges of children. Such forgiveness, as a living experience, is impossible without a forgiving spirit to others: as forgiven expresses the heavenward, so forgiving the earthward, relation of God's child. In each prayer to the Father I must be able to say that I know of no one whom I do not heartily love.

'And lead us not into temptation, but deliver us from the evil one.' Our daily bread, the pardon of our sins, and then our being kept from all sin and the power of the evil one, in these three petitions all our personal need is comprehended. The prayer for bread and pardon must be accompanied by the surrender to live in all things in holy obedience to the Father's will, and the believing prayer in everything to be kept by the power of the indwelling Spirit from the power of the evil one.

Children of God! it is thus Jesus would have us to pray to the Father in heaven. O let His Name, and Kingdom, and Will, have the first place in our love; His providing, and pardoning, and keeping love will be our sure portion. So the prayer will lead us up to the true child-life: the Father all to the child, the Father all for the child. We shall understand how Father and child, the Thine and the Our, are all one, and how the heart that begins its prayer with the God-devoted THINE, will have the power in faith to speak out the OUR too. Such prayer will, indeed, be the fellowship and interchange of love, always bringing us back in trust and worship to Him who is not only the Beginning but the End: 'FOR THINE IS THE KINGDOM, AND THE POWER, AND THE GLORY, FOR EVER, AMEN.' Son of the Father, teach us to pray, 'OUR FATHER.'

PRAYER 4

O Thou who art the only-begotten Son, teach us, we beseech Thee, to pray, 'OUR FATHER.' We thank Thee, Lord, for these Living Blessed Words which Thou hast given us. We thank Thee for the millions who in them have learnt to know and worship the Father, and for what they have been to us. Lord! it is as if we needed days and weeks in Thy school with each separate petition; so deep and full are they. But we look to Thee to lead us deeper into their meaning: do it, we pray Thee, for Thy Name's sake; Thy name is Son of the Father.

Lord! Thou didst once say: 'No man knoweth the Father save the Son, and he to whom the Son willeth to reveal Him.' And again: 'I made known unto them Thy name, and will make it known, that the love wherewith Thou hast loved Me may be in them.' Lord Jesus! reveal to us the Father. Let His name, His infinite Father-love, the love with which He loved Thee, according to Thy prayer, BE IN US. Then shall we say aright, 'OUR FATHER!' Then shall we apprehend Thy teaching, and the first spontaneous breathing of our heart will be: 'Our Father, Thy Name, Thy Kingdom, Thy Will.' And we shall bring our needs and our sins and our temptations to Him in the confidence that the love of such a Father cares for all.

Blessed Lord! we are Thy scholars, we trust Thee; do teach us to pray, 'OUR FATHER.' Amen.

THE PRAYERS OF ST. PAUL

By *REV. W. H. GRIFFITH THOMAS, D.D.*
(Originally published 1914)

TABLE OF CONTENTS

PREFACE

GRACE AND HOLINESS
1. His Prayer for Himself (ver. 11).
2. His Prayer for Others (vers. 12, 13).

CONSECRATION AND PRESERVATION
1. The Petition.
2. The Pre-Requisite.
3. The Prospect.
4. The Promise.

APPROBATION AND BLESSING
1. The Reason of the Prayer.
2. The Nature of the Prayer.
3. The Consequences of the Prayer.
4. The Guarantee of the Prayer.

LOVE AND PEACE
1. The Goal.
2. The Guide.
3. The Gift.
4. The Giver.

KNOWLEDGE AND OBEDIENCE
1. The Reason of the Prayer.
2. The Nature of the Prayer.
3. The Purpose of the Prayer.
4. The Character of the Prayer.

CONFLICT AND COMFORT
1. What Prayer Means.

2. What Prayer Brings.

WISDOM AND REVELATION
1. The Foundation.
2. The Appeal.
3. The Request.

STRENGTH AND INDWELLING
1. The Standpoint.
2. The Attitude.
3. The Address.
4. The Appeal.
5. The Standard.
6. The Petitions.

LOVE AND DISCERNMENT
1. The Definite Request.
2. The Immediate Purpose.
3. The Permanent Result.

APPENDIX

PREFACE

One of the most valuable elements in the Epistles of St. Paul is their revelation of the writer's spiritual life. While they are necessarily doctrinal and theological, dealing with the fundamental realities of the Christian religion, they are also intensely personal, and express very much of the Apostle's own experience. They depict in a marked degree the sources and characteristics of the spiritual life. This is especially seen when the various prayers, thanksgivings, doxologies, and personal testimonies are considered.

I

GRACE AND HOLINESS

"Now God Himself and our Father, and our Lord Jesus Christ, direct our way unto you. And the Lord make you to increase and abound in love one toward another, and toward all men, even as we do toward you: To the end He may stablish your hearts unblameable in holiness before God, even our Father, at the coming of our Lord Jesus Christ with all His saints."—*1 Thess.* iii. 11-13.

There are few more precious subjects for meditation and imitation than the prayers and intercessions of the great Apostle. He was a man of action because he was first and foremost a man of prayer. To him both aspects of the well-known motto were true: "To pray is to labour," and "To labour is to pray."

There is no argument for or justification of prayer; nor even an explanation. It is assumed to be the natural and inevitable expression of spiritual life. Most of the Apostle's prayers of which we have a record are concerned with other people rather than with himself, and they thus reveal to us indirectly but very really what St. Paul felt to be the predominant needs of the spiritual life.

In this series of studies we propose to look at some of these prayers, and to consider their direct bearing upon our own lives. Taking the Epistles in what is generally regarded to be their chronological order, we naturally commence with the prayer found in 1 Thess. iii. 11-13. In this passage we have what is not often found, a prayer for himself associated with prayer for others.

1. *His Prayer for Himself* (ver. 11).

Let us notice *Who it is to Whom he prays*—"God Himself and our Father, and our Lord Jesus Christ." The association of Christ with God as One to Whom prayer is addressed is of course very familiar to us, but it ought never to be forgotten that when the Apostle penned these words the association was both striking and significant. For consider: these words were written within twenty-five years of our Lord's earthly life and ascension, and yet here is this quiet but clear association of Him with the Father, thus testifying in a very remarkable and convincing way to His Godhead as the Hearer of prayer. And this fact is still more noticeable in the original, for St. Paul in this verse breaks one of the familiar rules of grammar, whether of Greek or English. It is well known that whenever there are two nouns to a verb the verb must be in the plural; and yet here the Greek word "direct" is in the singular, notwithstanding the fact that there are two subjects, the Father and Christ. The same feature is to be found in 2 Thess. ii. 17. It is evident from this what St. Paul thought of our Lord Jesus Christ, and it is in such simple, indirect testimonies that we find the strongest and most convincing proofs that the early Church believed in the Deity of our Lord.

Let us consider *what it is for which he prays*—"Direct our way." He asks for guidance. There had been certain difficulties in the way of his return to Thessalonica. He had been hindered, and now asks that God would open the way for him to go back to his beloved friends. Nothing was outside the Apostle's relationship to God, and nothing was too small about which to pray to God. As it has been well said: "Nothing is so small that we do not honour God by asking His guidance of it, or insult Him by taking it out of His hands." The need of guidance is a very real one in every Christian life, and the certainty of guidance is just as real. "The steps of a good man are ordered by the Lord" (Ps. xxxvii. 23); and this is as true now as ever. "I will guide thee with Mine eye" (Ps. xxxii. 8) is a promise for all time, and we may confidently seek guidance in prayer whenever it is needed. The answer to our prayer will come in a threefold way. God guides us by His Spirit, reigning supreme within our hearts. He also guides us by the counsels and principles of His Word. These two agree in one, for the Holy Spirit never guides contrary to the Word. And then, in the third place, He guides us by His Providence, so that when the Word, the Spirit, and Providence in daily circumstances agree we may be sure that the guidance has been given.

2. *His Prayer for Others* (vers. 12, 13).

Consider the *immediate request* he makes—"The Lord make you to increase and abound in love one toward another, and toward all men." He asks for *love* on their behalf, that God would grant them this greatest of all gifts—"the very bond of peace and of all virtues, without which whosoever liveth is counted dead before Him." Love in the New Testament is no mere sentiment, for it involves self-sacrifice. It is not limited to emotion; it expresses itself in energy. It does not evaporate in feeling; it expresses itself in fact. "Love is of God," for "God is love"; and the Apostle in praying this prayer asks for the supreme gift of their lives.

The measure of the gift is noticeable—"Increase and abound in love." The "increase" has to do with their inner life, their hearts being more and more enlarged in capacity to possess this love; the "abounding" has to do with their outward life, and points to the overflow of that love towards others.

Consider, too, the *objects* of this love—"Toward one another, and toward all men." There was, first of all, the special love to be shown toward Christians, according to the "new commandment" (John xiii. 34). In the New Testament the emphasis is laid again and again upon brother-love, or love of the brethren, and the brotherhood. This was something entirely new in the world's history—a new tie or bond, the union of hearts in Christ Jesus. To see how these Christians loved one another was a proof of this new affection based upon the new commandment. But, further, their love was to extend beyond their fellow-Christians—even to "all men," just as we have in St. Peter's Epistle, in that long chain of graces, first, love of the brethren, and then, love towards all (2 Pet. i. 7).

And yet it may perhaps be asked, How is it possible for us to love everybody? What about those who are not lovely and lovable—how can we love these? It may help us to remember that there is a clear distinction between *loving* and *liking*. While it is impossible to *like* everybody, it is assuredly possible to love everybody. A mother loves her wayward son, but she cannot like him, for there is practically nothing "alike" between them. In the same way we may love with the love of compassion if we cannot love with the love of complacency, and thus fulfil our Lord's command and realise the answer to the Apostle's prayers. This, we may be perfectly certain, is the supreme thing, and our Christianity will count for nothing in the eyes of men if it is not permeated and energised through and through with active, whole-hearted, Christ-like love.

Consider the *ultimate purpose* he expresses—"To the end He may stablish your hearts unblameable in holiness." The love for which he prays is to be expressed in holiness. The meaning of holiness throughout the Old and New Testaments is "separateness." The idea is that of a life separated unto God, dedicated, consecrated to His service. Wherever the words "holiness," "sanctification," and their associated and cognate expressions are found, the root idea is always that of separation rather than of purification. It involves the whole-hearted and entire dedication of the life to God. The cognate word "saint" does not strictly mean "one who is pure," but "one who belongs to God."

The sphere of this holiness is to be in "your hearts." It is always to be noticed that in Scripture the "heart" includes the intellect, the emotions, and the will. In a word, it is the centre of our moral and spiritual being; and when this is understood we can see at once the point and importance of the heart being holy, for it is only another way of saying that our entire being is to be separated from all else in order to be possessed by, and consecrated to, God.

The standard of holiness is also brought before us in this prayer—"Stablish your hearts unblameable in holiness." The Apostle prays that they may be steadfast, not weak and vacillating. The great need was for solidity and steadfastness, as it is in the present day, for it is only when the heart is established by grace and in holiness that it can in any true sense serve God. This emphasis on a fixed or stablished heart is brought before us several times in Holy Scripture (cf. Ps. lvii. 7, cviii. 1, cxii. 7; Heb. xiii. 9).

And steadfast hearts will be "unblameable" hearts, hearts that are not blameworthy. A clear distinction is to be drawn between unblameable hearts and unblemished hearts. A little child may perform a task which in the result is full of blemishes, though the child, having done his best, is entirely without blame. In like manner, though the believer is not free from blemish, it is nevertheless possible for him to live free from blame. This is the meaning of the Apostle, and the reason of his prayer.

In all this we can see the close connection between love and holiness. When our hearts are filled to overflowing with the love of God to us, and of our love to Him, the inevitable result is holiness, a heart separated unto God, "strengthened with all might," and "ready unto every good work."

Consider the *great incentive* he urges—"Before God, even our Father, at the coming of our Lord Jesus Christ with all His saints." The Apostle puts before his readers the great future to which they were to look, and he urges upon them this love and this holiness in the light of the coming of our Lord Jesus Christ, and all that it will mean to the people of God. St. Paul draws a wonderful picture of that day in a very few words. He speaks first of all of God's presence there: "Before God, even our Father." Then he reminds us of the presence of the Lord Jesus Christ. And last of all he tells us that "the saints" will be there also. Thus, surrounded by our fellow-Christians, and in the presence of our God and Saviour, we shall see as we are seen, and know as we are known, with hearts "unblameable in holiness."

This, then, is what the Apostle prays for his beloved friends in Thessalonica—abounding love and perfect holiness. This is Christianity and the normal Christian life. How simple it all is, summed up in the words Love and Holiness. And yet how searching it is! The simplest things are often the most difficult, and while it is possible for the believer to do great things and to shine in great crises, it is not always so easy to go on loving day by day, and to continue growing in grace and holiness, until the heart becomes so stablished in grace that our Christianity becomes the permanent character of our life. Yet this is God's purpose for each one of us. And the fact that the Apostle prayed for this is a clear proof that an answer was expected, and that the purpose can be realised.

II

CONSECRATION AND PRESERVATION

"And the very God of peace sanctify you wholly: and I pray God your whole spirit and soul and body be preserved blameless unto the coming of our Lord Jesus Christ. Faithful is He that calleth you, Who also will do it."—1 *Thess.* v. 23, 24.

As we consider these prayers of the Apostle, we become increasingly aware of what he felt to be the most important elements in the Christian life. The prayers all have reference to Christian living, and whether we think of the character of the life portrayed, or the standard held up in them, we can readily see their intense practical value for daily living. We may be pretty sure that those things for which he prayed on behalf of his converts were the things he regarded as most essential in Christian character and conduct.

The prayer that now calls for consideration is that found in 1 Thess. v. 23, 24.

1. *The Petition.*

He prays for their *sanctification*—"Sanctify you wholly." As already noted, the root idea of sanctification, and of its cognate expressions, "holiness," "holy," and the like, is *separation*. We see this very clearly in connection with buildings or things which are said to be "holy" or "sanctified." It is obvious that no thought of purification is applicable to buildings and inanimate objects. We must, therefore, understand sanctification in this case as equivalent to consecration. This is also the root-meaning of the word "sanctify" in relation to persons, and it may be questioned whether the word, as used in the original, ever really includes in it the idea of purification; the latter thought has another set of words altogether. The Apostle therefore prays that they may be consecrated, set apart from all else, for the possession and service of God. This meaning may be aptly illustrated from our Lord's words about Himself: "For their sakes I *consecrate* Myself, that they also may be *consecrated* through the truth" (John xvii. 19).

The *extent* of this consecration is very noteworthy—"Sanctify you wholly." The word rendered "wholly" is used in connection with the Old Testament sacrifices in the Septuagint, and implies the entire and complete separation of the offering for the purpose intended. The Christian life must be wholly, entirely, and unreservedly consecrated to God, no part being reserved or held back, but everything handed over and regarded as permanently and completely belonging to Him.

He prays for their *preservation*—"Preserved blameless." The consecration is to be maintained in continual preservation, in and for God. The consecration as an act is to be deepened into an attitude, so that, day by day, and hour by hour, the separated life may be maintained, and preserved in readiness for every call that God may make.

The *extent* of this preservation is also observable—"Your whole spirit and soul and body." The spirit is that inmost part of our life which is related to God. The soul is the inner life regarded in itself, as the seat and sphere of intellect, heart, and will. The body is the outward vehicle and expression of the soul and spirit through which we are enabled to serve God. The order of these three should be observed. It is not, as we often say, and sing in certain hymns, "body, soul, and spirit," but the very reverse—"spirit, soul, and body." The Apostle starts from within and works outward, thereby reminding us that if the spirit or deepest part of our nature is wholly surrendered to God, this fact will express itself in every part of our nature, and we shall be consecrated wholly. What a searching requirement this is, and what a solemnity and responsibility it gives to life! Whether in relation to God, or in relation to man, whether for worship or work, character or conduct, prayer or practice, we are to be wholly consecrated, and continually kept for the Master's use—

> "That all my powers with all their might,
> In Thy sole glory may unite."

2. *The Pre-Requisite.*

"The God of Peace Himself." The Divine title associated with this prayer as its definite presupposition and pre-requisite is very significant, as, indeed, is every title of God. There is always some special point of direct connection between the way in which God is addressed and the prayer that follows. In the present instance the prayer for consecration and preservation is addressed to "The God of Peace Himself."

The Apostle lays special stress upon the fact that it is God "Himself" Who consecrates and keeps us. As with salvation, so with consecration—it is and must be Divine. The work is entirely beyond any mere human power, and while there is a truth in our frequent reference to consecration as something that we ourselves have to effect, it is far more scriptural, and, therefore, much more helpful, to endeavour to limit the idea of consecration to the Divine side, and to think of it as an act of God, to which the corresponding human act and attitude is that of *dedication*. It is God Himself Who separates us, marks us off as His own, and designates us for His use and service. It is God Himself, and no one else, for we are here brought into personal and blessed association with the Divine power and grace.

Further, God is described as "The God of Peace," and we naturally ask what it means, and why peace is thus associated with consecration and preservation. This title, "The God of Peace," is found very frequently in the writings of St. Paul, and it deserves careful consideration in each passage. There is a twofold peace in Scripture, sometimes described as "peace with God" (Rom. v. 1), at others as "the peace of God" (Phil. iv. 7); and they both have their source in the "God of Peace" (Phil. iv. 9). Peace is the result of reconciliation with God. Our Lord made peace by the Blood of His Cross (Col. i. 20), and the acceptance of His atoning sacrifice through faith brings peace to the soul. This consciousness of reconciliation in turn causes a blessed sense of restfulness and peace to spring up in the heart, and thus we have the peace of God within us.

The connection between peace and holiness is close and essential. It is impossible for anyone to understand consecration until they have experienced reconciliation. Holiness must be based on righteousness, and righteousness is only possible to those who have accepted the Lord Jesus as God's righteousness through faith. So long as there is any enmity in the heart, or even any uncertainty as to our acceptance in Christ Jesus, holiness is an impossibility. May not the forgetfulness of this fact be the cause of surprise and disappointment at Christian Conventions from time to time? May it not be that many go to such gatherings longing to be made holy who have not settled this question of their standing before God and their peace as the result of acceptance of Christ's atonement? To understand and experience what holiness means before enjoying peace with God is like trying to take a second step before attempting the first. Only through peace can holiness come, and only as we have blessed personal experience of God as the God of peace can a prayer like this be answered.

3. *The Prospect.*

"Unto the coming of our Lord Jesus Christ." Once again the Apostle prays with special reference to that glorious day to which he was always looking and pointing his readers. As he looks forward to that day he uses again a favourite word, "blameless," and suggests to us the great and wonderful possibility of being so consecrated and preserved that we may lead a blameless life day by day until the coming of our Lord. Holiness is thus associated once again with the great future. The Apostle finds in the coming of the Lord one of the most potent reasons why Christians should be consecrated and preserved. This close and intimate connection between holiness, and what we term the Second Advent, needs much stronger emphasis in daily living and in church teaching than it often has in the present day. There is, in its way, nothing more powerful as a reason for holiness than the thought of the certainty and imminence of the Lord's coming.

4. *The Promise.*

"Faithful is He that calleth you, Who also will do it." Lest we should be tempted to think that so wonderful a prayer could not be fulfilled in daily experience, the Apostle adds this blessed assurance that God, Who puts this ideal before us, will enable us to realise it. The promise is undoubted—"Who also will do it." What He has promised He is also able to perform. If only our hearts are right with Him, and are willing to say, "Yea, let Him take all," God will, indeed, consecrate and preserve us blameless unto the end. The guarantee of this lies in His Divine faithfulness. "Faithful is He that calleth you." We are touching the bed-rock of Divine revelation when we contemplate the faithfulness of God. This phrase is often found in the New Testament: "God is faithful." "The Lord is faithful." "Faithful is He." "This is a faithful saying." If our hearts will only rest upon this we shall find in it, not only the most exquisite joy and assured peace, but also the ground of our perfect confidence that He will accomplish His purposes in us, and glorify Himself in our lives.

It is well and necessary from time to time to look at holiness from the human point of view, and to see our duty and responsibility; but it is equally essential and important that we should also dwell upon holiness, as in the passage before us, from the Divine standpoint, and keep well in view the glorious realities of God's faithfulness, God's power, God's grace. To be occupied unduly with self in the matter of holiness is to become self-centred, morbid, fearful, and weak; to be occupied with God is to be restful, quiet, strong, confident, and ever growing in grace.

III

APPROBATION AND BLESSING

"Wherefore also we pray always for you, that our God would count you worthy of this calling, and fulfil all the good pleasure of His goodness, and the work of faith with power: that the name of our Lord Jesus Christ may be glorified in you, and ye in Him, according to the grace of our God and the Lord Jesus Christ."—2 *Thess.* i. ii, 12.

Two words sum up the Christian life—Grace and Glory; and both are associated with the two Comings of the Lord Jesus Christ: Grace particularly with the first Coming, and Glory especially with the second. This twofold aspect of Christianity comes before us in the prayer of the Apostle which we now have to consider.

1. *The Reason of the Prayer.*

This thought is brought before us very clearly in the Revised Version: "*To which end we also pray.*" In the Authorised Version it is: "*Wherefore also we pray.*" Following the original, the R.V. refers definitely to what has preceded. The whole context is a reason for the prayer which now follows.

The *Triumphant Future* is part of the reason of his prayer. "When He shall come to be glorified in His saints, and to be marvelled at in all them that believe in that day." The Apostle looks forward to "the crowning day" that is coming, and bases upon this glorious hope the prayer that follows.

The *Testing Present* is another part of the reason for this prayer. The Church of Thessalonica was suffering persecutions and afflictions, and was passing through the fire of testing (vers. 4-7); and it was this fact—their then-existing severe experiences—that prompted the Apostle to pray for them, as well as to express the hope concerning their deliverance from the furnace of affliction.

Thus present and future are blended in his thought, and form the ground or reason of his intercession.

2. *The Nature of the Prayer.*

Two elements sum up this beautiful prayer.

He asks for the *Divine Approval* on their life: "That God may count you worthy of your calling." God's "calling" is His summons into His kingdom. The kingdom may be regarded both as present and future. In the Gospels it would seem as though the "calling" were limited to His invitation or appeal, while in the Epistles it appears to include the believer's response to the call. For this reason it is sometimes spoken of as God's "calling," and at others, as in this case, as "your calling." The thought of a Divine calling responded to by the believer is prominent in the teaching of St. Paul, and should be carefully studied. Even in these Epistles to the Thessalonians, the idea is frequently found (1 Thess. ii. 12, iv. 7, v. 24; 2 Thess. ii. 14).

"Count you worthy" is a notable phrase repeated from verse 5: "Counted worthy of the kingdom of God." Seven times this verb is used by St. Paul. As we ponder it we catch something of the wondrous glory of our life as contemplated by the King of Kings. Surely, it may be said, the believer can never be "worthy"; and this is true if he is considered in himself. But just as it is with justification, which means "accounted just," so with sanctification—by the unspeakable grace of God we are actually "counted worthy." Hooker's well-known words about justification may be quoted in this connection as illustrating the thought of worthiness in sanctification. "God doth justify the believing man, yet not for the worthiness of his belief, but for His worthiness Who is believed." So we may say, God doth count the believing man worthy, yet not for any personal worthiness, but for the worthiness which is wrought by grace. We must, however, not fail to notice that the believer is responsible for his use of grace, and that the very thought of God counting us worthy has included in it the thought of scrutiny with a view to decision.

He seeks the *Divine Blessing* on their life: "And fulfil every desire of goodness and every work of faith with power." This, which is the rendering of the R.V., seems, on the whole, the more intelligible and appropriate. It means, "all that goodness can desire, and all that faith can effect." It blends together the two ideas of *aspiration* and *activity*—the aspiration of goodness and the activity of trust—and it prays that God would fulfil *with power*, or powerfully, every aspiration that comes from goodness, and every activity that springs from faith. Just as in the familiar words of the Collect for Easter Day, God first puts into "our minds good desires," and then by His "continual help" we are enabled to "bring the same to good effect." By "His holy inspiration we think those things that are good, and by His merciful guiding we perform the same."

3. *The Consequences of the Prayer.*

Notice the twofold consequence here stated.

He expects that *God will be glorified in us*. Glory in the New Testament, and, indeed, in the whole Bible, is the outshining of splendour, and the Apostle seeks in answer to prayer that Christ may reveal in our lives the glory of His grace. This includes both our present and future lives. Christ is to be manifested by and glorified in us here, and He will be manifested by and glorified in us hereafter (ver. 10). What an unspeakable privilege and what a profound responsibility lie in this simple fact that Christ is to shine forth from our lives, and that men around us are to see something of Christ as they associate with us. One of the most beautiful testimonies ever given to a Christian was that of a poor dying outcast girl to a lady who had befriended her: "I have not found it hard to think about God since I knew you."

He also expects that *we shall be glorified in Christ*. This is, in a way, more wonderful still. There is to be a reciprocal glory; and, actually, marvellous though it seems, we are to have our share of glory in Christ. This, again, has its application to the present, as well as to the future, for every life that is loyal to Christ is glorified in union and communion with Him. And in the great future it will be seen and known on every hand who have been faithful to their Lord and Master. "Then shall the righteous shine forth as stars in the kingdom of their Father."

4. *The Guarantee of the Prayer.*

The Apostle scarcely ever prayed without reminding himself and his readers of the secret whereby prayer is answered. Accordingly he closes this prayer with a reminder that the guarantee of its fulfilment is the grace of God—"According to the grace of our God and the Lord Jesus Christ."

God is the *Source* of all grace. How lovingly the Apostle speaks of "our God" and "our Lord Jesus" in this verse! Elsewhere in his Epistles we also find this appropriating phrase, "Our God" (1 Thess. ii. 2, iii. 9; 1 Cor. vi. 11). As in the still more personal phrase, "My God," which we find about seven times in his writings, St. Paul expresses his consciousness of personal possession and the blessed reality of fellowship with God. "This God is *our* God," as the Psalmist says.

Christ is the *Channel* of grace. The Lord Jesus Christ being associated with God in this connection is a reminder that it is "the grace of our Lord Jesus Christ" as much as the grace of our God. He mediates grace to us, and through faith in Christ we are linked to God as the "God of all grace."

What a cheer and inspiration it is to have the assurance and guarantee that even a prayer like this, with its high standard and far-reaching possibilities, can and will be answered. Christianity provides not only an appeal, but a dynamic. He Who bids, enables; He Who calls, provides. The Gospel of Jesus Christ is at once a precept, a promise, a provision, and a power. The religions of the world often tell us to "Be good," but it is left for Christianity to proclaim that "He died *to make us good.*" As a result, the Christian can say with Augustine: "Give what Thou commandest and then command what Thou wilt." That is: "Only give me the spiritual power, and then I can do anything that Thou requirest of me." As the Psalmist cried: "I will run in the path of Thy commandments, when Thou hast set my heart at liberty."

Thus the Christian life is at once a life of Grace and a life of Glory. "First Grace, then Glory." "No Grace, no Glory." "More Grace, more Glory." "If Grace, then Glory."

"Grace, 'tis a charming sound,
 Harmonious to the ear;
 Heaven with the echo shall resound,
 And all the earth shall hear."

IV

LOVE AND PEACE

"The Lord direct your hearts into the love of God, and into the patience of Christ."—2 *Thess.* iii. 5, R.V.

"The Lord of peace Himself give you peace always by all means."—2 *Thess.* iii. 16.

It is striking to note the number of prayers in these two short Epistles to Thessalonica. They are probably the earliest of the Apostle's writings, and the frequency of his prayers is a significant testimony to his thought for his converts and their needs.

Hardly less striking is the variety of the prayers, of which we have already had several proofs. There are still two prayers to be considered in the second Epistle, very terse petitions, yet full of suggestiveness and importance. It will be convenient to consider these two together, not only because of their brevity, but also because of the spiritual connection between them.

1. *The Goal.*

The context of the prayer is noteworthy. The Apostle had been asking for their prayers, more particularly for deliverance from evil men. Then comes the strong assurance that God in His faithfulness would keep them from evil, together with the expression of his own personal confidence concerning them that they would be faithful to his counsels and commands. And then follows the prayer of our text in which he asks that their hearts may be directed to that Divine goal which is, and ever must be, the true home of the soul.

"*Your hearts.*" Once again does the Apostle lay stress on this central reality of their spiritual and moral being. The heart is the citadel of the life, and the usage of the term in the Word of God must ever be kept clearly before us. It includes, as we have already seen, intellectual, emotional, and volitional elements. There is no such contrast in the New

Testament between "the head" and "the heart" as we are now often accustomed to make, for intellect, feelings, and will are all comprised in the Biblical meaning. If, therefore, the heart is right, all else will be right. It was for this reason that Solomon gave the counsel to keep the heart "above all keeping," since "out of it are the issues of life."

"Into the love of God." The phrase seems to suggest the direction of the heart towards a goal—"*Into* the love." This must mean first and foremost the love of God to us, for this is the true goal and home of the soul. Home is at once a protection, a fellowship, and a joy. "There's no place like home;" and there is no place like the love of God as a home for the soul. In that love we find constant protection, for all the refuge and safety of a true home are experienced there. In that love we find the fullest, truest fellowship, for "truly our fellowship is with the Father, and with His Son Jesus Christ"; and we know also "the fellowship of the Holy Ghost." Not least of all, in this home of the soul, is perfect and permanent satisfaction. Just as when the door closes upon us and we know that we are within the privacy, comfort, cheer, and fellowship of home, we find blessed restfulness and satisfaction, so when the soul enters the home of God's love it soon realises the fulness of satisfaction, for it is "satisfied with favour, full with the blessing of the Lord." Love that is deep, unfathomable, constant, pure, unchanging, Divine, is our everlasting home. It is recorded that Spurgeon once saw a weathercock with the words on it, "God is love." On remarking to the owner that it was very inappropriate, since God's love did not change like a weathercock, he received the reply that the real meaning was, "God is love whichever way the wind blows." This is the experience of the believer. Whatever comes, wherever he is, he knows that "God is love."

It is possible, perhaps probable, that this phrase, "the love of God," may also include our love to God. At any rate, in several passages it is almost impossible to make a rigid distinction between the two ideas (cf. Rom. v. 5). The one is the source of the other, and "we love Him because He first loved us." Love from God begets love to God, and when once the soul has entered into God's love as its goal and home, love at once begins to be the spring, the strength, the sustenance, and the satisfaction of its life.

"Into the patience of Christ." The Authorised Version has somewhat misread this verse by translating it "into the patient waiting for Christ," which would need another expression in the Greek. It really refers to

active, persistent, steady endurance rather than to patient waiting. It refers to present patience, not to a future prospect. The patience of Christ must mean the active endurance which is like His, the endurance of which He is the pattern. How marvellously He "endured the contradiction of sinners against Himself"! How striking is the statement that "He set His face steadfastly to go to Jerusalem"! Whether in suffering or in service, our Lord "endured as seeing Him who is invisible"; and having endured to the end, He became our Saviour.

But "the patience of Christ" is also the endurance which comes from Him. He is not only our pattern, but also our power, since He enables us to endure with a like endurance to His own. As the Apostle says elsewhere: "I have power for all things in Him who is empowering me." To have a pattern without the power to realise it, to have our Lord's example without His efficacy and energy, would be of little practical use except to discourage and to mock us; but He who sets the standard supplies the strength, and our hearts are thus enabled to enter into and abide in the endurance of Christ.

The need of patient endurance is obvious. Those early Christians of Thessalonica were soon put to the test. A few days and their new-born experiences were severely proved. Persecution, ostracism, suffering, and, it may be, death put a real strain upon their Christian profession; yet they endured, and the Apostle's prayer was answered; for we know with what joy he received tidings of their endurance and continuance (ch. i. 4). The same endurance is needed to-day, though the circumstances are very different. Sin is still powerful, and trials, suffering, sorrow and death are found on every hand. Many things would tempt us from our allegiance and continuance. Like the Psalmist, we see the wicked prospering, and we are ready to burst out with the faithless cry: "I have cleansed my heart in vain, and washed my hands in innocency." Or we have been toiling in the vineyard for long without seeing any fruit, and like the prophet, we are tempted to cry: "I have laboured in vain, I have spent my strength for nought." Then we hear the voice of the Apostle reminding us of "the love of God" and "the patience of Christ."

The secret of patience is love. If only we live in the love of God we shall thereby find the grace of patience. The union of love and patience was exemplified in our Lord's earthly life. He kept His Father's commandments and abode in His love, and if only we will continue in

His love we shall thereby be enabled to keep His commandments, and endure as He endured.

2. *The Guide.*

"The Lord direct your hearts." We need direction. Sin has blinded us, and kept us from knowing the way home into the love of God, and into the endurance of Christ. Still more, sin has biassed our hearts, and kept us from going along the way. Thus we need nothing short of a Divine direction. If the Lord does not make straight our way home we never shall arrive there.

How does our Lord direct our hearts? First, by constant and ever-increasing experience of His love. "God is love," and as it is of the essence of love to communicate itself, God is ever revealing to our hearts and bestowing upon them His own Divine love. Along the straight pathway He guides the soul into deeper and fuller experience of His unchanging, unerring, and unending love.

He also guides by bestowing upon us an ever-fuller experience of the power of Christ. Patient endurance is not learned all at once, and the Lord leads us as we are able to bear His disclosures and His discipline. Every lesson of testing brings with it a fresh experience of grace, and every call to endure carries with it the assurance of sufficient strength and power.

The means used for our direction, as we have already seen, are three in number, but the truth is so important that it needs renewed emphasis. The Lord directs us *by His Word*. Its examples, its counsels, its promises, its warnings, it anticipations, its incentives all come with force and blessing upon the heart, impelling it to go the right way home. He also directs us *by His Holy Spirit* dwelling within us. The Divine Spirit possesses and purifies our thoughts, cleanses and clarifies our motives, freshens and fertilises our soul, sanctifies and sensitises our conscience, guides and guards our will; and thus "every virtue we possess, and every victory won, and every thought of holiness" are the work of the Holy Spirit of God in guiding and directing our hearts into the love of God and into the patience of Christ.

The Lord also guides *by His Providence*. He uses the circumstances of our daily life to indicate His will. The discipline, the thousand and one little events and episodes, the ordinary experience of daily duty, the shadows and the sunshine, are all part of His providential guidance as He leads us along the pathway home into the love of God. All things are continually working together for good to them that love God.

Now we pass to consider the second and complementary prayer.

3. *The Gift.*

In this concluding prayer of the Epistle the Apostle sums up by speaking of that which is in some respects the greatest gift of God in Christ, the gift of perfect and perpetual peace.

Our first need is *peace of conscience*. The burden of sin weighs heavily upon the awakened soul, and the condemnation of the law consciously weighs upon it. As we look back over the past, and realise what it has been, we long for rest in the removal of condemnation and the bestowal of forgiveness. Our hearts cry out for peace with God.

Our second need is *peace of heart*. The soul set free from the burden of condemnation and guilt soon finds the need of a new strength, new interests, new hopes. The past has been obliterated by mercy, but the present looms large with difficulty. Temptations to fear and discouragement arise, and the soul longs for peace. Peace with God by reconciliation must therefore be followed by the peace of God through restfulness of heart day by day.

Our third need is *peace of fellowship*. The true Christian life is never solitary, but is lived in association with others. Our relationship to Christ necessarily carries with it a relationship to those who are in Christ with us, and as a consequence the peace which is ours in Christ is expressed in peace and fellowship with our fellow-believers. The context of this prayer shows that the Apostle had this aspect of peace in mind, and no true peace can be enjoyed with God that is not shared with our fellow-Christians. Our Lord has broken down the wall of partition between us; He has made us all one in Himself, for He is our peace.

4. *The Giver.*

The source of this threefold peace is *"The Lord of peace Himself."* By His death He brings us peace of conscience, by His Resurrection life peace of heart, by His Holy Spirit peace of fellowship. "Peace I leave with you" is the legacy of His Death. "My peace I give unto you" is the gift of His Spirit. On the Resurrection evening He came with this twofold peace. First, He said, "Peace be unto you," and "showed them His hands and His side," thus assuring them of peace of conscience through His Death. Then He said unto them *again*, "Peace be unto you," and bestowed upon them His Holy Spirit, thus guaranteeing to them peace of heart. His own peace, which had been so marked a feature of His own life and ministry, was now to be theirs. He, the possessor of peace, was now to be the provider of peace to them.

The title, "The Lord of peace," in this passage is very noteworthy. It is only found here, though the title "God of peace" occurs several times. What are we to understand by it? Surely it is a hint to us that only in His Lordship, acknowledged and experienced by us, can we find peace. In very significant words we read in the prophet of "His government and peace." First government and then peace, since peace is only possible as a result of government. In like manner we read in the psalm of "righteousness and peace," for it is only as He is "the Lord our righteousness" that He becomes the Lord our peace. When the government is upon His shoulder, and He is the Lord of our life, the inevitable and blessed result is "peace, perfect peace."

The continuity of this peace is very noteworthy—"Give you peace *always*." It is a constant peace. It is independent of circumstances, and does not change with changing experiences, since it is independent of our variableness, and depends entirely upon the Lord of peace and His Divine gift. Peace is associated with our permanent relationship to God in Christ, and a relationship of this kind is unalterable by any experiences or circumstances. The Lord gives peace always.

The channels of this peace are also significant—"Peace always *by all means*." "In every manner," by all conceivable channels and methods this peace comes. No circumstance or condition of life can be ours which does not give some opportunity for the bestowal, experience, and enjoyment of peace. Not only does peace come "always," but "all ways."

Love, Patience, Peace—how beautiful and suggestive the combination and association! Patience is the fruit of love, and peace is the fruit of patience. When the soul is dwelling in the love of God patience and peace flow naturally into the life, and are as naturally exemplified in it. And so the heart rejoices in the love, reproduces the patience, and reposes in the peace of the Lord of peace, because it is ever at rest in the presence and grace of "the God of love and peace."

V

KNOWLEDGE AND OBEDIENCE

"For this cause we also, since the day we heard it, do not cease to pray for you, and to desire that ye might be filled with the knowledge of His will in all wisdom and spiritual understanding; that ye might walk worthy of the Lord unto all pleasing, being fruitful in every good work, and increasing in the knowledge of God; strengthened with all might, according to His glorious power, unto all patience and long-suffering with joyfulness; giving thanks unto the Father."—*Col.* i. 9-12.

The Epistles of the (first) captivity of the Apostle (Philippians, Ephesians, Colossians, Philemon) represent his maturest experiences. As a consequence the prayers found in them are particularly noteworthy, revealing some of the deepest things of the writer's spiritual life. In this respect they are at once tests and models for us; and it is perhaps not too much to say that careful and prolonged prayerful meditation on the prayers found in these Epistles will prove one of the most valuable and helpful methods of deepening the spiritual life. The first of these we now consider.

1. *The Reason of the Prayer.*

Colosse was one of the Churches which Paul had neither founded nor visited (ch. ii. 1). Christianity was brought there by Epaphras, one of his disciples (ch. i. 7). But the Apostle was as keenly interested in its spiritual welfare as if he had been instrumental in founding it. So when he had heard of their faith and love (ch. i. 4), and the fruitfulness of their life (ch. i. 6), he thanked God on their behalf (ch. i. 3), and prayed this prayer. Deep interest in the spiritual life of others was one of the prominent marks of the Christian character of St. Paul. His was no self-centred life, for he was ever keenly alert to appreciate the marks of grace in others. This is a test, and at the same time a rebuke, for us. How unlike we are to a Christian of the type of Barnabas, of whom we read: "Who, when he came, and had seen the grace of God, was glad" (Acts

xi. 23). This is only possible by having "a heart at leisure from itself"; and when we are thus deeply interested in the marks and manifestations of the Divine working in other people's lives we shall not only praise God on their behalf, but also, like the Apostle, pray for them; and thus the blessing will extend and deepen.

2. *The Nature of the Prayer.*

The main point of his prayer was that they might be "*filled with the knowledge of His will.*" The will of God known and done is the secret of all true living. It was the key-note of our Lord's earthly life. He came to do the will of the Father, and in one of the deepest experiences of His life He said: "Not My will, but Thine be done." He told His disciples that His meat was to do the will of Him that sent Him; and He taught them to pray, "Thy will be done in earth as it is in heaven." The will of God is the substance of revelation, for what is the Bible from beginning to end but the revelation of God's will for man? Perhaps the most all-embracing prayer is: "Teach me to do Thy will"; and certainly the ideal life is summed up in the phrase, "He that doeth the will of God abideth for ever." Well might the Apostle pray for these Christians of Colosse to be filled with the knowledge of God's will.

The word rendered "knowledge" means "mature knowledge," and is one of the characteristic words of these four Epistles written from Rome. The Apostle evidently regarded mature knowledge, or deep spiritual experience, as the pre-eminent mark of a ripening Christian. In this respect St. John bears the same testimony, in his reference to the three stages of the Christian life represented by "little children," "young men," and "fathers." The little children *have*; the young men *are*; the fathers *know* (1 John ii. 12-14). This spiritual knowledge or experience is the great safeguard against error, in that it gives power to distinguish between good and evil, between truth and falsehood.

The measure of this knowledge is to be carefully noted—"*filled with* the knowledge of His will." The word also implies a fulness which is realised continually—not a bare knowledge, but its completeness; not an intermittent stream, but a perpetual flow. When the soul experiences this it is provided not only with the greatest safeguard against danger, but also with the secret of a strong, growing, powerful Christian life.

The characteristics of this knowledge should be observed: "*In all wisdom and spiritual understanding.*" "Wisdom" is a general term which implies the capacity and faculty for adapting the best means to bring about the best ends in things spiritual. "Spiritual understanding" is the specific coming or putting together of principles by means of which true action is taken. It really means "putting two and two together," comparing ideas and principles, for the purpose of adopting the best in any given course of action. Of the importance and necessity of wisdom and spiritual understanding scarcely anything need be said. Christian wisdom, Christian understanding, Christian perception in the thousand and one things of life—this surely is one of our greatest necessities and choicest blessings. How many errors would be avoided, how many wanderings checked, by means of this spiritual wisdom! Still more, how much joy would be experienced and how much genuine service rendered, if we were always saying and doing the right thing, at the right time, in the right way.

"*Filled with the knowledge of His will in all wisdom and spiritual understanding.*" This means for its complete realisation constant touch with that Book which presents the clearly expressed will of God. The will of God is in that Word, and when the Word is illuminated by the Spirit of God we come to know His will concerning us. No one will ever have the full knowledge of that will, no one can possibly be mature in experience, if the Word of God is not his daily, definite, direct study and meditation. It purifies the perception of the faculties by its cleansing power; it illuminates the moral faculties with its enlightening power; it controls the emotional faculties with its protective power; it energises the volitional faculties with its stimulating power; and thus in the constant, continuous use of the Word of God in personal practice, with meditation and prayer, we shall become "filled with the full knowledge of His will in all wisdom and spiritual understanding."

3. *The Purpose of the Prayer.*

Knowledge is not an end in itself, but the means to an end; and so the Apostle states the purpose for which he asks this knowledge of God's will: "*That ye might walk worthy of the Lord unto all-pleasing ... fruitful ... increasing ... strengthened ... giving thanks.*"

Their life is to be influenced by this knowledge—"*walk worthy of the Lord.*" Knowledge is to be translated into practice. "Walking" is the characteristic Bible word descriptive of the character of the Christian life, the full expression of all our powers. As it presupposes life, so it means energy, movement, progress; and for this, knowledge is essential. How can we walk unless we know why and whither we go? The knowledge of God's will gives point and purpose to the activities of life.

"*Walk worthy of the Lord.*" What a profound and searching thought is here—"Worthy of the Lord." Surely this is impossible; yet these are the plain words of the inspired writer. To walk worthy of the Lord—it is almost incredible, and yet this is one of the possibilities and glories of grace. The Apostle is fond of the word "worthy." We are to walk worthy of our vocation (Eph. iv. 1), worthy of the Gospel (Phil. i. 27), worthy of the saints (Rom. xvi. 2), worthy of God (1 Thess. ii. 12). We may be perfectly sure that Paul would not put such an ideal before us if it could not be realised. God's commands always imply promises.

"*Unto all pleasing.*" Bishop Moule beautifully renders this phrase: "Unto every anticipation of His will" (Colossian Studies). "Teach me to do the thing that pleaseth Thee" (P. B. version). What a glorious ideal! We are so to walk as to please Him in everything. Not only doing what we are told, but anticipating His commands by living in such close touch with Him that we instinctively know the thing that will please Him. These words sound a depth of the spiritual life with which comparatively few are familiar; and yet here they are, facing us definitely, with their call to realise that which God has placed before us.

The specific details of this worthy walk are next brought before us in four pregnant phrases:

"*Being fruitful in every good work.*" Notice every word of this sentence. Our life is to be characterised by good works, and in each and every one of these we are to be fruitful, manifesting the ripeness, and, if it may be so put, the beauty and lusciousness associated with fruit. Mark, too, that it is "fruitful *in* every good work," that is, in the process of doing the work, and not merely as the result or outcome of it. The very work itself is intended to be fruitful apart from particular results. There may be very few results of our service for God, but the service itself may and should be fruitful.

"Increasing in the knowledge of God." Notice the difference between the knowledge of His will and the knowledge of Himself. "That I may know *Him*" (Phil. iii. 10); "They might know *Thee*" (John xvii. 3); "Ye have known *Him*" (1 John ii. 13). The knowledge of His will will lead us to the knowledge of Himself, and beyond this it is impossible to go.

"Strengthened with all might, according to His glorious power, unto all patience and longsuffering with joyfulness." The Apostle's thought pours itself out in rich abundance in these words. It seems as though he could not adequately express the possibilities and characteristics of the Christian life about which he prays. They are to be "strengthened," and not only so, but "with all might." The principle or standard of it is "according to His glorious power," and the end of it is "unto all patience and longsuffering with joyfulness." The man of the world might see in this phrase an anticlimax, when it is said that the end of strength is patience and longsuffering; and yet Christianity finds its ideal in energy expressed in character, activity manifesting itself in passivity, and might in meekness.

Notice, too, the suggestive addition, *"with joyfulness."* Patience and longsuffering without joy are apt to be cold, chilly, unattractive. There is a stern, stoical endurance of suffering which, while it may be admired sometimes, tends to repel. But when patience and longsuffering are permeated and suffused with joyfulness, the very life of Christ is lived over again in His followers. Resignation to the will of God is only very partially a Christian virtue; but when we take joyfully the things that come upon us we are indeed manifesting the very life of God Himself.

"Giving thanks unto the Father." This is the crowning grace for which the Apostle prays—thankfulness. How much it means. The heart full of gratitude and gladness, the life full of brightness and buoyancy, the character full of vitality and vigour. The joy of the Lord is, indeed, the strength of His people, and when this element of thanksgiving characterises our life, it gives tone to everything else, and crowns all other graces.

4. *The Character of the Prayer.*

We have seen what the Apostle desired for the Christians of Colosse, and in so doing we have learnt some of the deepest secrets of Christian living. It remains to notice the characteristics of this prayer, in order that our prayers may be taught and guided and inspired with power.

His prayer was *urgent*—"*Since the day we heard.*" From the moment the tidings came by Epaphras of the Christian life in Colosse the Apostle's heart went up to God in prayer.

His prayer was *incessant*—"*Do not cease to pray.*" Again and again he asked, and kept on asking, so fully was his heart drawn out in prayer for these Christians whom he had never seen.

His prayer was *intense*—"*And to desire.*" This was no mere lip service. His heart had evidently been stirred to its core by the tidings of the Christian life at Colosse, and as he heard of their faith, their love, their hope, their holiness, their service, a deep, intense, longing desire came into his soul to seek for still fuller and deeper blessing on their behalf. What a man he was, and what prayers his were!

His prayer was *offered in fellowship with others*—"*Since the day we heard.*" Timothy was associated with the Apostle in these petitions. United prayer is one of the greatest powers in the Christian Church. "If two of you shall agree as touching anything that they shall ask, it shall be done." Personal prayer is precious, united prayer is still more powerful.

Thus in these verses we have one of the fullest, deepest and most precious of the Apostle's prayers, and as we consider its union of thought and experience, of profound teaching and equally profound revelation of Christian life, we learn two of the most urgent and necessary lessons for the Christian life to-day.

The first of these shall be given in the words of Bishop Moule: "Beware of untheological devotion." If devotion is to be real it should be characterised by *thought*. There is no contradiction between mind and heart, between theology and devotion. Devotional hours do not mean hours when thought is absent. Meditation is not abstraction, nor is devotion dreaminess. "Thou shalt love the Lord thy God with all thy *mind*" is an essential part of the commandment. If genuine thought and equally genuine theology do not characterise our hours of devotion, we lose some of the most precious opportunities of grace and blessing. A piety which is mere pietism, an evangelicalism which does not continually ponder the profound truths of the New Testament, can never be strong or do any deep service. We must beware of "untheological devotion."

We must also beware of "undevotional theology." This is the opposite error, and constitutes an equally great danger. A hard, dry, intellectual study of theology will yield no spiritual fruit. Accuracy in knowledge of Greek, careful balancing of aspects of truth, large knowledge of the doctrinal verities of the New Testament, are all essential and valuable; but unless they are permeated by a spirit of devotion they will fail at the crucial point. *Pectus facit theologum*—it is the heart that makes the theologian; and a theology which does not spring from spiritual experience is doomed to decay, to deadness, and therefore to disaster.

When, therefore, our devotions are theological, and our theology is devotional, we begin to realise the true being, blessing, and power of the Christian life, and we go from strength to strength, from grace to grace, and from glory unto glory.

VI

CONFLICT AND COMFORT

"For I would that ye knew what great conflict I have for you, and for them at Laodicea, and for as many as have not seen my face in the flesh; that their hearts may be comforted, being knit together in love, and unto all riches of the full assurance of understanding, to the acknowledgment of the mystery of God, and of the Father, and of Christ."—*Col.* ii. 1, 2.

Although he was in prison the Apostle was constantly at work for his Master, and not least of all at the work of prayer. If ever the words *orare est laborare*, "to pray is to labour," were true, they were true of St. Paul, for to him to pray was to work with all his might, as we shall see from a study of another of the prayers offered in his Roman prison.

1. *What Prayer Means.*

Prayer is described as a *conflict*. We have a similar expression used of the prayers of Epaphras, in the words "labouring fervently" (Col. iv. 12). The same word "conflict" is associated with faith, "the good fight of faith" (1 Tim. vi. 12), and with the "good fight" of the Apostle's entire life (2 Tim. iv. 7). Prayer regarded as a conflict includes the two ideas of toil and strife.

The toil of prayer shows us the work involved in it. Sometimes we hear the expression, "If you can do nothing else, you can pray," as though prayer were the easiest of all things. As a simple fact, it is the hardest. No man knows what prayer means unless he knows what it is to "labour" in prayer. The strife involved in prayer implies opposition—the opposing force of one who wishes above all things to check and thwart our prayers. We discern something of this opposition in the well-known words, "We wrestle" (Eph. vi. 12); and the words of the hymn are as true as they are familiar—

> "And Satan trembles when he sees
> The weakest saint upon his knees."

The Apostle knew by spiritual experience that to pray was to rouse up against himself a mighty opposition, and it was this force that made his prayer such a "great conflict." No believer should be surprised at his prayers "being hindered" (1 Pet. iii. 7). It is evidently one of Satan's main objects to get the Christian to restrain prayer. The Christian man or the Christian Church that continues instant in prayer may rest assured of malignant opposition from the hosts of spiritual wickedness in high places. On the other hand, we may be sure that Satan scarcely troubles himself about the believer or congregation whose private, family, and public praying is neglected or thought little of. Prayer is, therefore, a "great conflict." It is not solicitude only, but a struggle; not merely anxiety, but activity. As Bishop Moule says: "Prayer is never meant to be *indolently* easy, however simple and reliant it may be. It is meant to be an infinitely important transaction between man and God. And therefore very often, when subjects and circumstances call for it, it has to be viewed as a work involving labour, persistency, conflict, if it would be prayer indeed" (*Colossian Studies*, p. 124). The Bishop goes on to quote a familiar incident which illustrates this great truth: "A visitor knocked betimes one morning at the door of a good man, a saint of the noblest Puritan type—and that was a fine type indeed. He called as a friend to consult a friend, sure of his welcome. But he was kept waiting long. At last a servant came to explain the delay: 'My master has been at prayer, and this morning he has been long in getting access.'"

The practical question for us is whether this is our idea of prayer, or whether we are merely playing at prayer, and not regarding it with true seriousness. If we know what it is to have "great conflict" in prayer, happy are we. If we do not, we may well ask God to search our hearts and change our minds about prayer.

Prayer is characterised by *unselfishness*. The conflict of the Apostle was not self-centred. It was on behalf of others: "Great conflict I have for you, and for them at Laodicea." This is the essence of prayer—intercession on behalf of others. If our seasons of prayer are largely taken up with prayers for our own needs, however genuine, we are failing at a crucial point; but if our time is mainly taken up with prayers for others, we shall soon find that our own blessings begin to abound. "There is that scattereth and yet increaseth."

Prayer also implies *sympathy*. The Apostle was praying for people whom he had never seen, and probably never would see. This is not easy—indeed, is very difficult—but it is a real test of spirituality. "Out of sight, out of mind." We are tempted to limit our prayers to friends whom we know, causes in which we are interested, subjects spiritually near and akin to us. Not so the Apostle, whose heart went out to the whole Church of God in every place where he knew through friends that little bodies of Christians were to be found. His sympathy was at once quick, wide, and deep, and it is one of the supreme tests of true spirituality to have a sympathy possessed of all these three characteristics. Our sympathy may be quick and yet narrow, or wide but not deep, or even deep and not wide; but to be at once quick, wide, and deep in sympathy is to be a true follower of Christ.

As we ponder these things—conflict, unselfishness, sympathy—do not our hearts condemn us? Instead of conflict, how easy-going have been our prayers! Instead of unselfish, how self-centred, instead of sympathetic, how contracted! Thus the Apostle searches and tests us as we dwell on his wonderful life of prayer.

2. *What Prayer Brings.*

What were the objects for which the Apostle prayed so earnestly on behalf of these unknown Christians? What were the precise gifts that he sought for them from God? This is no unnecessary question, for the same gifts will surely be suitable to us.

He asked for spiritual *strength*: "That their hearts might be comforted." St. Paul always went to the very centre and core of things, and so we find him constantly praying with reference to the "hearts" of these Colossian Christians. Since, as we have seen, the "heart" in Scripture is the centre of our moral and spiritual being, if the heart is right, all will be right, for "out of it are the issues of life." He prays that their "hearts" might be comforted—that is, in the full sense of the word, encouraged, exhorted, strengthened. "Comfort" includes the three elements of strength, courage, and consolation. We must be strong, brave, and cheery. This is the full meaning of the term "Comforter" as applied to the Holy Spirit. He is the One Who gives strength, courage, and consolation. This, too, is the true meaning of the familiar phrase of the English Prayer Book, "Comfortable words"—words that minister strength, fortitude, and cheer. The fact that this thought of "hearts comforted" was often in the mind and on the lips of the Apostle shows the importance he attached to it (2 Thess. ii. 17; Eph. vi. 22). With hearts made strong, courageous, and cheerful, Christians can face anything; while with hearts that remain weak, fearful, and sad the Christian life is a prey to all the temptations of the Evil One. It is exactly similar with a Church or a congregation of Christians, for one of the supreme needs in any community is comforted hearts—the centres of life made strong, courageous, and happy. Then it is that Churches live, grow, extend, and witness for Christ in the demonstration of the Holy Spirit the "Comforter."

He asked for spiritual *unity*: "Being knit together in love," or, quite literally, "having been compacted in love." He prayed that these Christians might be kept together, knit together, joined together in a spirit of love. Solitary Christians are always weak Christians, for "union is strength." If Christians are not knit together, the cause of Christ must necessarily suffer, for through the severances caused by division the enemy will keep thrusting his darts. That is why the Apostle elsewhere urges them "earnestly to strive to keep the unity of the Spirit" (Eph. iv. 3). One of the greatest powers that Satan wields to-day is due to the disunion among the people of God. It is true of the Christian home, congregation, and denomination. The wedge of discord is one of the enemy's most powerful weapons. On the other hand, where the brethren dwell together in unity, the Lord commands His blessing. In almost every Epistle the Apostle emphasises unity, and we can readily understand the reason.

This unity is only possible "in love." It is the love of God *to* us that unites us to Him, and it will be the love of God *in* us that unites us to our brethren. There is no power like love to bind Christians together. We may not see eye to eye on all aspects of truth; we may not all use the same methods of worship and service, but if we love one another God dwells in us and among us, and adds His own seal of blessing to the work done for Him. Let every Christian be fully assured that in so far as he is striving, praying, and labouring for the union of God's people in love, he will be doing one of the most powerful and blessed pieces of work for his Master, and one of the greatest possible pieces of disservice to the kingdom of Satan. Contrariwise, the Christian man or Christian Church that stands out for separateness and exclusiveness is one of the best allies of Satan, and one of the most effective workers for the kingdom of darkness.

He asked for spiritual *certitude*: "Unto all riches of the full assurance of understanding." Wealth is a favourite metaphor of St. Paul, and is used to denote the fulness and abundance of the Christian life as conceived by him. Mark how he piles phrase upon phrase—"understanding," "fulness of understanding," and then "wealth of fulness of understanding." To the Apostle, the mind was one of the essential powers and principles of the Christian life. So far from thinking according to a modern fashion that the less one uses the mind the better Christian one is, St. Paul, following his Master, ever emphasised the duty and glory of loving God "with all the mind." This wealth of the fulness of "understanding" means an abundance of conviction, both intellectual and moral, that Christianity is what it claims to be, and that the Christian life is the perfect satisfaction of all the different parts of man's nature. He prays that they may "rise to the whole wealth of the full exercise of their intelligence" (Moule). Just as we find elsewhere "the fulness of faith" (Heb. x. 22), "the fulness of hope" (Heb. vi. 11), and "much fulness" (1 Thess. i. 5), so here the Apostle desires them to enjoy to the full the intelligent grasping of assurance of Christian truth which was theirs in Christ.

In the same spirit Luke writes to Theophilus: "That thou mightest know the certainty of those things wherein thou hast been instructed." A firm conviction of the understanding is one of the greatest needs, as it is also one of the greatest blessings, of the Christian life. If a Christian cannot say, "I know," "I am persuaded," he is lacking in one of the prime essentials of a vigorous experience. Let us ponder, then, this remarkable phrase, "the whole wealth of the fulness of intelligence," and see in it one of the absolute necessities of daily experience.

But how does it come? It is the result of the foregoing "comfort" and "love." Hearts made strong mean minds fully assured. Hearts full of love mean intellects full of knowledge and conviction. Let no one say that love is blind: on the contrary, it is love that sees and knows. It was the Apostle of love who was the first with spiritual insight to say, "It is the Lord," on that memorable early morning on the Lake of Galilee. It is the Christian with a heart strong and full of love who will have the "wealth of the fulness of intelligence." The same is true of a Church, for when it is strong and united in love, there will come such an influx of conviction and certitude that the world will be impressed by the demonstration of the truth of the Christian Gospel.

He asked for spiritual *knowledge*: "To the full knowledge of the mystery of God and the Father, even Christ" (not as A.V.). Here, again, we have a favourite word of these Epistles, "full knowledge," that is, ripe, mature experience; and it means the experience of all that is summed up in the one word "Christ." In view of the dangerous errors, then rife and increasing, of a special knowledge confined only to a few, to an intellectual aristocracy, the Apostle lays stress upon the possibility of every Christian becoming acquainted in personal experience with all the knowledge of God that is stored up in Christ. He declares Christ as the Image of God (ch. i. 15), as the Head of the Church (ch. i. 18), as the One in Whom all fulness dwells (ch. i. 19), as the Redeemer from sin (ch. i. 20), as the Hope of glory (ch. i. 27), as the One in Whom are hid all the treasures of wisdom and knowledge (ch. ii. 3). There is no mistiness here, no vagueness, no hesitation, no limitation, but a full, free, open opportunity for all believers to become acquainted with Christ in His Divine fulness. This is the crowning-point of the Apostle's prayer, for in the full knowledge of Christ everything else is included. This knowledge, at once intellectual, moral, and spiritual, is the safeguard from all error, the secret of all progress, and the guarantee of all blessing.

Let this prayer, then, be our constant and careful study. We shall find in it much to rebuke the shallowness, the selfishness, the dulness, and the sluggishness of our prayers; and we shall also find in it a model of instruction, and the inspiration of all true petition and intercession. The Christian who learns from the prayers of the Apostle will learn some of the deepest secrets of the Christian life.

VII

WISDOM AND REVELATION

"Wherefore I also, after I heard of your faith in the Lord Jesus, and love unto all the saints, cease not to give thanks for you, making mention of you in my prayers; that the God of our Lord Jesus Christ, the Father of glory, may give unto you the spirit of wisdom and revelation in the knowledge of Him: the eyes of your understanding being enlightened; that ye may know what is the hope of His calling, and what the riches of the glory of His inheritance in the saints, and what is the exceeding greatness of His power to us-ward who believe, according to the working of His mighty power."—*Eph.* i. 15-19.

If prayer for others is a barometer of our own spiritual life, we can realise what St. Paul felt was necessary for himself by his prayers for others. In Ephesians there are two petitions, and nothing fuller and deeper is found in any of the Apostle's writings. This Epistle represents the high-water mark of Christian privilege and possibility.

1. *The Foundation.*

We see from verse 15 that his prayer is closely and definitely based on what precedes, and this introduces us to a feature not hitherto found. Up to now the prayers at the opening have been recorded almost immediately after the personal greetings. But here a long paragraph intervenes, and the prayer is not recorded until after fourteen verses full of spiritual teaching have been given. This section deserves special attention because it is the basis of the prayer. Let us review it briefly in order to obtain the true perspective of the petition.

The key-thought is in verse 3, where the Apostle praises God for having actually blessed them "with all spiritual blessings in heavenly places in Christ." Then comes a wonderful statement of the way in which these blessings had become their own. (*a*) They had been eternally purposed in God the Father (vers. 3-6*a*); (*b*) they had been historically mediated through God the Son (vers. 6*b*-12); (*c*) they had been spiritually applied by God the Spirit (vers. 12-14). And in connection with each Person of the Sacred Trinity practically the same phrase occurs in this paragraph, showing that all the blessings were given in order that they might be used for the Divine glory: "To the praise of the glory of His grace" (ver. 6); "To the praise of His glory" (ver. 12); "To the praise of His glory" (ver. 14).

Now it is upon this wealth of provision that the Apostle bases his prayer: "On this account." God had so wonderfully blessed them in Christ by His Spirit, and this fulness of blessing was so clearly intended to be used to the praise and glory of God that he could pray, as he does here, assured that the answer would come. God's revelation of Himself is invariably and inevitably the foundation of our prayers. Because of what He has done and is doing we can be sure of grace. Because His power has provided "all things that pertain to life and godliness" we can be certain of power for daily living.

2. *The Appeal.*

The names and titles of God are particularly noteworthy and are always full of spiritual significance, shedding light on the passages in which they occur. St. Paul prays to "the God of our Lord Jesus Christ." This title as it stands is unique, though already he has referred to "the God and Father of our Lord Jesus Christ" (ver. 3), and will refer again to "the Father of our Lord Jesus Christ" in connection with prayer (ch. iii. 14). "The God of our Lord Jesus Christ" seems to suggest the highest point and peak of power and grace. God, as the God of Christ, is the primary source of all blessing.

He is also "the Father of Glory." This, too, is a phrase not found elsewhere. He is the Father to Whom all glory belongs as its Divine source. In Acts vii. 2 He is "the God of glory," and in 1 Cor. ii. 8 Christ is "the Lord of glory." In Rom. vi. 4 Christ is said to have been raised from the dead "by the glory of the Father." Glory is a characteristic quality of God. It is the manifestation of His splendour and the outshining of His excellence. All radiance, all brightness, all magnificence come from Him and are intended to be returned to Him in praise. The glory of God in Romans is threefold: it is God's proof for man's past life (ch. iii. 23); it is God's prospect for man's future life (ch. v. 2); it is God's principle for man's present life (ch. xv. 7). And the association of glory with prayer seems to suggest that the praise of His glory which is to characterise our life can only come from God Himself as the Father of glory. If our lives are to be lived "to His praise," His must be the power. If our lives are to manifest His glory, His must be the grace. "Thine is the kingdom, the power, and the glory."

3. *The Request.*

Now we come to this profound prayer which teaches the inmost secrets of the spiritual life.

(1) A Divine Gift. "May give to you a spirit of wisdom and revelation." He has spoken of the wealth of blessing stored up in Christ (ver. 3), and of God's grace abounding to us in all wisdom and prudence (ver. 8). Now he asks for wisdom and illumination to perceive all this for themselves as a personal experience. The word "spirit" seems to refer to their human faculty, though of course as indwelt and possessed by the Divine Spirit. But the absence of the definite article from the word "spirit" seems to suggest a gift rather than a Person. The Holy Spirit of God enters into our spirit, and the result is wisdom and revelation. These two words refer to general illumination and specific enlightenment. He desires his readers to enter fully into the meaning of these great realities to which he has given such full expression (vers. 1-14).

(2) But this Divine gift is only possible by means of a simple yet important condition. It is "in the full knowledge of Him." The word rendered "knowledge" is characteristic of these prison epistles, and always means "full knowledge," the mature experience of the spiritual man. It is invariably connected with God; it refers to the deep, growing, ripening consciousness which comes from personal fellowship with Him. Philosophy can only say "Know thyself," but Scripture says, "Know God." This is how wisdom and revelation become ours, and Christian history and experience testify abundantly to the simple yet

remarkable fact of spiritual insight and moral understanding which are due solely to fellowship with God. Nothing is more striking than the fact of a deep, spiritual apprehension and appreciation which are independent of intellectual conception and verbal expression. Believers can have a true spiritual consciousness of God without the possession of great capacity or attainments. Many whose natural education and intellectual opportunities have been slight have had this spiritual perception in an uncommon degree, and it always marks the spiritually ripe Christian. It is not the one whose intellectual knowledge is critical, scholarly, and profound, but he whose spiritual insight is suffused with grace, love, and fellowship. This does not mean that natural knowledge or culture is to be despised or avoided as evil, but that the two kinds of knowledge should be carefully distinguished. The Christian Church has at least for the last three hundred years set great store by knowledge and science, but deeper than all this is the spiritual instinct, insight, knowledge, and illumination which constitute the supreme requirement of the true Christian life. We can see this spiritual perception in its various stages in several passages of the New Testament. We have seen how St. John divides believers into three classes (1 John ii. 12-14). But while in his repetition the Apostle can vary the description of the "children" and the "young men," when he has to speak the second time of the "fathers" he has nothing new to say, for they cannot be otherwise or more fully described than as those who "know Him Who is from the beginning."

(3) The immediate consequence of this fellowship is that the eyes of the heart become permanently enlightened (Greek). Keeping in view the Scripture truth of the "heart" as including the elements of Mind, Emotion, and Will, the result of fellowship with God is that every feature of the inner life becomes purified and enlightened. The mind is illuminated to perceive truth, the emotions are purified to love the good, and the will is equipped to obey the right. It is not that new objects meet the gaze so much as that a new and deeper perception is given to enable the heart to see and understand what had hitherto been dark and difficult. This illuminated heart is one of the choicest blessings of the spiritual life and one of the greatest safeguards against spiritual error. "Ye have an unction ... and ye know" (1 John ii. 20). "The Son of God hath come, and hath given us an understanding" (1 John v. 20). Many of the problems affecting the spiritual life are solved only in this way. Criticism, scholarship, intellectual power may be brought to bear upon

them, but they will not yield to this treatment. The illuminated heart of the babe in Christ is often enabled to understand secrets which are hid from the wise and prudent.

(4) The outcome is a permanent spiritual experience. "That ye may know," *i.e.* possess an immediate, instinctive, direct knowledge (εἰδέναι). Three great realities are thereupon mentioned as the objects and substance of our spiritual knowledge.

(*a*) The first is "What is the hope of His calling." "His calling" is the appeal and offer of the Gospel with all its Divine meaning and purpose, and "the hope of His calling" is that which is intended by and included in the offer of God. This "hope" is either that *to* which God calls us, or *by* which He calls; either objective or subjective; either the substance or the feeling. Hope when regarded as objective, as the substance of our experience, is full of promise, on which the believer fixes his faith. Hope when regarded as subjective, as the possession of the soul, is full of inspiration, as it encourages and confirms belief that "He is faithful that promised." Hope as an objective reality is fixed on Christ, and since God has a purpose in calling us, we can exercise hope. Hope as a subjective realisation is based on the fact of experience. God calls us by the Gospel, and therefore hope becomes possible. Hope is the top-stone of life and follows faith and love (cf. ver. 15). Faith draws the curtain aside; hope gazes into the future; while love rejoices in the present possession of Christ. Faith accepts; hope expects. Faith appropriates; hope anticipates. Faith is concerned with the person who promises; hope with the thing that the person promises. Faith is concerned with the past and present; hope with the future alone. Hope is invariably fixed on the future and is never to be regarded as merely a matter of natural temperament. It is specifically connected with the Lord's Coming, and we are thus reminded that the calling of God covers past, present, and future. It starts from regeneration and culminates in the resurrection of the body at the Coming of Christ.

(*b*) The second is "The riches of the glory of His inheritance in the saints." This may mean the wealth which God possesses *for* them or *in* them; our wealth in Him or His in us. If we take it in the former sense it will mean that God is the inheritance and we are the heirs; that the saints now possess imperfectly, and anticipate in its fulness, the inheritance of grace, the spiritual Canaan which they are to enjoy here and hereafter. If, however, we take it, as is more likely, in the latter sense, it will mean that we are the inheritance and God is the Possessor and Heir. We must never forget that the Biblical ideas associated with "heir" and "inheritance" always refer to possession, and not, as in ordinary phraseology, to succession. In the Bible the heir does not merely expect, but already enjoys in part that which he will possess in full hereafter. Adopting, then, the second of these interpretations, the saints belong to God and are precious in His sight. They are His *peculium*, or special treasure, like Israel of old (Deut. iv. 20). They have been formed for Him and are to show forth His praise (Isa. xliii. 21). He sets store by them, as is suggested by the significant words, "Hast thou considered My servant Job?" There are several indications in Scripture that God values and trusts His people; "I know him, that he will command his children and his household after him" (Gen. xviii. 19). "The Lord taketh pleasure in His people" (Ps. cxlix. 4). "The steps of a good man are ordered by the Lord: and He (that is, God) delighteth in his way" (Ps. xxxvii. 23). And the "wealth" is a further proof of the value placed on believers by God. Five times in Ephesians the Apostle uses this metaphor of "riches," showing his thought of those who have been "bought with a price" (1 Cor. v. 20). Believers are God's riches, wealth, treasure; they belong to Him in view of that day on which He will enter in full upon His inheritance when He comes to be glorified and admired in them that believe (2 Thess. i. 10). And we are to see this, to know it, to realise the spiritual possibilities of each believer and all God's people together as God's own inheritance.

(*c*) The third is "the exceeding greatness of His power to us-ward who believe." In this marvellous association of almost inexpressible thoughts the dominant note is "power" (δύναμις), and the Apostle prays that the Ephesian Christians may know what this means. Power is a characteristic word of St. Paul as expressive of Christianity. The Gospel is "the power of God unto salvation" (Rom. i. 16). By the Resurrection Christ was designated "the Son of God with power" (Rom. i. 4). He is "the power of God" (1 Cor. i. 18). Man needs power, not merely a philosophy or an ethic, but a dynamic, and it is the peculiar privilege of His Gospel to bring this to us. But let us try to analyse this power. There are no less than four comparisons stated or illustrations given. (1) It is exactly the same power that God wrought in Christ at the Resurrection. Nothing less than this is the standard of the Divine working. We are to possess and experience the spiritual and moral dynamic exercised by God on Christ when He raised Him from the dead. This is described as "the exceeding greatness of His power." The same adjective is used of grace (ch. ii. 7), and of love (ch. iii. 19), and it is intended to express the superabundance of that power which was put forth in the Resurrection and is now exercised on our behalf. Then the four words used for power are particularly noteworthy: "power," "energy," "strength," "might." Each conveys an aspect of this great spiritual force. "Might" is power in *possession*; "strength" is power as the result of *grasping*, or of coming into contact with the source of that power; and "energy" is a power in *expression*. (2) Not only so, but the power exercised by God in the Ascension is also intended to be bestowed on and experienced by us. When we are told that Christ was set at God's right hand far above all powers, we can understand something of the Divine might exercised. (3) Still more, it is the same power by means of which God put all things under the feet of Christ. This, too, is the Divine force and energy for believers. (4) Not least of all, it was Divine power that gave Christ to be "the Head over all things to the Church," and it is exactly this power that is exercised on our behalf. When we contemplate all this as intended by God for us, we can see something of the vigorous and victorious life He can and will enable us to live.

As we review this wonderful prayer it is impossible to avoid noticing that the first petition refers mainly to the past ("His calling"); the second mainly to the future ("His inheritance"); and the third mainly to the present ("His power"), though of course each petition has its bearing on the other two points of time. Every part of our life is thus adequately supplied and intended to be abundantly satisfied. Nor may we omit to observe that all through the prayer the emphasis is on God: *His* calling; *His* inheritance; *His* power. Everything is regarded from the Divine standpoint, because we are not our own but His. The contemplation of this glory of the Divine love and grace overwhelms the soul with "wonder, love, and praise."

In the presence of such a prayer, dealing with such profound realities, three thoughts naturally arise in our minds. (*a*) How little we know, and how much we might and should know. (*b*) How little we are, and how much we might and should be. (*c*) How little we do, and how much we might and should do. And yet if we will but remind ourselves of the simple secret of true living, as here described, we might become and accomplish infinitely more than we have ever experienced up to the present. "To us-ward who believe." Faith is the simple yet all-sufficient secret. Trust relies on God and receives from Him. It puts us in contact with the source of blessing, and in union with Him we shall find spiritual illumination, spiritual insight, spiritual experience, and spiritual power that shall all be lived and exercised to His praise and glory.

VIII

STRENGTH AND INDWELLING

"For this cause I bow my knees unto the Father of our Lord Jesus Christ, of Whom the whole family in heaven and earth is named, that He would grant you, according to the riches of His glory, to be strengthened with might by His Spirit in the inner man; that Christ may dwell in your hearts by faith; that ye, being rooted and grounded in love, may be able to comprehend with all saints what is the breadth, and length, and depth, and height; and to know the love of Christ, which passeth knowledge, that ye might be filled with all the fulness of God."—*Eph.* iii. 14-19.

"In no part of Paul's letters does he rise to a higher level than in his prayers, and none of his prayers are fuller of fervour than this wonderful series of petitions. They open out one into the other like some majestic suite of apartments in a great palace-temple, each leading into a loftier and more spacious hall, each drawing nearer the presence chamber, until at last we stand there" (*Maclaren*).

The second prayer in Ephesians possesses remarkable affinities with the first; indeed, the two are complementary, and many of the expressions call for close comparison.

1. *The Standpoint.*

"For this cause" (ver. 14). To what does this phrase point back? Some associate it with verse 1, "For this cause," thinking that St. Paul, having been diverted from his main teaching in verses 1-13, here resumes it in the form of a prayer. But perhaps it is still better to regard the resumption of the main teaching as coming in ch. iv. 1, where the Apostle again speaks of himself as "the prisoner." This would make ch. iii. wholly parenthetical, so that instead of the present prayer being based on the teaching of ch. ii. the Apostle is led here to speak of his ministry (ch. iii. 1-13) and its outcome. His ministry is a gift, a trust, a stewardship, and its purpose is the proclamation of the Gospel and its results in the accomplishment of God's purposes for Jew and Gentile.

On this view the standpoint of the prayer is associated closely with his ministry and its effects, as seen in the immediately preceding verses. It is because of his remarkable ministry, given to him by God, and all the spiritual privileges brought to the Gentile Christians thereby that he is able to work for them (ver. 13), and also to pray for them (ver. 14). Thus, while the prayer in ch. i. looks at their life from the standpoint of the Divine purposes, this prayer will be occupied with their spiritual privileges in Christ.

2. *The Attitude.*

"I bow my knees unto the Father" (ver. 14). The intense reverence of the Apostle in this allusion to bowing his knees is particularly noteworthy. As a rule the Jews stood for prayer (Luke xviii. 11-13), and prostration seems to have been an exceptional posture. But in connection with Christians, kneeling is mentioned (Acts vii. 60, ix. 40, xx. 36). Nothing could more beautifully express the true attitude of the soul before God than this posture of the body. At the same time the use of the word "Father" indicates the other side of the truth and confidence with which we approach God. He is at once our God and our Father (ch. i. 17), and our attitude must be expressive both of our adoration and of our assurance. He is great and good, and we approach Him as the Holy One and the Loving One.

3. *The Address.*

"The Father from Whom every family in heaven and earth is named." It is interesting that the title "God" is not associated with this prayer as in ch. i., although the thought of Deity is found in the allusion to bowing the knees. And in addition to God as the Father He is described as the One "from Whom every family (Greek, 'fatherhood') in heaven and earth is named." This seems to mean that whatever element of family life exists, it comes from God, that all true spiritual life in heaven or earth has its origin in the Father. The scope of the prayer is particularly noteworthy, as we contemplate God as the Fount of every fatherhood and the Parent of all men everywhere. Such a statement will do more than anything else to guard us against narrow or purely selfish desires as we approach God in prayer.

4. *The Appeal.*

"That He would grant you" (ver. 16). As in the former prayer, the Apostle is clear that what he is about to ask is essentially a Divine gift. It comes from above, whether he is seeking knowledge (ch. i. 17) or power (ch. iii. 16). At every step God must give and the believer must receive. It would be well for us in our Christian experience to emphasise this simple but searching truth. "Every good and every perfect gift comes from above."

5. *The Standard.*

"According to the riches of His glory" (ver. 16). Here again we begin to realise something of the fulness of the prayer to be offered. The measure of the Apostle's desire is not our own poverty, but God's wealth; we are to look away from ourselves to the infinite riches of the Divine glory. In the former prayer he asked that we might know the riches of God's glory. But here there is something more; we are to experience them in our heart and life.

6. *The Petitions.*

In general St. Paul asks for two great spiritual blessings, the inward strength of the Holy Spirit and the indwelling presence of Christ. These are inseparable, and we may regard the first as essential to the second, and the second as the effect of the first. But the prayer goes into detail and each part of the petition calls for careful meditation.

(1) "Strengthened with power through His Spirit in the inward man" (ver. 16, R.V.). As wisdom was the burden of the former prayer (ch. i.

17), so strength is the main thought here. The order, too, is significant; wisdom and power, since power without knowledge would be highly dangerous. This strength comes from the Holy Spirit; He is the Agent of God's enabling grace. And the strength is to extend "into the inward man." The contrast seems to be between the inward and the outward, as in 2 Cor. iv. 16; Rom. vii. 22. The strength is not of the body, or of the mind, but of the soul. The "inward" is not exactly identical with the "new" man, but emphasises the inner essential life of the spirit as contrasted with the outer life of the body. "The hidden man of the heart."

(2) "That Christ may dwell in your hearts through faith" (ver. 17, R.V.). This is the outcome of the inward strength of the Spirit, and almost every word needs attention. The indwelling of Christ is virtually identical with that of the Spirit (ch. ii. 22), although of course Christ and the Holy Spirit are never absolutely identified in Holy Scripture (2 Cor. iii. 17, 18). It is only in regard to the practical outcome in the believer's experience that the indwelling of Christ and the Spirit amount to the same thing. This is to be a permanent indwelling and not a mere passing stay, just as believers together are described as a temple for God's permanent habitation (ch. ii. 22, Greek). This permanent indwelling of Christ is to be "in your hearts." Almost every prayer is thus concerned with the "heart," the centre of the moral being, and the Apostle prays that Christ may make His home therein. This is no mere influence, but a Personal Presence, the Living Christ within, and it is to be "through faith." It is faith that admits Christ to the heart, allowing Him to enter into every part of the "inward man." And the same faith that admits Him permits Him to remain, reside, and rule. Faith, in a word, is the total response of the soul to the Lordship of Christ.

(3) "That ye, being rooted and grounded in love" (ver. 17). Here again the original expressions imply permanent results, and the two words "rooted" and "grounded" are beautifully complementary. The one refers to a tree, the other to a house, and the expressions point to those hidden processes of the soul which are the result of Christ's indwelling and the Holy Spirit's working. The power of the Spirit and the indwelling of Christ tend to our permanent inward establishment in the element and atmosphere of Christian love. This is one of the seven occasions in this short Epistle where we find the Pauline phrase, "in love," referring to the sphere and atmosphere of our fellowship with God. The love no

doubt means primarily and perhaps almost exclusively God's love to us, as that in which we are to "live, and move, and have our being."

(4) "May be strong to apprehend with all the saints what is the breadth and length and height and depth" (ver. 18, R.V.). Here again the emphasis is on strength, and the Apostle prays that we may have full strength to grasp, may be quite able to accomplish this purpose. Spiritual ideas can never be appropriated by intellectual action alone. It is not by brilliant intellect but by spiritual insight that we become "able to comprehend." Although there is now no specific reference to love, it would seem as though the idea of verse 19 is already in view, and, assuming this to be the case, we have four aspects of the Divine love which we are to be strong to grasp. Its "breadth" means that there is no barrier to it, reminding us of the extent of the Divine counsels; its "length" tells us of the Divine foreknowledge and His thought of us through the ages; its "height" points to our Lord in heaven as the goal for the penitent believer; its "depth" declares the possibility of love descending to the lost abyss of human misery for the purpose of redemption. And the ability to grasp the Divine love in this fourfold way is to be experienced with "all the saints." It is impossible to accomplish it alone; no spiritual exclusiveness is thinkable in this connection, to say nothing of the lower forms of egotism and selfishness. Twice in this brief writing does the Apostle refer to "all the saints" (ch. vi. 18), thereby reminding us of the place and power of each saint in the spiritual economy of God. One saint will be able to comprehend a little, another saint a little more, and so on, until at length all the saints together are "strong to grasp" the Divine love. The wider our fellowship the fuller and firmer our hold of the love of Christ. This is doubtless why public worship is so strongly emphasised in the New Testament. "Where two or three are gathered together in My Name, there am I." The experiences of our fellow-worshippers are always intended to be, and usually will be, of help to our own fuller realisation of our Lord and Master. The soul is justified solitarily and alone, but it is sanctified only in the community of believers.

(5) "And to know the love of Christ which passeth knowledge" (ver. 19). If we are correct in interpreting verse 18 of the Divine love, the present verse will be the climax of this part of the prayer, and it has been helpfully suggested that we have here the "fifth dimension" of the love of Christ after the four already mentioned. Not only are they to

experience breadth and length and height and depth but also the inwardness; they are to know by personal experience the love of Christ as it can only be known by those who have fellowship with Him. It is a love that surpasses knowledge, just as His power surpasses everything (ch. i. 19). The paradox of knowing that which surpasses knowledge will not be misunderstood from the standpoint of spiritual experience, because it is the difference between apprehending and comprehending. We know, and know deeply, increasingly, blessedly, and yet all the while there are infinite stretches of love beyond our highest experiences.

(6) "That ye may be filled unto all the fulness of God" (ver. 19, R.V.). This is the climax of the prayer and is the culminating purpose of the work of the Spirit and the indwelling of Christ. Strength, indwelling, love, and knowledge are to issue in fulness, and we are to be "filled unto all the fulness of God." In the former prayer this fulness is associated with Christ and with His body the Church (ch. i. 23), but here it is specifically associated with God and ourselves as believers in Christ. When these two passages are associated with ch. v. 18, which speaks of the fulness of the Spirit, we have the word "fulness" connected with each Person of the Blessed Trinity. What it means for the soul to be filled to overflowing with the presence of God itself is beyond our comprehension; it can only be a matter of personal experience as we seek to fulfil the proper conditions. Such a prayer for the fulness of God is best expressed in Miss Havergal's words—

> "Lord, we ask it, scarcely knowing
> What this wondrous gift may be;
> But fulfil to overflowing,
> *Thy* great meaning let us see."

IX

LOVE AND DISCERNMENT

"And this I pray, that your love may abound yet more and more in knowledge and all judgment: that ye may approve things that are excellent; that ye may be sincere and without offence till the day of Christ; being filled with the fruits of righteousness, which are by Jesus Christ, unto the glory and praise of God."—*Phil.* i. 9-11.

One of the most beautiful elements in the Pauline Epistles is the intimate relation which evidently existed between the Apostle and his converts. This is especially the case in the Epistle to the Philippians, for in no other writing is there such a full revelation of the heart of St. Paul and of his love to those with whom he was united in Christ. As, therefore, he knew them so intimately, so he prayed for them, the prayer revealing at once their need, and his conviction as to essential things. Prayer is always strong in proportion to our acquaintance with the spiritual life of others, and feeble so far as we are ignorant of their needs.

1. *The Definite Request.*

Let us mark the opening words: "this I keep on asking" (Greek). There was one thing for which he asked continually, and this seemed to him to sum up everything in their life.

(1) He prayed for love; "your love." As they already possessed life, he wished it to be expressed in love. The Epistle is full of this subject. No writing is so truly characterised by the love of St. Paul for his converts, or of his converts for St. Paul (see ch. iv. 14-18). Let us again remind ourselves that love in the New Testament is something definite, tangible, strong, practical, intense. It is more than sentiment, though of course it includes that; it is more than emotion, though undoubtedly it includes that; it is more than desire, though obviously it includes that. Love is the outgoing of the entire nature in self-sacrificing service. It is the sympathy of the heart and the devotion of the life to its object. As such it is the supreme proof of the reality of our Christian profession. "If ye

love Me, ye will keep My commandments" (John xiv. 15, R.V.). "Lovest thou Me ... feed My sheep" (John xxi. 16). "Seeing ye have purified your souls ... love one another from the heart unfeignedly" (1 Pet. i. 22, R.V.). It was with no cynicism, but with a wonderful astonishment, that the heathen used to say, "See how these Christians love one another." When therefore the Apostle prayed for love he was asking that the Philippian Christians might possess and manifest the very finest, truest, most powerful, and most attractive proof of their Christian life.

(2) He prayed for abounding love; "that your love may abound." Not only some, but abundant love; not a little, but much. Love to be real must be kept full, intense, overflowing; it calls for continual reinforcement, replenishing, and the abundance of love is the measure and proof of the possession of abundant life.

(3) He prayed for increasing love; "that your love may abound yet more and more." Expression is piled upon expression in order to emphasise the importance of love and its progress. Love is intended to grow and not to remain stationary. Just as life makes progress, so must its result similarly develop in love. The motto for the Christian is "more and more." This is why there is so much in the New Testament about growth, for just as it is with natural life so it must be with spiritual. Constant increase, development, progress, extension, expansion must mark it at every step.

(4) He prayed for discerning love; "that your love may abound yet more and more in knowledge and all discernment" (R.V.). The two words "knowledge" and "discernment" are particularly noteworthy. One expresses the principle, the other the application. Again we observe this word "knowledge" as a characteristic expression of the Apostle in these prison-epistles. "Full knowledge" (Greek) is one of the marks of a growing Christian life, and is proved by spiritual perception, spiritual feeling, spiritual discernment. There is a world of difference between intellectual ability and spiritual insight. Many people are clever, but not spiritual, while many people are often truly spiritual without being possessed of much intellectual capacity. Much is said in Scripture about *sight* in regard to things spiritual. "Except a man be born again, he cannot *see*" (John iii. 3). "Blessed are the pure in heart, for they shall *see* God" (Matt. v. 8). There are many people in our congregations of average intellect, and perhaps with mental powers decidedly below the

average, who are nevertheless full of profound spiritual wisdom because love to Christ has given them keenness of vision and depth of insight.

2. *The Immediate Purpose.*

This constant progress and abundance of love was intended for a very practical purpose; "so that ye may approve the things that are excellent" (ver. 10, R.V.). The discernment already mentioned was intended for spiritual discrimination. They were to be enabled to distinguish, to prove, and thereby to approve. As Lightfoot points out, "love imparts a sensitiveness of touch, a keen edge to the discriminating faculty in things moral and spiritual." In things spiritual at least love is not blind, but keen-sighted. It is endowed with a spiritual discernment which is able to distinguish not only between good and bad, but between good and better, between better and best, and between best and excellent. The words, "approve the things that are excellent," occur also in Rom. ii. 18, and the meaning seems to be first that they were to "distinguish the things that differ," and then as a result they were to "approve the things that transcend." This spiritual discernment is particularly needful to-day, as the Christian soul is surrounded by so many views and voices. Much that appears on the surface to be attractive and charming contains within it the elements of spiritual danger and disaster, and it is only by spiritual discernment which comes from abounding and increasing love to Christ that the soul is safeguarded against evil and led to approve and follow the things that are superior. It is a vivid picture that the prophet gives of the Messiah when he describes Him as endowed by the Spirit of God and made of "quick scent in the fear of the Lord" (Isa. xi. 3, Hebrew). It is this "quick scent" that by the same Spirit the Lord Jesus Christ bestows upon those who love Him with all the heart.

3. *The Permanent Result.*

Every Christian grace is intended for practical and permanent effect in character. Our lives are not to be intermittent, but continuous in their expression of grace and blessing, and all that the Apostle has been praying for and desiring on behalf of his Philippian Christians was intended to develop and express in them the solid and permanent realities of Christian character.

(1) Sincerity; "that ye may be sincere" (ver. 10). This has to do with motives. The word is thought to mean "tested in the sunlight." Our lives are to be manifestly true, genuine, sincere, "transparent." "Motive makes the man," and from time to time it is essential that we should allow ourselves to be tested and judged in the sunlight of our perfect fellowship with Christ, just as St. Peter, when asked by his Master, said, "Lord, Thou knowest all things." Sincerity is one of the essential features of the true Christian life. The believer, if he is to do the will of God and commend the Gospel to others, must have no doubtful *arrière pensée* but a life lived moment by moment in the perfect brightness of the presence of perfect holiness.

(2) Consistency; "void of offence" (ver. 10, R.V.). This has to do with conduct. Not only are we to be inwardly true, but outwardly sure. Our lives must not hinder others, or put a stumbling-block in their way. Just as the Master said, "Blessed is he whosoever is not put to stumble by Me," so must it be with every follower of Christ. Our lives are to be stepping-stones, not stumbling-blocks.

(3) Character; "being filled with the fruits of righteousness." This has to do with our permanent life both within and without, though the emphasis is on being rather than on doing. Character is the highest point and peak of the Christian life, for just as fruit is the outcome of the life of a tree, so character is the fruit of Christian living, and is the best proof of its existence. The Apostle's word suggests that we are to be "permanently filled" (Greek) with the fruits of righteousness, those things that are right, straight, true, correct, upright, without any deflection on either side. The Lord Who is our Righteousness works in us the fruits of righteousness by the indwelling of the Holy Spirit.

4. *The Ultimate Object.*

The Apostle looks forward "unto the day of Christ" (ver. 10, R.V.), and then speaks of the Christian life being lived "unto the glory and praise of God" (ver. 11). Everything is to tend towards the manifestation of the splendour of God in human life whereby others will be led to acknowledge and praise Him (Matt. v. 16). And this will reach its culminating point in the "day of Christ," that time when Christian people will stand before their Master and receive the reward of their life and service rendered to Him (ch. i. 6, ii. 16). This was the Apostle's constant thought, and towards this he strained every nerve (ch. iii. 11-21). It expresses the highest ideal of Christian living, for day by day we are to live with this wonderful thought of "the glory and praise of God," and day by day we are to look forward to the coming of Christ as that day in which our life will find its fullest realisation, its complete satisfaction, and its unending joy. And all this reminds us of the essential simplicity of life, for there is nothing complex, or involved, or mysterious, or difficult in a life lived day by day to the praise of God and in the light of the coming of our Master.

As we review this prayer we may feel perfectly sure that the Apostle meant it to be answered, and indeed, he himself gives us the hint of how this may come to pass when he tells us that the fruits of righteousness are "through Jesus Christ." This is only another way of expressing what he has already shown, his confidence that the possession of the Christian life is the guarantee of its complete realisation and full perfection by the indwelling presence and work of the Lord Jesus Christ Himself (ch. i. 6). Let us therefore take heart of grace as we contemplate this prayer and the other prayers of the Apostle. We must not be depressed, or disheartened, or discouraged, as we ponder the marvellous details and contemplate the stupendous heights of the Christian life as depicted by St. Paul's wonderful spiritual insight. On the contrary, we must remind ourselves that he would not have prayed these prayers unless he had been certain that God would answer them, and they will assuredly be answered as we set ourselves resolutely, humbly, lovingly, trustfully to fulfil the required conditions, "through Jesus Christ our Lord."

APPENDIX

Considerations of space have prevented the inclusion of all the Prayers of St. Paul, but for the treatment of the prayer in Rom. XV. 13 reference may perhaps be permitted to the author's *Royal and Loyal* (ch. v.) and to his Devotional Commentary on *Romans* (vol. iii. p. 103 ff.). And a fuller treatment of 2 Thess. iii. 16 is given in his *The Power of Peace*.

For the thorough exegetical foundation of the passages included in these prayers of the Apostle special attention should of course be given to the various modern standard Commentaries. The following have proved of particular value in the preparation of these pages. On Thessalonians: Milligan, Frame, Eadie, and Ellicott. On Romans: Sanday and Headlam, Godet, and the Notes by Lightfoot. On Ephesians: Armitage Robinson, Westcott, and Eadie. On Philippians: Lightfoot and Ellicott. On Colossians: Lightfoot and Ellicott. Preachers will find it nothing short of an education in Greek to ponder the passages under the guidance of these master-minds. The first step in all true expository preaching is the consideration of the words and phrases in order to elicit their full exegetical value. Following this, and based upon it, will come the spiritual teaching and personal application, and for this purpose the following books will be found of great value. On Thessalonians: Denney in the *Expositor's Bible*. On Romans: Bishop Moule in the same series. On Ephesians: G. G. Findlay in the *Expositor's Bible*, with R. W. Dale's well-known Lectures. On Philippians: Rainy in the *Expositor's Bible*, and Jowett's *The High Calling*. On Colossians: Maclaren's peerless treatment in the *Expositor's Bible*, with Bishop Moule's *Colossian Studies*, and a useful American work, *Oneness with Christ*, by Bishop Nicholson. The subject of this book is definitely treated in *The Prayers of St. Paul*, by W. B. Pope, D.D.; *The Pattern Prayer Book*, by E. W. Moore; *Preces Paulinæ*, a valuable old book by an anonymous author, which is now only obtainable second-hand.

On the general subject of Prayer, which will naturally be given attention in the expository preaching and teaching on this special topic of St. Paul's petitions, the following among other books may perhaps be mentioned: *Waiting on God*, by Andrew Murray; *The Hidden Life of Prayer*, by D. M. M'Intyre; *Prayer*, by M'Conkey; *Praying in the Holy Ghost*, by G. H. C. Macgregor; *Quiet Talks on Prayer*, by S. D. Gordon; and *Prayer: Its Nature and Scope*, by H. C. Trumbull.

www.ingramcontent.com/pod-product-compliance
Lightning Source LLC
Chambersburg PA
CBHW071331080526
44587CB00017B/2802